NESTED SECURITY

NESTED SECURITY

LESSONS IN CONFLICT MANAGEMENT
FROM THE LEAGUE OF NATIONS
AND THE EUROPEAN UNION

ERIN K. JENNE

CORNELL UNIVERSITY PRESS   *Ithaca and London*

First published 2015 by Cornell University Press
Printed in the United States of America

Library of Congress Cataloging-in-Publication Data

Jenne, Erin K., author.
   Nested security : lessons in conflict management from the League of Nations and the European Union / Erin K. Jenne.
      pages cm
   Includes bibliographical references and index.
   ISBN 978-0-8014-5390-8 (cloth : alk. paper)
   1. Security, International—Europe. 2. Conflict management—Europe. 3. Pacific settlement of international disputes. I. Title.
   JZ6009.E85J46   2015
   341.5094—dc23   2015020426

Cornell University Press strives to use environmentally responsible suppliers and materials to the fullest extent possible in the publishing of its books. Such materials include vegetable-based, low-VOC inks and acid-free papers that are recycled, totally chlorine-free, or partly composed of nonwood fibers. For further information, visit our website at www.cornellpress.cornell.edu.

Cloth printing   10 9 8 7 6 5 4 3 2 1

CONTENTS

ACKNOWLEDGMENTS

This book is the product of over a decade of thinking, researching, and writing about how civil conflicts can be alleviated when they are embedded in international conflict-resolution processes. Along the way, I have accumulated a significant debt to scholars, policy analysts, and policy makers, as well as colleagues, friends, and family. I will never be able to thank adequately all those who contributed to this project, but I nevertheless attempt to do so briefly here.

I would certainly never have attempted a project of such scope without the generous backing of the Carnegie Corporation. Their support made possible numerous research trips to the headquarters of the High Commissioner on National Minorities (HCNM) in The Hague, the archives of the Organization for Security and Cooperation in Europe (OSCE) in Prague, successive trips to the Balkan and the Baltic states, and the League of Nations archives in Geneva. Special thanks go to my former PhD supervisor, David Holloway, for supporting my application to the Carnegie Corporation. The Open Society Institute funded additional research trips to the League of Nations archives to complete my research on conflict management in interwar Europe.

Those who helped with my fieldwork in Europe are far too numerous to thank here, but I received invaluable support in The Hague from John Packer, who also commented helpfully on early draft chapters on preventive diplomacy. Nicu Popescu, Michael Merlingen, and Neil Melvin each provided useful connections and advice for my research at the NATO headquarters and European Commission in Brussels; Alexander Astrov assisted me in locating useful informants in Riga and Tallinn; and James Lyon and Elissa Helms gave me interview contacts in Podgorica and Belgrade. Natalia A. Peral helped me with contacts in Pristina, Kosovo; and Dane Taleski assisted me in Skopje, Macedonia. Throughout, Rhodri Williams and Charles Philpott offered useful insights into the workings of the OSCE and HCNM, which greatly assisted my contemporary case analysis.

I wrote up my research findings with a Fernand Braudel Fellowship from the European University Institute, in Florence, Italy, where I received invaluable advice and feedback from a number of colleagues—most especially Rainer

Bauböck, Dorothee Bohle, Béla Greskovits, Peter Mair, Philippe Schmitter, and Pascal Vennesson. The historical parts of my book benefited greatly from comments I received from Patricia Clavin, Susan Pederson, and other historians at a League of Nations conference sponsored by the Graduate Institute of International and Development Studies in Geneva, Switzerland. In the final stages of write-up, I profited from the comments of attendees at conferences and invited talks at Queens University in Belfast, Uppsala University in Sweden, and Leiden University in the Netherlands.

I generated more versions of the chapters of this book than I care to admit, and I owe an enormous debt of gratitude to colleagues and researchers at Central European University—in particular, members of the Conflict and Security Research Group, including Alexander Akbik, Artak Galyan, Natalia A. Peral, Milos Popovic, Vujo Ilić, Hanna Kirvas, Beata Huszka, Nicu Popescu, Roland Schmidt, Miriam Hänni, Tina Magazzini, Matteo Fumagalli, and Robert Sata, who read successive draft chapters. I am particularly indebted to Levente Littvay and Milos Popovic, whose collaboration yielded the quantitative analysis in chapter 7. Alexander Akbik, Magdalena Bernaciak, Dane Taleski, Kinga Koretta Sata, and Ilir Kalemaj provided excellent research assistance.

I am grateful to colleagues and friends who have read various versions of the chapters in the book, including Bill Ayres, Kristin Bakke, Jóhanna Kristín Birnir, Zsuzsa Csergő, Nitsan Chorev, Kathleen Gallagher Cunningham, Tanja Ellingsen, Jan Erk, Erika Forsberg, Nils Petter Gleditsch, Carol Harrington, Patrick James, Nicole Lindstrom, Peter Trumbore, Manus Midlarsky, Will Moore, Harris Mylonas, Ephraim Nimni, Stephen Saideman, Carsten Schneider, Ulrich Sedelmeier, Ivan Szelenyi, and Monica Duffy Toft. Particular thanks go to Barry O'Neill, Stefan Wolff, and Stuart Kaufmann, who each read several chapters and gave me feedback, as well as Gregory Mitrovich and Idean Salehyan, who generously read the final draft manuscript for clarity and organization. Finally, considerable thanks go to two anonymous reviewers for excellent constructive feedback, Bill Nelson for the maps, and Susan Specter and Glenn Novak for excellent editorial assistance. Finally, I thank Roger Haydon at Cornell University, who pushed me throughout the writing process to clarify my central argument and rethink the theoretical scope of analysis. Without Roger's persistent prodding and patient guidance, this book could not have become what it now is.

The usual caveats apply concerning any mistakes contained herein. I share credit for the successes of the book with all those mentioned above, in addition to many others whose ideas have inspired theoretical insights and who have helped to clarify my thinking. Above all, I am deeply grateful to my friends and family for encouraging me and helping me maintain focus on completing the book, particularly my mother, to whom this book is dedicated.

ABBREVIATIONS

ANA	Albanian National Army
ARF	ASEAN Regional Forum
ASEAN	Association of Southeast Asian Nations
AU	African Union
CEE	Central and Eastern Europe
CIS	Commonwealth of Independent States
CoE	Council of Europe
COW	Correlates of War
CSCE	Conference on Security and Co-operation in Europe
DPA	Dayton Peace Agreement
DPKO	Department for Peacekeeping Operations, United Nations
DUI	Democratic Union for Integration (Albanian party in Macedonia)
ECOMOG	Economic Community of West African States Monitoring Group
ECOWAS	Economic Community of West African States
EU	European Union (formerly EC, European Community)
EUFOR	European Union Force (Bosnia Herzegovina)
EULEX	European Union Rule of Law Mission in Kosovo
HCNM	High Commissioner on National Minorities (under OSCE)
ICFY	International Conference on the Former Yugoslavia
IFI	international financial institutions
IGO	intergovernmental organization
IMF	International Monetary Fund
ISIS	Islamic State of Iraq and Syria
KFOR	Kosovo Force (NATO)
KLA	Kosovo Liberation Army
LN	League of Nations
MENA	Middle East and North Africa
MILC	Uppsala Dataset on Managing Intrastate Low-Intensity Conflict

NATO	North Atlantic Treaty Organization
NLA	National Liberation Army
OAS	Organization of American States
OAU	Organization of African Unity
OFA	Ohrid Framework Agreement (Macedonia)
OIC	Organization of the Islamic Conference
OSCE	Organization for Security and Co-operation in Europe (formerly CSCE, Conference on Security and Co-operation in Europe)
UCDP	Uppsala Conflict Data Program
UNDP	United Nations Development Programme
UNHCR	United Nations High Commissioner for Refugees
UNMIK	United Nations Mission in Kosovo
UNPREDEP	United Nations Preventive Deployment Force
UNPROFOR	United Nations Protection Force in Croatia and Bosnia Herzegovina
UNSC	United Nations Security Council
WTO	World Trade Organization

Nested Security

INTRODUCTION

When the dust finally settled from the 2014 civil rebellion in Ukraine, with freshly deposed Ukrainian president Viktor Yanukovych having fled to the east, the country's transitional leaders turned their attention to the secessionist threats in Eastern Ukraine and Crimea. To head off internal violence that might draw in neighboring Russia, the Ukrainian government invoked a provision in the Organization for Security and Co-operation in Europe (OSCE) Vienna Document that permitted member countries to invite military observers onto their territory to monitor emerging threats of inter-state conflict.[1]

The results were less than inspiring for the prospects of containing unrest through peaceful means. Although the OSCE did organize negotiations between the two governments, and international military observers eventually deployed to Ukraine, they failed to achieve much beyond fueling further international controversy and tensions. The first team, invited by the Ukrainian government, was briefly held hostage in the Eastern Ukrainian town of Slovyansk until its members were released after international outcry.[2] A second team, approved at a subsequent meeting in Geneva, was not even allowed into Crimea, blocked as it was by pro-Russian forces. Russia, an OSCE member, had used the organization's consensus rule to prevent the team's entry to the breakaway territory until after Moscow annexed Crimea through military intervention and a controversial referendum. Crimea has since been incorporated into the Russian Federation, and widespread pro-Russian protests in the east led to a bloody insurgency against the Ukrainian government.

These events prompted R. Spencer Oliver, former secretary-general of the OSCE Parliamentary Assembly, to observe, "If the OSCE were working the way it's supposed to, the Ukraine crisis should never have happened in the first place."[3] He pointed out that the OSCE's consensus rule prevents the organization from defusing such conflicts when one of its members wishes to block preventive action. Armenia, for example, undermined OSCE efforts to resolve the separatist conflict involving its co-ethnics in Azerbaijan, and Russia played a similar "spoiler" role in OSCE conflict management in Moldova, Georgia, and Azerbaijan. In the words of High Commissioner on National Minorities

(HCNM) political adviser Mihai Gribincea, "Everything depends on Russian actions. If Russia doesn't want the intervention to go forward, everything stops."[4]

In this book, I address the conundrum presented by the 2014 crisis in Ukraine, the 2008 conflict in Georgia, the 1990s conflict in Kosovo, the 2001 insurgency in Macedonia, as well as spillover effects from the Syrian war into Iraq today. My research is based in Europe, the site of two of the best-known international security regimes[5] that used minority protections to de-escalate conflicts in their early stages. Using comparative historical analysis, I investigate the conditions under which international conflict managers[6]—operating with limited resources and no firepower—succeeded in defusing civil disputes in Europe before they led to full-blown civil war. These interventions worked as follows: when communal tensions were detected within a given state, conflict monitors such as the OSCE approached the target state with a set of recommendations for managing these tensions. Major powers such as the United States, Britain, or France often backstopped their recommendations, giving cooperative interventions teeth. Such engagements were clearly preferable to sanctions or military force insofar as they minimized the costs of intervention (for both intervenors and the target state), did not violate international norms of sovereignty, and were unlikely to generate new conflicts or exacerbate existing ones. I show, however, that although soft-power conflict management has assumed greater importance since the end of the Cold War, it has failed to bear fruit so long as the wider conflict environment remained unchecked.

Why Study Europe?

European rulers have long established international security regimes in the wake of war or political transition—regimes based on the principles of minority protection. For most of the past five centuries, these regimes have included mechanisms for ensuring the protection of certain minorities that found themselves on the wrong side of new borders. In every regime, a handful of national minorities were singled out for special focus because its architects believed the grievances of certain groups lay at the heart of internecine struggles, fueling inter-state warfare.

The 1648 Peace of Westphalia, concluding the Thirty Years' War, provided a prototype for such regimes, mandating that signatory states respect the liberties of particular religious minorities upon their territory. It was embryonic in the sense that it included no formalized mechanism for third-party mediation. Instead, signatories made mutual promises to protect one another's religious minorities in return for agreements of nonintervention in one another's sovereign affairs.[7] In return for respecting one another's sovereignty, European princes contracted among themselves to protect the rights of certain religious minorities within their borders.[8] Because each state had coreligionists in other states, the contracts were enforced through mutual deterrence. As such, the regime constituted little more than a set of contractual obligations among states.

The Concert of Europe was the first regional security regime that included mechanisms for continuous third-party mediation of emerging armed conflict. The 1815 Treaty of Vienna—designed to dismember the Napoleonic empire—affirmed that the Great Powers should work together to resolve future instabilities in Europe. With this provision, the Concert acquired a far more institutionalized status and served as an early blueprint for modern security regimes. Although the Concert was basically conservative and pro-establishment, it promoted certain minority rights in order to maintain the peace of the Continent. For example, although Poland remained partitioned and occupied by Russia, Prussia, and Austria, the Congress of Vienna established a degree of independence for the Poles on the basis of "national rights."[9] It was believed that limited "autonomy" would mollify the local population while maintaining the fragile status quo among occupying powers. In the first decades, the Concert powers achieved numerous diplomatic victories. They quickly resolved Allied occupation of post-Napoleonic France, restoring the country to equal status with other European powers. The Concert also facilitated the peaceful independence of Belgium and Greece in 1830–31 and achieved its greatest success at the 1878 Congress of Berlin, where the Concert powers negotiated recognition for new states in the Balkans (Serbia, Romania, and Montenegro), decided the status of Bosnia and Cyprus, and negotiated a division of Africa between competing European metropoles.[10]

Nonetheless, there were problems with the Concert regime. First, it was wholly ad hoc, with no requirement that signatory states meet on a regular basis or submit to Concert arbitration. Moreover, the Concert was primarily aimed at arbitrating differences *between states*. Very little attention was directed at de-escalating *internal* conflicts—indeed, the Concert actually *assisted* European states in repressing the 1848 national movements. Most important, the Concert was not designed to cope with military conflicts among the powers themselves and failed to prevent the Crimean War (1853–56), the Second Italian War of Independence (1859), the Austro-Prussian War (1866), and the Franco-Prussian War (1870–71). That one member's obstruction could hamstring the regime turned out to be its Achilles heel; the Concert failed to check Bismarck's attacks on Denmark and Austria, or France's war against Germany. Neither could the Concert, many years later, forestall Austria's declaration of war against Serbia, which ultimately led to World War I. This critical decision-making flaw continues to plague international security regimes today—not only within Europe. It is therefore understandable that the international community views the lack of enforcement power and the consensus rule as the most important handicaps to soft-power conflict management.

Subsequent European leaders strove to overcome these problems with the interwar League of Nations Minority Protection System (MPS) and, fifty years later, the EU/OSCE system for conflict prevention.[11] Both systems had well-elaborated mechanisms of monitoring, early warning, and preventive diplomacy—mechanisms designed to give the regimes teeth in the face of great-power resistance. The bulk of this book is dedicated to examining the historical record of these systems to see how well they managed emerging tensions in the absence of coercive power. In doing so, I examine cooperative interventions under both regimes to determine why some interventions succeeded, while others did not.

Snapshot of the Two Security Regimes

At the close of World War I, the victorious Allied powers—Britain, France, Italy, and the United States—fashioned nation-states out of the wreckage of the German, Ottoman, and Habsburg Empires at a series of conferences. The Allies supported the unification of smaller Slavic nations into Czechoslovakia and the Kingdom of Yugoslavia; Poland was restored after more than a century of partition; and the borders of Greece and Romania were enlarged. Wherever possible, the Allies used national geography as a template for the new state boundaries. Nonetheless, national communities were often bisected to give the new states defensible borders and access to important waterways and trade routes. By giving them strategic territories and mandating that they protect the rights of their new national minorities, the Allies hoped that their client states would prevent revisionist challenges by Germany, Bulgaria, and Hungary, while forestalling military alliances among revisionist states. To this end, Czechoslovakia received the German-speaking Sudetenland in the west and Hungarian territory in the southeast, while the reconstituted Polish state obtained vast Belarusian and Ukrainian territories in the east and large German territories in the west. Romania received the eastern region of Hungary as well as a large chunk of Bulgarian territory. The Allies thus formed a *cordon sanitaire* in Central Europe, isolating the revisionist powers from one another through the creation of buffer states.

The peace settlement created an enormous potential for violence. The new borders separated almost one hundred million people from their prewar states; over twenty-five million people were now stranded outside their national homelands.[12] Millions of Greeks and Turks woke up on the wrong side of the border, as did millions of ethnic Germans and Hungarians in Central Europe. The new and enlarged states now boasted the largest ethnic minorities in the region. Indeed, fully 85 percent (22.5 million) of people belonging to national minorities in Central and Eastern Europe resided in the new and enlarged states of Poland, Czechoslovakia, Romania, and Yugoslavia; one out of every three people in the region now belonged to a minority.[13]

Western leaders recognized the volatility of the situation. U.S. president Woodrow Wilson declared at the Paris Peace Conference: "Nothing, I venture to say, is more likely to disturb the peace of the world than the treatment which might in certain circumstances be meted out to minorities."[14] With this in mind, the Allies established a security regime under which the new and enlarged states pledged to observe the rights of certain restive minorities.[15] The treaties signed by these states in 1919–20 were fairly limited, consisting mostly of negative rights, such as the right to nondiscrimination, the free exercise of religion, and the right to form minority associations. In a few cases, minorities were promised linguistic and cultural rights and even the right to political autonomy or self-government. These promises were to be taken as "basic law" (Article 1) by the signatory state, meaning that the state could not pass laws to contravene them. The treaties also provided for monitoring and enforcement by the League. Far from creating universal minority protections, the treaties covered only revisionist borderland minorities that threatened to foment inter-state war.[16]

The Allies also compelled former belligerent powers (Austria, Bulgaria, Germany, and Hungary) to sign treaties with the League pledging that they would not attempt to regain lost territories—compliance would later be rewarded with League membership. The "top-down" regime established in 1920 was formal, centralized, and hierarchical. Individuals, organizations, and governments were permitted to submit complaints of discrimination to the League, which was authorized to rule on these petitions. The Supreme War Council (and its successor, the Conference of Ambassadors, which represented France, Britain, Italy, and Japan, with the United States in an advisory role) would be called upon to enforce League decisions if necessary.

Although the interwar regime scored important victories in the 1920s, it began to break down in the mid-1930s, as League interventions failed to prevent civil conflicts from escalating into international conflicts between revisionist states (Hungary, Germany), on the one hand, and new and enlarged client states (Yugoslavia, Czechoslovakia, Poland, Romania) on the other. Worse, Germany's Nazi leadership actually managed to subvert the system of minority protections, using the pretense of beleaguered German co-ethnics abroad to justify Germany's territorial expansion. By the 1930s, the League was increasingly bypassed by all parties and became a virtual dead letter after Nazi Germany invaded Poland and Czechoslovakia.

At the end of World War II, the victorious powers eschewed collective security regimes and instead divided Europe into two competing zones of political dominance. The territorial settlements after the war were established through force—driven by the emerging dynamics of a tight East-West bipolarity where Central Europe served as a critical battleground. There was no Paris Peace Conference to establish a postwar order once major hostilities had ended in Europe. Instead, the terms of the settlement were hammered out behind closed doors between Franklin Delano Roosevelt, Winston Churchill, and Joseph Stalin. A new balance of power had already emerged between the United States and the Soviet Union in the final year of the war; each side had begun to regard its erstwhile ally warily, recognizing that whoever managed to "liberate" the countries of Central Europe would also have considerable influence over their foreign and domestic policies. As the East-West rivalry began to heat up, the region remained divided and physically occupied by both Soviet and Western forces.

Focused on their bipolar contest, the Great Powers were rather less concerned with the status of minorities in the region, much less with redrawing the borders of the states of East Central Europe to approximate the idealized one-to-one nation-state fit. Instead, the countries' borders were largely restored to their prewar locations, returning the territories that had been reannexed by Bulgaria, Hungary, and Germany to their prewar owners. The most dramatic adjustments involved populations, not borders. The Central and East European states assumed a more homogeneous character as a result of the systematic exterminations and killings of Jews, Slavs, and Roma prior to and during the war; reprisal killings by formerly victimized groups after the war; expulsions of groups both during and after the war; and voluntary migration, expulsions, and population exchanges after the war.[17]

The principles of minority protection that undergirded the League regime fell into ill repute. Political leaders had seen how minority rights and self-determination could be used to justify the territorial expansion of revisionist states; Nazi Germany had openly used the League of Nations minorities regime to justify its incursions into Poland and Czechoslovakia. Averse to collectivist ideologies, now associated with National Socialism and fascism, Western leaders decided that recognizing group and minority rights in international institutions was unlikely to stabilize the postwar order and might even undermine peace and security. Consequently, minority rights appeared nowhere in the United Nations documents that laid the groundwork for the postwar order.[18] Population transfers, political repression, and foreign occupation kept the peace in Europe for forty-five years, not cooperative conflict management.

At the end of the Cold War, a new regional security regime began to take shape in Central and Eastern Europe, looking in some ways like a return to the past. Similar to the interwar League regime, the post–Cold War regime was a response to the implosion of large, ethno-federal states—namely Yugoslavia and the Soviet Union. As these states began to fragment, a number of national conflicts—involving the Croats, Muslims, and Serbs in Bosnia; the Serbs in Croatia; and the Albanians in Kosovo and Macedonia—threatened to escalate into inter-state conflicts. Restive Hungarian minorities in Yugoslavia, Romania, and Slovakia, as well as aggrieved Russian-speakers in Latvia and Estonia, appeared to pose additional threats. Western leaders watched these events with considerable apprehension, while policy makers and scholars alike warned of a wave of nationalism that threatened to destabilize the Eurasian continent, if not the world at large. U.S. president Bill Clinton proclaimed that the end of the Cold War "lifted the lid from the cauldron of long-simmering hatreds. Now the entire global terrain is bloody with such conflicts."[19] Observers, too, believed that the collapse of the Soviet Union would lead to significant violent conflict and confidently predicted that we would soon be longing for the bad old days of the Cold War.[20]

Fearing the spread of anarchy, Western governments attempted to shore up the territorial integrity of the existing states for as long as they possibly could. In 1991, the European Community (EC) announced "a common position on the process of recognition" of new states: the EC was committed to the principle of self-determination and minority rights so long as they were exercised within "*existing frontiers which can only be changed by peaceful means and by common agreement.*"[21] Unsurprisingly, this proclamation did little to halt the dissolution of Yugoslavia. The EC failed even to prevent its own member states from adhering to this position, as Austria and Germany openly supported the independence of Slovenia and Croatia; Macedonia and Bosnia-Herzegovina declared independence soon afterward.[22]

As the Bosnian war escalated, European leaders resolved to establish a new security regime to monitor and de-escalate minority conflicts in the region. The Conference on Security and Co-operation in Europe (CSCE), originally a Cold War institution for promoting East-West dialogue, was reconfigured to manage emerging sectarian conflicts in postcommunist Europe.[23] To fulfill its mandate, the CSCE established the High Commissioner on National Minorities, which would use back-door diplomacy to *prevent* sudden crises from devolving into civil and inter-state violence. The High Commissioner would be "an instrument of conflict prevention at the earliest possible stage" by focusing "on disputes involving national minorities that have an international character and that have the propensity to cause inter-State tension or to ignite international armed conflict."[24]

Two additional European organizations would serve as monitors under the new regime. In 1992, the Council of Europe (CoE) adopted the Framework Convention for the Protection of National Minorities—the first legally binding instrument for enforcing group rights. Signatory states were required to report periodically to the CoE Committee of Ministers concerning the treatment of ethnic minorities in their borders.[25] The third, and by far most consequential, monitor was the European Union (EU). In 1993, the EU set out its "Copenhagen criteria"—a set of standards on human and minority rights that EU candidate countries would have to meet in order to obtain membership.[26] Indeed, it must be said that these criteria, and the power of EU membership conditionality more broadly, have given the EU something close to enforcement capabilities for target countries that are also candidates for EU accession.

Meanwhile, NATO, the United States, and other powerful Western states have served as the de facto enforcers of the post–Cold War security regime. Particularly during the Balkan wars of the 1990s, NATO acted as principal enforcer, peacemaker, and peacekeeper of Europe. A natural division of labor soon emerged—with NATO undertaking "hard" interventions and the CoE, the OSCE, and the EU employing "soft" interventions with the cooperation of the conflict parties—all under the rubric of UN-mandated missions. In postwar Bosnia and Kosovo, the EU has since assumed many of the tasks of "enforcer"—insisting that the accession countries fulfill standards on minority rights, among other things, before being admitted as full members of the EU. The post–Cold War regime is widely regarded as a success, at least in Central Europe and the Balkans.

Scholars have yet to exploit the opportunity for comparative discovery afforded by the two security regimes. In the case of the League of Nations, scholars focused disproportionately on its ultimate demise. Having failed to contain Nazi aggression in the 1930s and '40s, the League is commonly written off as an overly idealistic experiment in cooperative conflict management.[27] However, this overlooks the many victories achieved by the League in the 1920s, including effective arbitration of inter-state conflicts over Teschen, Silesia, and Mosul. One scholar wrote during the 1930s, "There are many, I myself one of their number, who do not believe that the system [of minorities protection] was foredoomed either to failure or to success. . . . We think that here, as in other vital questions of peace, there will be a long struggle against the anarchical factors in the Family of Nations, and the success or failure will be constantly in the balance."[28]

By contrast, scholars and policy makers have, if anything, *overstated* the potency of the contemporary European regime, crediting the OSCE and the High Commissioner with de-escalating conflicts in the Baltics and Macedonia in the 1990s.[29] Observers have also extolled the OSCE and the HCNM for their capacity to engage in sensitive and secretive preventive diplomacy, helping to ward off more violent bloodshed in the region.[30] U.S. secretary of state Warren Christopher averred that "OSCE's innovative work on crisis management and conflict prevention is one of the most promising experiments underway in Europe today."[31]

The analysis in this book shows that the success of cooperative interventions under both regimes depended to a significant degree on the stabilization of the external conflict environment. For instance, the OSCE and EU were able to achieve satisfactory technocratic solutions to minority conflicts in the Baltics and the Balkans because of U.S. and NATO management of destabilizing factors in the wider neighborhood. The same technocratic solutions were undermined in 1990s Kosovo and Macedonia because of the *lack* of regional stability. At the same time, the EU/OSCE security regime spectacularly failed to manage emerging conflicts in Chechnya, Georgia, Ukraine, and elsewhere in the Commonwealth of Independent States (CIS) region because of Western reluctance to manage Russian intransigence or check conflict spillover effects from neighboring states.

To serve as a corrective and tease out broader policy lessons for conflict management in general, I take a more granular view of the two regimes' intervention records. This means disaggregating the regimes into multiple interventions to be judged on their own terms. I exploit the variation of success *across* regimes and *within* interventions over time to identify the conditions that are broadly associated with successful conflict management—conditions that transcend the identity of the mediator, the stage of conflict, and the interests and perceptions of the conflict participants.

The argument developed in these pages is that conflict managers of *both* regimes were far more likely to achieve a successful outcome if powerful third parties acted to *nest the domestic disputes in a stable regional environment*. Put another way, cooperative (or soft-power) conflict management requires hard-power backing to achieve success. One scholar wrote that the League system "was not a substitute for great-power politics . . . but rather an adjunct to it. It was only a mechanism for conducting multinational diplomacy whose success or failure depended on the willingness of the states, and particularly the most powerful states, to use it."[32] Stephen Krasner likewise contended that the League system failed because "outcomes were the result of power and interests."[33] If they are right, then the failure of the League to de-escalate internal conflicts was due more to lack of Great Power interest in supporting League interventions than the institutional design of the League itself. France, Britain, and the United States (never a member of the League) failed to intervene proactively to stabilize the regional environment once Germany regained its dominant position in Central Europe. The proactive engagement of great powers is no less important today, with Russia, Ukraine, Serbia, Macedonia, Georgia, and Azerbaijan embroiled in border conflicts that threaten to escalate into regional conflagrations.

It is not enough that great powers be involved; they must also be involved intelligently. In other words, *what* these actors do may be just as important as *who* is doing it. I argue that effective civil conflict management requires building security from the outside in—that is, stabilizing the external environment before (or at the same time as) reconfiguring domestic institutions. If sectarian conflicts are securely "nested" in a stable regional and hegemonic environment, they are likely to become far more tractable; *cooperative* conflict management in particular is far likelier to meet with success. For the conflicts in Georgia, Ukraine, and Transnistria, this means deterring Russian cross-border involvement; for the Kashmir conflict, it means resolving the Indian-Pakistan border conflict and blocking Pakistani intervention; for many internal conflicts in the Middle East and North Africa (MENA) region, it means managing refugee flows and disrupting state sponsorship of terrorist organizations such as al Qaeda, the Islamic State of Iraq and Syria (ISIS), Hamas, and Hezbollah. Contrariwise, *failing* to securely nest sectarian struggles in a stable external environment may be setting peacemakers and peacekeepers up for an impossible task.

1

THE PROMISES AND PITFALLS OF COOPERATIVE CONFLICT MANAGEMENT

The end of the Cold War brought many changes to global governance, not least of which was a technocratic revolution in the management of intra-state conflict.[1] During the 1990s, the world powers resolved to work together to achieve a lasting peace, which partially meant refocusing their energies from ending civil war to preventing mass violence in the first place.[2] A leading authority on peace research decried the international community's "myopic focus on crisis negotiation," proclaiming that "too little attention is paid to the prevention of conflicts in the latent stages."[3] UN secretary-general Kofi Annan avowed, "For the United Nations but also for me, personally, as Secretary-General there is no higher goal, no deeper commitment, and no greater ambition than preventing armed conflict."[4] The 2000 Report of the Panel on United Nations Peace Operations concluded, "Prevention is clearly far more preferable for those who would otherwise suffer the consequences of war, and is a less costly option for the international community than military action, emergency humanitarian relief or reconstruction after a war has run its course."[5] In this spirit, a number of international organizations emerged to facilitate peaceful ends to emerging wars, including the International Crisis Group, International Alert, the Crisis Management Initiative, the Centre for Humanitarian Dialogue, Swisspeace, Conciliation Resources, and numerous regional organizations.[6] These and other actors have sought to suppress conflicts in their early stages—using early warning mechanisms, preventive diplomacy, mediation, arbitration, conditionality, and other methods of cooperative conflict management to ameliorate internecine struggles around the world.[7]

In a related trend, states and international organizations (particularly the UN and the United States) have increasingly favored cooperative over coercive techniques of managing intra-state conflict.[8] Cooperative conflict management is "a form of third-party intervention in a conflict . . . [that is] not based on the direct use of force and is not aimed at helping one of the participants to win . . . [but] to bring the conflict to a settlement that is acceptable to both sides."[9] Preventive diplomacy is a variant of cooperative conflict management that aims to defuse low-intensity conflicts before they lead to widespread violence. Michael Lund describes preventive diplomacy as "actions or institutions

that are used to keep the political disputes that arise between or within nations from escalating into armed conflict"; Stephen Stedman describes it as
"concerted action designed to resolve, manage, or contain disputes before they
become violent."[10] In practical terms, this means offering incentives for peace
to the parties in conflict, such as membership in international organizations,
financial aid, or "good offices" through which settlements can be negotiated in
lieu of war.[11]

There are several reasons why cooperative techniques are particularly well
suited for defusing *low-intensity* conflicts.[12] First, and most obviously, addressing nascent disputes before they escalate is best accomplished through skillful backdoor diplomacy. Second, participants are likely to be more open to
diplomatic solutions in the early stages of conflict than after years of warfare,
at which point negotiated settlements become exponentially more difficult
to achieve. Third, cooperative conflict management seeks out positive-sum
solutions that improve the status of at least one side of the dispute without leaving either side worse off. This stands against zero-sum interventions
that leverage one side against the other, creating a moral hazard that perversely exacerbates internal tensions.[13] Such a conservative approach is ideal
for de-escalating minor conflicts, where the aim is to bring calm rather than
dramatically change facts on the ground. Finally, whereas violent intervention
tends to undermine state capacity, a cooperative approach is more likely to
enhance state institutions—a critical assist to weakened or transitioning states
that must suddenly deal with challenger groups at the same time that they face
other pressing domestic or international concerns.

While much of the conflict-resolution literature focuses on how to conduct (relatively short-term) coercive interventions, relatively little is known
about the conditions for successful *cooperative* conflict management. This is
all the more striking given the growing centrality of this approach in the
peace-building toolbox since the end of the Cold War.[14] The interwar and
post–Cold War European regimes are two of the most highly institutionalized experiments in soft-power conflict management, yielding a voluminous
archival record—including both primary and secondary data—compiled by
historians and security studies scholars. It therefore makes sense to mine the
history of these regimes to explain their variable success, and thus the variable
success of mediation in general. Using structured-focused comparative analysis, I examine these data closely, finding that *building nested security from the
outside in* (that is, containing turbulence in the external environment) is critical to containing emerging communal conflict, particularly where the third
party has a limited coercive capacity. This is because mediators have neither
the tools nor the mandate to contain conflict spillover from the neighborhood or to prevent a neighboring state from sending in troops. In the absence

of military occupation or some other application of force, global or regional powers must back third-party mediations by neutralizing the external conflict environment at the same time that the third party conducts its mediation. Otherwise, cross-border flows of refugees, guns, and fighters and/or neighbor state interventions may upset any peaceful settlement that is brokered at the domestic level. The upshot is that in the absence of regional stability, cooperative techniques may not succeed *even when conditions on the ground are optimal for conflict mediation.* Throughout the book, I explore an even bolder claim that domestic peace can be built from the outside in, even when conditions on the ground are *sub*optimal for conflict mediation.

The remainder of this chapter lays the groundwork for this argument. The first section outlines the puzzle that takes center stage in the book—why soft-power conflict management appears to work in some places, but not in others. Next, I present a theory of nested security to account for this puzzle, showing that the wider conflict environment can account for a great deal of domestic conflict. I then explain the role of regional security regimes in managing these "nested" conflicts. This is followed by an outline of the research design, including the metric used to gauge intervention "success." Finally, I explain my focus on conflicts in Europe and lay out the plan of the book.

What Explains Variation in Mediation Success?

I seek to explain why, over the course of a single intervention, communal tensions on the ground can vary—sometimes dramatically—over time. I measure "success" as a marked *reduction in the level of collective tensions* between the minority and dominant group (or majority).[15] This is a departure from more conventional measures of success, which is the *nonoccurrence* or cessation of violence in a given hot spot. There are a number of reasons why it makes practical sense to measure "success" as the reduction of communal tensions. First, as a general rule, the line that separates success from failure is fairly arbitrary, so dichotomization is best avoided wherever possible. Second, it is highly problematic to attribute the cause of a nonevent (the absence of civil war) to any factor in particular. This is because the nonoccurrence of mass violence cannot be definitively connected to the presence or absence of any given factor. By focusing instead on the *level* of conflict over time, I locate the point at which the shift occurred and apply backward induction to trace the chain of events that instigated the reduction or escalation of conflict. Third, dichotomized outcomes imply that once success is achieved, the conflict is terminated. However, mediations are often long-term affairs in which communal tensions are sometimes contained, but rarely decisively resolved; they usually fluctuate over time. Much as domestic law enforcement manages (but does not eliminate) violent crime in society, third-party mediators (particularly those operating under regional security regimes) must engage in long-term "policing" of communal conflicts that, once left alone, could re-escalate at a later date.

For these reasons, I use "success" and "failure" as shorthand for the de-escalation and escalation of communal tensions over the course of a single mediation. In practice, I focus on explaining *shifts* in communal conflict, beginning at the point when the intervention has begun. By combining process tracing and comparative historical analysis, I unpack the causal chain of events that connects the level of conflict on the ground with events in the state, the mediator, and the wider neighborhood. To do so, I periodize multiyear mediations into higher and lower conflict phases and trace the micro-processes that alter the level of communal tensions from one period to the next. This allows me to identify the conditions at time t = 0 that precipitate a reduction (or escalation) in conflict at time t = 1. If the theory of nested security is correct, then the *de*stabilization of the wider environment should lead to conflict escalation—even if domestic-level factors are ripe for peace. By contrast, the neutralization of conflict dynamics in the wider environment is expected to reduce the level of conflict on the ground, all other things being equal. If the model is generalizable, I expect to observe a similar general pattern across different cases, historical periods, mediators, domestic institutions, and conflict participants.

The Argument

The theory of nested security holds that successful cooperative conflict management requires a neutralized external environment. Indeed, nested security may be not just a necessary, *but also a sufficient*, condition for domestic conflict reduction. The theory rests on the observation that protracted internal conflicts are rarely confined to the borders of a single state—what Buhaug and Gleditsch call the "closed polity" thesis of civil wars[16]—but are instead horizontally and vertically "nested" in regional and/or global conflict processes. As George Modelski once put it, "Internal wars occur not only within a political system but also within an international system."[17] Gary Goertz likewise argues that internal conflicts are nested within a wider international context.[18] In fact, fully three-quarters of the civil wars waged since the end of the Cold War featured intervention by foreign governments—most often neighboring states with a significant stake in the outcome.[19] Domestic conflicts are also bound up in transnational conflict processes, such as diaspora activism (either transnational or transborder); the actions of external interest groups, networks, or multinational corporations; conflict spillover from neighboring states; wider events such as financial crises, regional war, and political transition; and demonstration effects from conflicts in other states.[20]

There are numerous ways that the regional environment can accelerate a domestic conflict, even when it is undergoing third-party mediation. One is through *contagion*, where civil war in one state pushes refugees, weapons, and warriors across state borders.[21] Examples include the 1994 Rwandan war, when Hutu refugees fleeing the Rwandan Patriotic Front sparked a vicious civil war in neighboring Congo; also, the 1997 civil unrest in Albania, which produced a flood of weapons that were trafficked over the border for use in the Kosovo Liberation Army (KLA) insurgency. Weapons and fighters have considerable longevity and may turn up in numerous wars in a given region. For instance, U.S. weapons transferred to the mujahedeen during the Soviet occupation of Afghanistan in the 1980s later turned up in the 1990s wars in Bosnia and Kosovo; the mujahedeen themselves participated in these conflicts as volunteers and mercenary soldiers. Most recently, the civil conflict in Syria gave rise to the so-called Islamic State insurgents, who captured territory in eastern Syria before moving across the border to seize oil-rich areas of northern Iraq. Regions plagued by conflict spillover are sometimes described as "bad neighborhoods."[22] Idean Salehyan has identified three uniquely dangerous neighborhoods or "conflict clusters" in West Africa, the Middle East, and Southeast Asia where cross-border flows of refugees, weapons, and warriors serve to perpetuate civil violence in an endless feedback loop.[23] In 2001, former KLA fighters slipped over the Kosovo border into Macedonia, igniting a violent conflict between Skopje and the Albanian minority. Cross-border ethnic ties, too, can escalate domestic conflict when the political leaders of the first state attempt to "rescue" a domestic constituency's transborder kin as a means of securing their electoral support.[24] A rebel movement in one state can likewise use the territory of a second state as a physical sanctuary, escalating conflict in the first state, as seen when the Tamil Tiger rebels used the Indian state of Tamil Nadu as a safe haven from which to strike back at the Sri Lankan government.[25]

Second, the regional environment might prolong or exacerbate domestic conflict through *diffusion* or demonstration effects, as a successful movement in one place inspires activists in another place to mimic these tactics in hopes of achieving the same result.[26] Methods of resistance in one conflict are routinely copied by groups that find themselves in similar situations elsewhere. Mark Beissinger, for example, demonstrated that the momentum triggered by 1980s independence movements in the Baltics led to a cascade of independence movements in other Soviet republics, including Georgia, Armenia, and Azerbaijan. A similar cascade effect through social media could be seen in the

2011 Arab Spring conflicts in the Middle East and North Africa.[27] Although diffusion need not occur at the regional level, it is often confined to a given region owing to proximity, cultural similarities, and other network effects.

Third, bilateral conflicts between the host state and another state in the region can greatly fuel internal disputes, in what Gary Goertz and Paul Diehl have called "enduring rivalries."[28] In fact, many civil wars began as border conflicts between rival states, including the 1970s Ethiopian-Somali war over Ogaden, the 1960s and '70s Greco-Turkish conflict over Cyprus, the 1990s Croatian-Serbian war over territory in Croatia and Bosnia, the periodic Indian-Pakistani conflict over Kashmir, recurrent Israeli-Lebanese conflict over South Lebanon, and so on. In many of these border conflicts, the disputed regions are rarely ordinary pieces of land, but have significant economic or geopolitical value to the disputant states. In decades past, control over south Lebanon and the Golan Heights, for example, offered important strategic advantages to the regional rivals of Lebanon, Syria, and Israel.

Nearly all the civil conflicts considered in this book were exacerbated and prolonged by conflicts and actors at the regional level. Through the first half of the twentieth century, the Åland Islands were sought by Finland, Sweden, Germany, and Russia, as control over the islands offered states a decisive advantage in the event of naval warfare in the Baltic Sea. After the First World War, the Teschen region was claimed by both Czechoslovakia and Poland because it was rich in coal and contained a vital railway from the Czech lands to southern Slovakia. The contested Saar Basin and Upper Silesia were mineral-rich regions that were invaluable for developing industrial economies in the region. Finally, Memel and Danzig were sought by Lithuania, Poland, and Germany, as important shipping outlets to the Baltic Sea.

Border disputes are typically driven by competing claims to the land rather than by co-ethnics residing on the land. What separates contested from uncontested border regions is not violations of national self-determination, but the value of the territory itself.[29] This does not, however, mean that such conflicts take place merely at the international level. They also have an important local or substate component, involving another set of conflict parties (here, the minority and state majority). The complexity of such conflicts—with numerous "veto players" standing in the way of peaceful resolution[30]—is what makes them unusually protracted or intense; it is for this reason I call them "nested conflicts."

"Nested *In*security" and the Path to Conflict Escalation

But how do the different layers of conflict interact? In the field of international relations, much of the scholarship argues for a feedback loop or *bidirectionality* of international and domestic-level conflict processes, where foreign patrons exacerbate civil wars while civil wars draw in external patrons, leading to a wider regional conflagration.[31] Indeed, the very notion of "internationalized" civil war suggests that internal conflicts spread beyond state borders like contagious disease vectors and thence become internationalized. While it is true that contagion and spillover effects from neighboring civil wars (cross-border flows of refugees, guerrilla fighters, and movement activists) *do* move in both directions, active interventions by kin states or major powers are generally driven by their own agendas. Foreign governments are rarely "pulled into" conflicts against their will to "rescue" their beleaguered ethnic brethren. While it is true that homeland governments routinely pay lip service to the status of cross-border ethnic kin, they seldom intervene to help unless they perceive it to be in their geopolitical interest. Indeed, quantitative analysis has shown that homeland states are no more likely to intervene on behalf of their co-ethnics when they are repressed than when they are not.[32] Governments instead intervene for their own geopolitical reasons or to satisfy domestic political pressures—for example, to serve the interests of their ethnic constituents or powerful economic or political elites.[33]

Kin state interventions may even take place *against* the wishes of their co-ethnics. A particularly poignant example is provided by the Bosnian war. As Serb-dominated Yugoslav units and Croatian forces pushed into Bosnia in 1992, local activists and political leaders led peace marches to avert the coming proxy war between Zagreb and Belgrade over Bosnian territory. The upshot of this is that local intergroup compromises—achieved through informal brokerage or electoral engineering—may be insufficient for resolving internal conflicts so long as wider conflict processes remain unchecked. This is because regional or international conflict dynamics operate according to a distinct logic, often disconnected from the stakes of conflict at the local level. What this means is that peace mediators ignore the interests of regional players, and the dynamics of the wider conflict neighborhood, at their peril.

None of this is to say that so-called internationalized civil wars do not have domestic drivers. Very often, secessionist struggles are driven either by a fight between the state majority and local minority over state resources such as oil, diamonds, or otherwise valuable land (consider the examples of Iraqi Kurds, the Cabindans in Angola, the Aceh in Indonesia, the South Sudanese, the Ibo in Nigeria, European or Chinese minorities in various sub-Saharan African countries, and the like). Sometimes, too, conflicts rage over the exclusion of one or more groups from state power or discrimination (Tamils in Sri Lanka, Catholics in Northern Ireland, blacks in South Africa, and so on). The point is that, once external conflict dynamics interact with internal conflict dynamics, these conflicts tend to reinforce one another, making it exponentially harder to suppress or contain an emerging civil conflict through soft-power conflict management.

"Nested Security" and the Path to Conflict Reduction

Mediators are usually aware that regional conflict processes pose a threat to their efforts to suppress emerging conflicts. They therefore sometimes try to neutralize or *exogenously stabilize* conflict dynamics in the neighborhood by recruiting powerful states or international organizations to broker a pact between the rival states. This effectively de-triangulates the conflict, making it easier to resolve. They may also seek the assistance of major powers in containing ongoing wars in neighboring states or controlling the borders of the target state. As regional rivals withdraw from the conflict state and the borders are more effectively policed, the civil conflict will become easier to contain through soft power. Still, the conflict participants may remain mobilized because the peace has been externally (rather than internally) induced through pressure or conditionality by powerful states or organizations. The combatant parties understand that once the third party withdraws, regional rivalry may reemerge, reigniting tensions at the domestic level. As a result, internal cleavages are likely to remain salient, increasing the likelihood of conflict recurrence.

A more stable peace becomes possible when the participants in the conflict (including rival neighboring states) have *endogenous* incentives to broker a settlement. For instance, the Catholics and Protestants in Northern Ireland became much more amenable to a power-sharing solution once Ireland and Britain agreed to work together to end the conflict. A permanent de-escalation of tensions at the domestic level can occur once the combatants expect to gain a joint peace dividend from the deal, rendering it self-enforcing. Assuming these incentives are sustained over time, the domestic divide can gradually lose political salience.[34]

In short, the theory of nested security calls for an "outside-in" approach to cooperative conflict management. It says that mediation is most likely to succeed when minority-majority relations are "nested" in a stable external environment. Hence, mediators are advised to stabilize the wider conflict setting before, or at the same time as, they attempt to reduce tensions at the domestic level through electoral engineering and the like. This book demonstrates that "nested security" is a key background condition for successful conflict reduction, regardless of the resources of the third party, the intervention strategy, and the attitudes of the government and minority representatives.

Regional Security Regimes

Cooperative conflict management aims to de-escalate conflicts using neither military force nor economic "compellence," but by offering technical solutions to policy problems.[35] Jacob Bercovitch defines mediation as a "process of conflict management . . . whereby the disputing parties or their representatives seek the assistance, or accept an offer of help from an individual, group, state or organization to change, affect or influence their perceptions or behavior, without resorting to physical force, or invoking the authority of the law."[36] As noted earlier, such mediation may be undertaken by any number of third parties, including states, international organizations, nongovernmental organizations, or even private citizens. Powerful states and individuals routinely engage in one-off cooperative interventions, as seen in Norwegian peace envoy Erik Solheim's initiative to broker a peace deal between the Tamil Tiger rebels and the government of Sri Lanka in the 2000s. Other examples include the serial mediations in Sudan, especially following the Comprehensive Peace Agreement of 2005; U.S. efforts to mediate the sectarian conflict in Northern Ireland in the late 1990s; and Russian mediation of civil conflicts in Nagorno-Karabakh and Transnistria.

In recent decades, intergovernmental organizations (IGOs) and nongovernmental organizations (NGOs) have been increasing their capacity for soft-power conflict management at the global level. The UN has numerous agencies that now engage in mediation, including the Department for Peacekeeping Operations, the International Peace Institute (formerly the International Peace Academy), the UN Department of Political Affairs, and the United Nations Development Programme. As early as the mid-1950s, Secretary-General Dag Hammarskjöld called for developing such tools—a call repeated by Secretary-General Boutros Boutros-Ghali in his *Agenda for Peace*, which he delivered to the UN Security Council in 1992. Secretary-General Ban Ki-Moon followed in his predecessors' footsteps by calling on the Security Council to build a stronger preventative capacity for the UN.[37] Since 2000, the secretary-general's list of special representatives and advisers to troubled regions or countries has included more than one hundred people; a new UN mediation support unit was created in 2006 and now has a standby team of mediation experts to handle especially difficult disputes.[38] While these are welcome developments, I argue that there are compelling reasons for building conflict prevention capacities at the regional level.

A *regional security regime* is a set of norms and practices established within a certain territorial remit to halt the escalation of violent conflict within and/or between states.[39] Katarina Engberg writes that such regimes have advantages that facilitate mediation success because of their "closeness to the conflicts."[40] They also possess instruments that can be used to de-escalate emerging violence, including forums where creative solutions to disputes can be developed and shared with other peacemakers. Bercovitch and Gartner argue that regional organizations (the principal mediators in regional security regimes) are most effective at containing emerging conflicts because of their "proximity, cultural similarity, and comparative informality."[41]

There are other reasons why regional security regimes can be expected to succeed where global regimes fail. First, organizations and states are more inclined to invest the necessary resources to manage conflicts that take place in their own backyard. Moreover, managing latent conflict requires long-term involvement by third-party mediators—and this is most likely under the auspices of regional security regimes. High levels of institutionalization—also common to regional organizations—tend to enhance mediation success, as they establish roles, and coordinate the activities, of monitors and enforcers in each conflict setting.[42] For instance, regional security regimes often establish a division of labor between monitors who evaluate the degree of tensions in designated "hot spots" or "danger zones" and enforcers who implement the judgments of the monitors. Nearly a century ago, the Minorities Section and League Council acted as conflict monitors while the Allied powers served as enforcers. Today, the OSCE and European Union act as monitors while NATO and major powers serve as enforcers. These monitors and enforcers are in turn subject to oversight bodies, adding an additional layer to the process. In this way, regional security regimes lock in third-party mediators and enforcers, institutionalizing the process of conflict management for the long haul.

In fact, there has always been a place for regional regimes in the global security architecture. Chapter VIII (Article 52:2) of the UN Charter reads in part that member states shall "make every effort to achieve pacific settlement of local disputes through . . . regional arrangements or by . . . regional agencies before referring them to the Security Council." This suggests a division of labor between the UN and regional security institutions where regional bodies handle low-intensity conflicts, while the UN steps in when violence escalates (although in practice, Chapter VIII has not precluded distressed states from appealing to the UN Security Council from the very beginning).

The end of the Cold War has coincided with the growing centrality of regional regimes, as major powers become increasingly reluctant to engage in global conflict management—either unilaterally or through the United Nations.[43] The wars in Rwanda, Bosnia, and Somalia during the 1990s caught the UN flat-footed in response, while vetoes in the Security Council and the lack of resources have prevented the UN from developing timely reactions to the crises in Kosovo and Iraq, among other places. At the same time, regional organizations have increasingly taken on the tasks of *intra*-state conflict management, with ever greater success,[44] while some (such as the EU, OAS, and AU) have developed a hard-power capacity. Altogether, this has meant that regional security regimes have taken over many of the responsibilities of conflict management that were earlier relegated to superpowers and their allies during the Cold War. Since that time, we have also seen increasing "multilateralization" of peace missions, where the UN or major powers delegate many peace-building tasks in a conflict state to organizations such as the EU, the Economic Community of West African States (ECOWAS), the African Union (AU), the Intergovernmental Authority of Development (IGAD), and the Arab League—who have become "regional subcontractors to UN-mandated missions."[45] Lake and Morgan write, "In the foreseeable future . . . efforts to cope with violent conflicts, as well as to achieve order and security, will primarily involve arrangements and actions devised and implemented at the regional level."[46]

Indeed, regional regimes have proliferated around the world to address unmet security needs. Wallensteen and Bjurner counted some thirty-one regional organizations that are involved in peacemaking.[47] The most developed and institutionalized of these is the contemporary EU/OSCE regime in Central and Eastern Europe. Other regional regimes include the AU; the quasi-formalized regime in Latin America associated with the Organization of American States (OAS); the Association of Southeast Asian Nations (ASEAN) Regional Forum (ARF); and the Shanghai Cooperation Organization (SCO) and Collective Security Treaty Organization (CSTO) in Eurasia.[48] Although several of these were originally economic organizations, a few have developed hard military power, and even more have established a mechanism for conflict prevention within their respective territorial remits. For instance, the AU changed its doctrine from noninterference in member states' internal affairs to a principle of "non-indifference" in the face of imminent security threats.[49] Article 1 of the OAS Charter stipulates that the organization create "an order of peace and justice [among member states], to promote their solidarity, to strengthen their collaboration, and to defend their sovereignty, their territorial integrity, and their independence." At the same time, new regional regimes have been added to the mix, including the Union of South American Nations, now active in the area of preventive diplomacy, and the Biketawa Declaration of the Pacific Island Forum (2000), which called for a diplomatic response to conflicts in the Pacific Islands. There is also the Organization of the Islamic Conference (OIC), which helped mediate the separatist conflict in the Philippines and which recently established a conflict prevention arm called the Peace, Security and Mediation Unit at its headquarters in Jeddah, Saudi Arabia.[50]

Although cooperative intervention lies at the heart of such regimes, coercive backing plays a critical role in their success. Indeed, the more entrenched the conflict, the more indispensable hard-power backing becomes—partly so the mediators themselves will be perceived as credible in the eyes of the conflict participants. When it comes to regional security regimes, hard power is usually provided by the region's major powers or hegemons (for example, Germany, the UK, and France for the EU/OSCE; Nigeria and South Africa for the AU). This is because regional powers have both the resources and strategic incentives to monitor at-risk states in the neighborhood as well as the capacity and willingness to resolve nascent conflicts within close proximity. One need only consider the fact that Germany, France, and Britain invested far more in managing the conflicts in the western Balkans than they have in West Africa—the management of which has been largely relegated to resource-poor IGOs such as the United Nations.[51] Hamstrung by weak mandates and the lack of hard power, the UN has often proved incapable of preventing major bloodletting, as seen in Rwanda in 1994 and more recently in South Sudan.[52] Insofar as UN peacekeeping missions have succeeded in containing violence in remote hot spots of the world, it is often because one or more major powers provided critical backing. Paul Diehl wrote that "Major powers have the military capacity and political influence to prod recalcitrant disputants to cooperate with the peacekeeping force" while offering key political support to the organizing agency and "contributing money, logistical support, and other forms of help to the peacekeeping operation."[53] This is the very reason why regional security regimes—which usually have the backing of a motivated regional hegemon—may be better equipped than the UN to undertake conflict prevention.

Since the management of low-intensity civil conflicts is the focus of this book, I have chosen to investigate two experiments in soft-power conflict management in interwar and post–Cold War Europe. Using a rich empirical record, I explore historical and contemporary sources to answer why some of these engagements appear to have succeeded while others failed spectacularly.

Case Selection

There are a number of reasons for conducting this research in Central and Eastern Europe. To begin with, Europe is the site of not one, but two, of the most institutionalized systems of cooperative conflict management in the world. In contrast to the well-elaborated League Minority Protection System and the EU/OSCE system of conflict prevention, other regional security regimes are less institutionalized. The security arm of ASEAN is relatively weak and informal, basically amounting to ad hoc consultations by state governments to resolve conflicts in the region. Africa's Economic Community of West African States Monitoring Group (ECOMOG) consists mainly of a formal arrangement whereby West African militaries organize ad hoc military interventions to resolve civil wars in the region. The AU, IGAD, and the

OAS have neither the institutional infrastructure nor a strong track record of containing emerging civil conflicts.[54] By contrast, third-party mediation in Europe is highly institutionalized, invasive, vertically integrated, and aimed at long-term management of communal conflicts at the substate level.

Second, Europe's security regimes have made conditionality and diplomacy the centerpiece of conflict management in the context of highly regularized, decades-long mediation of emerging substate disputes. Therefore, these mediations are "most likely" cases for showcasing the power of cooperative mediation. If, under even the most auspicious conditions, the stability of the wider neighborhood remains a central facilitator for conflict management, these cases serve as "tough tests" of the theory of nested security, suggesting that cooperative conflict management can be significantly compromised by the state of the external environment, even under the best of circumstances.

A third reason for focusing on the region is that doing so offers quasi-experimental controls. Since both security regimes were established to manage conflicts in twentieth-century Central and Eastern Europe, the region's pre–World War I institutions and legacies can be effectively ruled out as explanations for variable mediation success. Varying effectiveness across the two regimes cannot be put down to a history of Ottoman, Habsburg, or German rule, nor can it be attributed to the location of these states in the buffer zone between East and West, nor to the fact that the countries in question endured serial foreign occupations over the centuries. Neither can such variation be explained by the region's relative backwardness vis-à-vis major West European states. In other words, pre-twentieth-century experiences cannot be invoked to explain differential success rates either between or within the two regimes.[55]

My case selection also facilitates *intra*-regime analysis. Conflict managers in both periods engaged in two strategies of cooperative intervention: *preventive diplomacy* and *induced devolution* (see chapter 2). Under preventive diplomacy, mediators persuade target states to implement integrationist minority rights—including affirmative action or education or language rights—to placate, and hence demobilize, rebelling minorities. Under induced devolution, mediators persuade the target states to solve the conflict through territorial solutions such as federalism or autonomy. Because the two strategies were used in both interwar and post–Cold War regimes, instances of each strategy may be fruitfully compared both within and across the two regimes to explain why some applications of the strategy met with success while others did not.

The two regimes also had a similar raison d'être, which was to stabilize regions undergoing massive political transition. This has meant managing nationalistic host states, separatist national minorities, and revisionist neighboring kin states; in so doing, they hoped to prevent civil and, ultimately, inter-state war. In both periods, the host or target states were also motivated to comply with third-party mediators—Central and East European governments consistently sought closer economic and political union with powerful Western governments—both to protect against neighboring revisionist states and improve their prospects for economic development. Because the target states sought closer relationships with the intervenors, conditionality became a powerful technique for inducing compliance in both periods.

Despite these apparently favorable starting conditions, cooperative conflict management yielded variable success not only across each regime, but also within interventions over time. I show that this variation is largely attributable to *variable nested security* in each case (that is, whether the internal conflict was nested in a peaceful or conflictual regional/external environment). This analysis demonstrates that the nested security propositions hold up for both regimes, suggesting there are general conditions for success that are untethered to a given set of historical circumstances. If this is true, it means that nested security is a precondition of successful mediation across time as well as space.

Policy Importance and Plan of the Book

This book is aimed at students and practitioners of security studies—particularly those who work on peace research, conflict mediation, security regimes, and conflict prevention. The nested security model implies that hard power may be indispensable to conflict management success because—while mediators may have the technical expertise to negotiate solutions to conflict—major powers provide the necessary power and clout to contain cross-border conflict contagion and induce regional rivals to broker compromises, giving them incentives to credibly commit to peace at both the international and domestic levels.[56] While the existing scholarship shows that regional instability is an important contributor to civil war, nested security spells out the concrete implications for effective third-party mediation. The central claim is intuitive, yet novel: third-party mediations are unlikely to de-escalate sectarian conflicts so long as the regional environment is not first (or simultaneously) stabilized. This is the foundation of the "outside-in" model of cooperative conflict management. I show that in the absence of this critical background condition, third-party mediation is likely to founder. What follows is a summary of subsequent chapters of the book.

Chapter 2 presents the full logic of nested security. The theory holds that protracted low-intensity conflicts are very often nested in rivalries between states or conflict-prone regions, and further, that external events and actors have an asymmetric impact on domestic-level conflicts. This means that major powers must "nest" low-intensity conflicts in a stable external environment before mediations can have a real chance of success. The chapter concludes by outlining the research design used to test this model against competing theories of mediation success using cases from interwar and post–Cold War Europe.

The empirical core of the book consists of qualitative process-tracing of cooperative mediations in both interwar and post–Cold War Europe. Chapter 3 explores cases of preventive diplomacy under the League of Nations regime. Here, I compare four of the most troubled minority conflicts undertaken by the League's Minorities Protection System—German minorities in Poland and Czechoslovakia, and Hungarian minorities in Romania and Czechoslovakia. Chapter 4 investigates the results of League interventions using induced devolution—to resolve conflicts over the Åland Islands and the free cities of Memel and Danzig.

The final two empirical chapters examine the record of cooperative conflict management under the post–Cold War security regime. Chapter 5 investigates cases of preventive diplomacy in the postcommunist period. During the 1990s, the OSCE HCNM focused its efforts primarily on the Russian-speaking minorities in Latvia and Estonia, as well as the Albanian minorities in Kosovo and Macedonia. Chapter 6 examines the use of induced devolution in postcommunist Europe. In the 2000s, the EU and NATO achieved variable success in managing the conflicts in Serbia and Montenegro, Macedonia and northern Kosovo by insisting that autonomy and power sharing be given to restive minorities in these countries.

Chapter 7 then tests the transportability of the nested security model beyond qualitative case studies in Europe using quantitative analysis of mediated low-intensity conflicts around the world from 1993 to 2004. The analysis is drawn from a coauthored paper that uses the Mediated Intra-State Conflicts (MILC) dataset, housed at the Uppsala University Department of Peace and Conflict Research. In the final chapter, I sketch the implications of this analysis for designing more effective regional security regimes both inside Europe and beyond.

Europe boasts a long history of cooperative conflict management, dating back to the 1815 Congress of Vienna. European powers made mediation the core of not just one, but two regional security regimes in the last century alone. Their architects hoped that these regimes would address the dual instabilities of imperial collapse and nation-state creation following totalizing wars in the heart of Europe. Both interwar and post–Cold War regimes were marked by successes as well as failures, begging the question: What accounts for the variable success of soft-power conflict management within and across regional security regimes?

To answer these questions, I conduct longitudinal analysis of individual mediations in designated "hot spots" of emerging communal violence within each period. Analysis over time of interwar and post–Cold War cases demonstrates that—regardless of the mediation strategy, the identity of the mediator, the historical circumstances, and the nature and incentives of conflict participants—successful cooperative conflict management requires the condition of "nested security." Put differently, third-party mediations are likely to bear fruit only *after* minority-majority relations on the ground are nested in a stable regional environment, which should in turn be nested in a secure hegemonic or global environment—much like Matryoshka nesting dolls. If the disputes remain embedded in these wider struggles or are subject to conflict spillover from the neighborhood, then even the best-designed mediations are likely to founder.

There are vital practical benefits to identifying the determinants of successful conflict mediation, as it remains the single best hope for arresting conflict spirals before they trigger widespread violence. Since the upsurge of violence that engulfed Eurasia and sub-Saharan Africa in the early 1990s, the United Nations and other conflict mediators have urged practitioners and scholars to devise early warning systems and routinized methods of shuttle diplomacy to enable mediators to contain substate tensions before they escalate to full-blown war. Once there is significant bloodshed, internal conflicts become much more difficult to resolve because of the dangerous path dependencies created by warfare. Ethnic cleansing and separatist violence generate powerful institutional interests in prolonging the violence: warlords and other war profiteers have strong incentives to maintain a state of perpetual conflict so they can reap the rewards of criminal enterprises and patronage networks established under conditions of war.[57] If internal tensions are contained in their early stages, through routinized methods of conflict prevention, such harmful path dependencies might be avoided.

2

THE THEORY OF NESTED SECURITY

How can third parties defuse emerging conflicts before they lead to large-scale violence? One possibility is that you need the right intervenor—one who is taken seriously and enjoys legitimacy in the eyes of conflict parties on the ground. To some, this means that the third party should be disinterested in the outcome of the dispute and operate by a set of commonly accepted rules.[1] Stephen Krasner has argued that the League of Nations minorities system "proved futile" because it was imposed on the target states rather than being entered into voluntarily through a self-enforcing contract. The logic follows that the new and defeated countries perceived the League as illegitimate, which is one reason it failed to prevent conflict escalation in the 1930s.[2] The problem with this explanation is that successful conflict management does not always require third-party legitimacy. Indeed, the League's most important achievements were racked up in the 1920s—when the new and enlarged states of Central Europe were most resentful of the minority treaties and openly questioned the League's authority to regulate their internal affairs. Others contend that mediations are most likely to yield success when the third party is *biased* or "interested" in the outcome, because its involvement is therefore seen as consequential by the combatants, and the third party is seen as committed to ensuring peace.[3] However, neither argument can explain the variable success of conflict mediation in Central Europe, since the identity and perceived interests of the mediators did not change over time, even though their effectiveness *did*.

Perhaps mediators are more likely to succeed when they employ skillful persuasion and diplomacy, or when the third party enjoys a certain degree of leverage over the conflict parties.[4] For example, Steve Ratner has argued that the High Commissioner on National Minorities "eased tensions between states . . . by influencing and persuading actors in situations of ethnic conflict to solve their dispute in a norm-based way."[5] Likewise, Konrad Huber observed that "the role of the High Commissioner . . . was instrumental in limiting further escalation of tensions and keeping options for further dialogue largely open."[6] I argue that scholars have probably overestimated the impact of the high commissioner, while underestimating the importance of background conditions, such as the promise of entering NATO and the EU, in yielding peace.[7] Indeed, it is precisely because of these background conditions that the high commissioner appears to have been quite influential in the Baltics, where prospects of joining NATO and the EU were credible and imminent, but not in the Caucasus or Central Asia, where governments have had little hope of joining western organizations.

Others contend that third parties can de-escalate low-intensity conflicts through "conditionality"—offering material rewards to the target states in return for implementing institutions calculated to reduce internal tensions. Indeed, numerous scholars have argued that external incentives, so long as they are highly valued, enhance a mediator's odds of success. In postcommunist Europe, both NATO and the EU have used political conditionality to pressure states in Central and Eastern Europe (CEE) to adopt liberal minority legislation. For example, Judith Kelley claims that "membership conditionality"—offering accession to valued organizations such as the EU and NATO in exchange for concessions—induced CEE governments to enact minority legislation in the 1990s, effectively reducing the potential for ethnic violence.[8] Milada Vachudova likewise argues that external pressure was a key motivator for implementing minority protections, as "passive" leverage (socialization) and "active" leverage (conditionality) led the Baltic and Central European countries to liberalize their policies, paving the way for domestic harmony.[9] Indeed, there is a qualified consensus in the literature that third-party conditionality played a key role in promoting minority protection and consequently peace in the region.[10] However, conciliatory minority policies *do not always* reduce internal tensions. History provides many examples of minority leaders that continually radicalized their positions—even against an accommodating government—so long as they believed they could extract substantial concessions by doing so. A textbook case is interwar Czechoslovakia, where Sudeten Germans were encouraged by Nazi Germany to rebel against the Prague government, despite being offered extensive territorial autonomy.[11]

It is also possible that successful mediation depends on domestic-level factors. Zsuzsa Csergő argues, for example, that toxic domestic politics exacerbated Hungarian minority conflicts in Romania and Slovakia during the 1990s. The Council of Europe and the OSCE were able to promote ethnic peace only *after* moderates had prevailed over extremists on both sides of the conflict—a political shift that occurred internally rather than in response to external conditionality.[12] Concessions such as power sharing and territorial autonomy reassure the minority (as well as the minority's homeland state) that the majority has neither the intent nor the capacity to discriminate against the minority, reducing its incentives to mobilize.[13] In this view, a domestic culture of tolerance and domestic reconciliation is essential for conflict reduction, and this cannot be induced by outside actors.[14]

The problem with these explanations is that they focus disproportionately on the government side of the equation.[15] Although the actions of the government are critical to internal peace, so too are the actions of the minority. Government liberalization (through new or enhanced minority protections) cannot inoculate a country against violence so long as the minority is incentivized to pursue conflict. In Sri Lanka, for example, anti-Tamil discrimination long predated the emergence of a Tamil separatist movement in the 1980s (which in turn was fueled by the existence of cross-border military bases in the Indian state of Tamil Nadu), at which point the government had actually begun to *reverse* its discriminatory policies. New pro-minority policies did little to prevent the rapid growth of the Tamil insurgency, leading ultimately to a decades-long bloody civil war and tens of thousands of deaths. A textbook case of the dangers of minority leverage is given by the Sudeten Germans of interwar Czechoslovakia, who mobilized violently against Prague in the 1930s despite a decade of internal power sharing and extensive autonomy arrangements for German-speaking areas. The problem was that these minorities had few incentives to pursue peace, empowered as they were by a resource-rich diaspora in the first case and an aggressively revisionist homeland state in the second. Finally, wider *contextual or international* factors may also affect mediation success. Wars in neighboring states generate cross-border flows of weapons, refugees, and guerrilla fighters—intensifying communal conflicts in the target state, despite the presence of determined mediators.[16] National homelands, diasporas, rival states, or major powers may also intervene directly in the target state to tip the scales of conflict on one side or the other.

Table 2.1 lists the main rival theories for mediation success and derives predictions for each. In brief, cooperative conflict management is more likely to succeed if the third party enjoys legitimacy in the eyes of the conflict parties, has the support of major powers, can offer significant incentives for peace, and uses effective mediation strategies. Factors (4) and (5) relate to domestic-level conditions that promote peaceful outcomes. Namely, if the target government is moderate or offers the minority significant concessions, then a negotiated solution is more likely. Contextual factors are examined separately in the theory section, as they are broadly compatible with the nested security model.

Table 2.1 Competing explanations for mediation success

Determinants of mediation success	Prediction
THIRD-PARTY FACTORS 1. Third-party legitimacy/resources 2. Incentives for peace (big carrots) 3. Major-power support for intervention 4. Effective negotiation setting	When the third-party intervenor enjoys legitimacy in the eyes of all conflict parties, commands significant resources, has credible sticks and carrots to induce compliance, and/or uses an effective negotiation process, its mediations are more likely to succeed, all else equal.
DOMESTIC FACTORS 5. Government liberalization; moderate elites come to power 6. Power-sharing institutions; minority autonomy; electoral engineering	When host governments accommodate restive minorities through greater rights and access to economic and political power, and/or when moderates come to power, conflict mediation is more likely to achieve success, all else equal.
CONTEXTUAL / NESTED SECURITY FACTORS 7. Containing cross-border contagion or diffusion effects 8. Hegemonic leveling—inducing pacts between host government and external patrons	When aggressive kin states or other external spoilers[a] are neutralized, and regional conflicts contained, substate sectarian disputes will be easier to mediate.

[a] "Spoilers" are political or military factions or extremist groups who attempt to derail peace process in the context of conflict resolution. For more on the problem of "spoilers"—domestic actors who upset peace deals because they stand to gain from continuing the conflict—see Stedman 1997; Greenhill and Major 2006/7; Fortna 2008; Newman and Richmond 2006.

The Anatomy of Nested Civil Conflicts

To see why nested security is critical to mediation success, we must first review the anatomy of nested conflicts. Although civil conflicts are traditionally characterized as a dyadic dispute between a minority and majority at the substate level, much of the recent scholarship focuses on "internationalized" civil conflicts, which feature intervention by a "system member" or state.[17] External influences on internal conflicts may have increased over time. J. David Singer and his colleagues reckon that "internationalized" civil wars occur at more than double the rate after 1960 as before 1960.[18]

A domestic dispute takes on an international dimension when two or more foreign governments wage a proxy war in that state because they believe direct confrontation is too dangerous or risky (examples include U.S.-Soviet proxy wars in Afghanistan, Angola, Korea, and Vietnam).[19] A conflict may also become internationalized when neighboring states intervene to annex minority territory or because they wish to dominate the third state or the region as a whole (see the recent Russian interventions in secessionist conflicts in

Georgia and Ukraine). Interstate competition over territory, waterways, and other resources has been an important driver of inter-state conflict throughout history.[20]

Internal conflicts may also become internationalized laterally, as when transborder diaspora groups or transnational activist networks intervene in a civil dispute, exacerbating simmering communal struggles (see table 2.2). For example, the Kosovo conflict became much deadlier when the Albanian diaspora began to support the insurgents financially through the Homeland Calling Fund; likewise, the Tamil Tiger insurgency in Sri Lanka received a critical assist from diaspora fund-raising in Western countries.[21] The flow of weapons and soldiers across borders (contagion or spillover effects) and the flow of ideas (diffusion effects) can also spread conflict laterally across borders, internationalizing civil conflicts. Finally, major-power intervention into a civil dispute can greatly alter the dynamics of conflict. Gleditsch and Beardsley

Table 2.2 Notable nested conflicts since World War II

Minority-majority[a]	Regional conflict	Wider/hegemonic conflict
Protestants and Catholics of Northern Ireland	Great Britain-Ireland	
Greek and Turkish Cypriots	Greece-Turkey	
Israelis and Palestinians	Israel-Arab states	U.S.-USSR
Maronite Christians and Palestinians in Lebanon	Israel-Syria-Iran-Lebanon	U.S.-USSR
Hindus and Muslims in Kashmir	India-Pakistan	U.S.-USSR
Chinese and Tibetans	China-India	China-U.S.
Sinhalese and Sri Lankan Tamils	Sri Lanka-India	China-India
Ethiopians and Somalis in Ogaden	Somalia-Ethiopia	U.S.-USSR
Serbs and Albanians in Yugoslavia/ Serbia	Albania-Serbia; NATO-Serbia	NATO-Russia
Georgians and South Ossetians	Georgia-Russia	U.S.-Russia
Georgians and Abkhazis	Georgia-Russia	U.S.-Russia
Azerbaijanis and Armenians in Nagorno-Karabakh	Armenia-Azerbaijan	Russia-Turkey
Moldovans and Transnistrians	Moldova-Russia	
Latvians and Russophones	Latvia-Russia	U.S.-Russia
Estonians and Russophones	Estonia-Russia	U.S.-Russia
Ukrainians and Russians in Ukraine	Ukraine-Russia	U.S.-Russia
Saharawis and Moroccans	Morocco-Mauritania-Algeria	

[a] As noted in the introduction, I use the terms "minority" and "majority" to denote subordinate and dominant groups in a state; a majority may sometimes be a numerical minority of the state population.

demonstrate, for example, that the influence of the United States—owing to its vast resources—had a considerable impact on the trajectory of civil wars in Guatemala and El Salvador.[22]

A brief review of notable civil wars since World War II shows that many of these so-called domestic disputes were in fact nested in bilateral or regional conflicts (the second level). The conflict in Cyprus between the Greek and Turkish Cypriots was embedded in a century-long conflict between Greece and Turkey. The war in Northern Ireland was nested in a dispute over territorial sovereignty between Britain and Ireland. The Palestinian conflict has been fueled in part by regional conflicts between Israeli and neighboring Arab states; and the ongoing conflict in Kashmir is nested in a decades-long border dispute between India and Pakistan. Unsurprisingly—given that many bilateral disputes are waged over borders—many of the most entrenched civil wars of the modern era have been situated at the fault line of two rival states or coalitions of states. These include Northern Ireland, Cyprus, Kashmir, Palestine, Kosovo, Bosnia, Abkhazia, South Ossetia, Ogaden, Sri Lanka, Nagorno-Karabakh, Crimea and Eastern Ukraine, and Transnistria.

Three Levels of Nestedness: Domestic, Regional, and Systemic

The levels of conflict are defined as follows. The domestic conflict is waged between the majority-controlled state and one or more restive groups within the borders of the target state. The regional conflict environment generally extends to states that lie just outside the borders of the target state, encompassing states or actors that easily affect or are affected by events and/or actions in close proximity to the target state. For example, the regional conflict environment for Macedonia includes Bulgaria, Serbia, Kosovo, Albania, and Greece. Nested security implies that any efforts to mediate communal disputes in the target country should be accompanied or preceded by efforts to control the state's borders and mediate outstanding disputes between the target and neighboring states.

Domestic conflicts become all the more intractable when they are nested in an unstable regional conflict environment that is in turn nested in an unstable hegemonic or systemic conflict environment (the third level). The third, systemic level is more difficult to define and measure for model testing but basically extends to any extra-regional factor or actor (such as a military intervention by a major power) that can influence minority-majority relations in the target state. A paradigmatic example of nested conflict is the dispute between Palestinians and Israeli settlers in the West Bank, which is situated in a regional conflict between Israel and its Arabic neighbors. During the Cold War, this nested regional conflict was itself nested in the bipolar U.S.-Soviet conflict. Likewise,

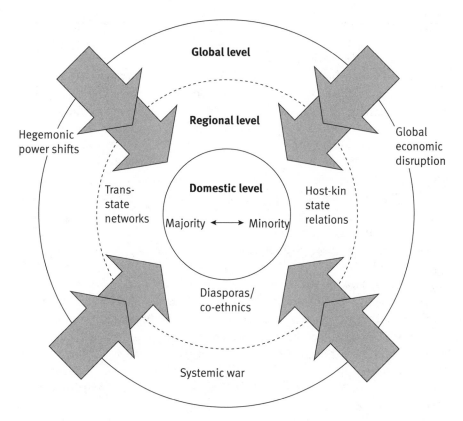

Figure 2.1 The nested security model

in the post–Cold War Balkans, the conflict between Serbs and Albanians in Kosovo was nested in a struggle between Belgrade and Pristina, which in turn was fueled by episodic conflict between the United States and Russia. A powerful state outside the region might also intervene *unilaterally* to tip one side of a civil conflict against the other, as in the case of the 2011 Libyan civil war. Successful mediation of the domestic conflict requires neutralizing any harmful external influences on the target state—be they from the regional level, the systemic level, or both.

Nested Conflicts Consist of Distinct but Interrelated Struggles

Scholars have argued that "internationalized" or nested conflicts are best treated as complex conflicts with both domestic and international components. Gleditsch and colleagues contend that the two levels are inextricably interwoven, noting, "the issues and dynamics surrounding the civil war are most often central to the international conflict."[23] Others take this even further, arguing that civil wars are merely international struggles or that the two (domestic and international disputes) are really two sides of the same coin.[24]

However, a cursory review of nested conflicts shows that internationalized conflicts are usually composed of two or more unique conflicts at the domestic and international level, where the interests, identities, and agendas of the conflict parties at times overlap but are nevertheless distinct. For instance, the Bosnian civil war consisted of both a sectarian dispute between Bosnian Muslims, Croats, and Serbs over control of the central government and an inter-state conflict between Belgrade and Zagreb over annexing or at least controlling parts of Bosnian territory. The civil wars in Georgia consist of a struggle between Tbilisi and the autonomy-seeking South Ossetians and Abkhazis as well as an international conflict between the Russian and Georgian governments over gas and oil pipelines and Tbilisi's controversial orientation toward NATO and the EU.

Likewise, the domestic struggles surrounding the Kurds in Turkey and Iraq have drivers that are distinct from those of the international conflicts between Turkey and Iraq. Although a domestic conflict party may at times share a common agenda with an international conflict party, such alliances are often fleeting and can easily collapse when circumstances change. Peace practitioners understand that communal conflicts are typically composed of multiple layers and issues, involving multiple stakeholders whose roles sometimes overlap, and therefore require separate negotiation tracks.

Asymmetrical Impact of the External Environment on an Internal Conflict

The next point to make is that, although domestic and international conflicts influence one another, conflict dynamics at higher levels tend to have a *disproportionate* impact on conflict dynamics at lower levels. This is because actors operating at higher levels of political order tend to choose their policies based on a wide range of inputs, interests, and constraints, whereas domestic-level disputants are more narrowly concerned with their relative share of state resources. Second, actors who operate at higher levels of political order, such as regional or global hegemons, usually command greater resources, which they use to influence political actors on lower levels (see figure 2.1). Douglas Lemke argued that major powers have an asymmetrical influence on local power structures or "hierarchies" because major powers have global reach, whereas minor powers do not. For these reasons, Lemke contended that "leading members in the top of the nested hierarchies can affect members below and not the other way around."[25] What this means is that external events and actors tend to have a greater impact on *intra*-state relations rather than vice versa.

To illustrate the disproportionate impact of higher on lower-level conflicts, intervening in a civil war is something that regional or global actors may or may not decide is in their interest, given their comparatively wide scope of interests and concerns; kin states often intervene in third states in order to satisfy the interests of domestic constituencies, which shift over time as a function of changing governments and "selectorates."[26] This means that a local conflict is unlikely to "pull in" intervenors as long as the outside actors in question are unwilling to participate. Indeed, research has shown that homeland states are no more likely to intervene on behalf of their kin when the minority is repressed than when it is not, suggesting that external patrons tend to call the shots.[27]

By contrast, domestic actors (involved in lower-level conflicts) *do* tend to be strongly influenced by the perceived intentions of external players, whose ongoing or prospective interventions greatly alter the expected cost-benefit calculations of continuing the conflict relative to brokering a peace. This means that external conflict processes are far more likely to influence the calculus of war on the ground than conflicts on the ground are to influence external conflict processes. Given the primacy of the wider conflict environment, peace mediators should address the external conflict processes *before* (or at least alongside) the domestic drivers of the dispute. Once the conflict dynamics in the wider environment are neutralized, then the domestic conflict is effectively "nested" in a stable regional and systemic environment (in Lemke's terminology, stable "sub-hierarchies" of regional powers are nested in a stable international hierarchy of global power),[28] at which point cooperative mediations are far more likely to succeed. All other things being equal, so long as the target state is situated in a turbulent neighborhood, internal conflicts will be much more difficult for third parties to address than if the target state is located in a stable region—even in the best-case scenario (for example, the mediator is resourceful and credible, and domestic-level factors favor peace).[29]

Likewise, neutralizing cross-border influences on a sectarian struggle is likely to *greatly enhance* the effectiveness of conflict mediation.[30] Sometimes, however, ending cross-border interventions can lead to short- or even longer-term conflicts at the substate level, such as when client groups or governments lose their source of support and other domestic actors respond to the weakening of the state with violence. For instance, although many believed that the end of the Cold War would help resolve many civil wars in the Global South as proxy wars between the United States and the USSR wound down, the 1990s actually coincided with *more* rather than less regional destabilization, as the Soviet Union and Yugoslavia collapsed and many client governments in Africa lost their support from Moscow. This destabilization led to conflict escalation in many parts of the continent.

Several caveats are in order at this point. First, I do not argue that *all* civil conflicts are nested in regional and/or global conflict processes.[31] Some internal conflicts are genuinely divorced from the wider external environment—particularly in their early stages. The Biafran war of 1967–70 and the Sudanese civil wars, for example, were rooted in internal ethnic disputes over the control of valuable territory and government; foreign actors became consequential only when the conflicts were internationalized later on. Second, I do not argue that domestic conflict dynamics are *un*important to the emergence and prolongation of internal war. On the contrary, intergroup relations have a critical influence on the shape, longevity, and fate of civil disputes; micro-level factors that incite sectarian violence include elite machinations, ethnic symbolism, intergroup competition over resources, political opportunism, and ethnic fears and grievances.[32] I claim only that third-party mediation is unlikely to succeed in reducing tensions on the ground *so long as the external dimensions of sectarian feuds remain unchecked*—either by major powers, international organizations, or regional peace deals. Where the external conflict dynamics *have* been stabilized, by contrast, third-party mediators are likely to find domestic conflict management a great deal easier.

In the section that follows I describe the nested nature of many protracted civil disputes, focusing in particular on how conflict processes on the regional (second) and systemic (third) levels disproportionately influence domestic (first) level conflicts, and further, how third-party mediation should be designed in light of this asymmetry.

Building Nested Security from the Outside In

An internal conflict is *securely* nested in a stable international environment when neither conflict party is leveraged or incentivized by external actors or events to challenge the other side through violence. Many mediators (such as the UN or the OSCE) have no coercive capacity, nor any other means to force regional rivals to withdraw from the conflict state or broker a bilateral or multilateral compromise with their government. In such cases, great powers or international organizations may need to backstop mediations by neutralizing the external environment—either through the threat of force or offer of inducements, creating the conditions of nested security that facilitate conflict reduction. For example, a great power might engage in "hegemonic leveling," by pushing through a bilateral deal to resolve a destabilizing regional environment in which a domestic conflict is embedded. Such a deal might consist of a formal or informal bilateral peace pact with provisions for minority protections. For instance, in 1920, Britain persuaded Sweden to withdraw its territorial claims on the Swedish-speaking Åland Islands (which Finland had declared to be sovereign Finnish territory) and normalize relations with Helsinki. With the internal dispute between the Finns and the Ålanders nested in a stable bilateral environment (normalized Swedish-Finnish relations), the dispute could be submitted to the League of Nations for arbitration. This resulted in the historic Åland Agreement of 1921, which gave the islands autonomy within Finland—an arrangement that remains in force to this day.

Alternatively, regional rivals may broker a peace of their own accord, obviating the need for hegemonic intervention. For instance, the 1998 Good Friday Peace Agreement, which ushered in the end of the thirty-year Northern Ireland conflict, was made possible by a prior bilateral deal between Irish prime minister Bertie Ahern and UK prime minister Tony Blair. Under that agreement, the two governments pledged not only to deny patronage to either side of the conflict, but also to facilitate a cease-fire and ultimately a peace agreement to end the war and resolve the status of Northern Ireland. This nested the domestic conflict in a stable bilateral partnership, creating strong *dis*incentives for the Nationalist and Loyalist factions to continue the struggle as well as strong positive incentives for them to sign the power-sharing agreement.

Creating the conditions of nested security also means *stabilizing an anarchical regional environment*—either spontaneously or through conscious policy decisions. For example, a sectarian conflict may be nested in a stable regional environment because wars or other violence in neighboring countries have ended—reducing the flow of arms and personnel over the borders as a consequence. Alternatively, intergovernmental organizations (IGOs) or regional or global hegemons can actively contain or arrest cross-border spillover (in the form of refugees, weapons, and refugees) by sealing or patrolling the target state's borders. During the Sri Lankan civil war, for example, the Colombo government sought to interdict rebel financing and weapons trafficking over its borders; meanwhile, foreign governments engaged in an international crackdown on diaspora fund-raising for the Tamil Tigers.[33] A third possibility is that a common threat or interest leads rival states to bury their hatchet over minority territory so they can realize joint security or economic dividends. For instance, Finland and Sweden were able to resolve their differences over the Åland Islands for good when they were forced into an alliance to defend against Nazi aggression in the late 1930s.

A domestic conflict may also be *insecurely* nested in an unstable regional conflict environment. For instance, hegemonic states or IGOs might create conditions of conflict by leveraging or "tipping" one side of the conflict, encouraging the empowered side to radicalize against or challenge the other side militarily. For instance, the U.S. government encouraged the Kurdish and Shiite minorities in Iraq to rise up against Saddam Hussein's government after the 1991 Gulf War with an implicit promise of support, leading to massive re-prisals against Shiites in the south when the United States failed to intervene. Regional players such as external homeland states may also incentivize one member of the domestic dyad to challenge the other by providing financial, lo-gistical, or direct military support to that side of the battle. Systemic events or regional disruptions such as spillover from a civil war in a neighboring country might also provide one side with the resources and incentives to attack the other. When such dynamics go unaddressed, cooperative mediations at the domestic level are likely to fail. Examples include the efforts by the OSCE to mediate between the Kosovo Liberation Army and the Yugoslav state in the 1990s, which failed utterly when internal unrest in Albania led to a flow of arms and fighters across the border, and particularly once the KLA gained the tacit support of NATO and the United States. Neutralizing these exter-nal influences would have meant border patrols to contain cross-border flows from Albania and cutting off Western military support to the KLA. As it was, continued military assistance to the Albanian insurgents initially led them to reject the proposed deal that came out of the Rambouillet peace negotiations in 1999—despite the fact that it gave Kosovo extensive autonomy, effectively meeting their demands. Even the moderate Kosovo leadership rejected a deal that it would have eagerly accepted in the mid-1990s, a time when the Kosovo Albanian side was relatively weak.

The above logic yields four broad predictions concerning the success of cooperative conflict management (table 2.3). First, the external environment in which an internal conflict is nested may be *destabilized* at any time because of power shifts or events on the regional or systemic level, creating a condi-tion of nested *in*security. There are two possible variants here. All else equal, external factors that generate perceptions of *increased minority leverage* against

Table 2.3 Nested security hypotheses

1. Destabilization　　　　　⟶	Nested *in*security
	Variant A: *If the minority is leveraged, the domestic conflict is likely to escalate as the leveraged minority mobilizes to obtain concessions from the center.*
	Variant B: *If the majority is leveraged, the domestic conflict is likely to escalate as the leveraged majority seeks to gain ground against a restive minority.*
2. Exogenous stabilization　⟶	Nested security *(the domestic conflict is likely to de-escalate, but both sides will remain mobilized)*
3. Endogenous stabilization　⟶	Consolidated nested security *(the domestic divide loses political salience; sustained inter-group cooperation may emerge)*

the state center are likely to produce minority radicalization or rebellion,[34] leading the center to offer the minority concessions or confront the minority through violence. An example of this dynamic is post–Cold War Montenegro, which began to push for ever-greater autonomy in the late 1990s in response to growing U.S. (and later EU) support. After threatening to intervene in Montenegro during the Kosovo conflict, the newly defeated Belgrade government had little choice but to offer the secessionist leadership ever-increasing concessions in return for promises to remain in the union. This resulted in a loose confederation that barely functioned, giving way to Montenegrin independence after a few short years.

Second, external conflict processes can *leverage the majority*, increasing the likelihood that the government will attempt to suppress a rebellious minority while it enjoys the upper hand. The early 1920s provides numerous examples of this, as the Polish and Czechoslovak governments (among others) had the implicit support of Allied powers for implementing nationalizing policies as a means of homogenizing their state populations. This led to significant violations of minority rights, most dramatically when Poland expelled thousands of ethnic German "optants" (Polish Germans who had opted for German citizenship) in the 1920s in order to "polonize" its border regions. Likewise, Romania expelled numerous ethnic Hungarian optants in order to "romanize" its new Transylvanian territory. In short, when the target government is empowered and has revisionist goals at the domestic level, cooperative mediation is extremely unlikely to succeed in de-escalating conflict (in this case caused by government-backed minority discrimination). Despite the League's attempts to halt expulsions of German optants, for example, Poland utterly ignored the League's directives and continued its polonization campaigns into the late 1920s.

On the positive side of the ledger, there are two variants of nested security that increase the odds of successful mediation of sectarian conflict. In the weaker version, regional rivalries between the host government and the minority's external patron are *exogenously* stabilized. This means that the conflict between the host and rival state or other conflict parties is held in check by external inducements or sanctions. Overt conflict at the substate level is thus effectively suppressed. However, the chances of intergroup cooperation remain minimal because inducements for peace are not self-enforcing. Kyle Beardsley argues similarly that when incentives for peace are wholly external—as when great powers pressure the combatants to reach a settlement—it will often be a "fragile peace" that can easily be undermined in the future if and when these incentives are later withdrawn.[35]

In other words, exogenous pressures may nest the conflict in a stable environment, but both conflict parties understand that once these external inducements disappear, the peace deal is likely to disintegrate. This was the case with the exogenously induced Åland Agreement between Finland and Sweden immediately after World War I, which terminated the conflict but did not end ethnic hostilities. The logic of exogenous stabilization can also be seen in the post–Cold War Balkans when NATO intervened to contain an emerging insurgency in Macedonia in 2001. Remnants of the former Kosovo Liberation Army had crossed the border to foment an Albanian minority rebellion against the Macedonian majority government in the tiny neighboring republic. Through quick action by NATO forces, the conflict was quelled, and both sides were induced to enter a cross-ethnic coalition government. The coalition arrangement has held up to this day, although deep divisions remain because the domestic pact largely relies on external incentives for peace, which may later change. This is the kind of fragile peace that can be obtained through exogenous stabilization.

Third-party mediation is most likely to achieve lasting success under conditions of *endogenous* stabilization. This is when the relevant regional actors stand to gain substantial rewards for bilateral cooperation, such as a valuable trade agreement or a bilateral security alliance against a common enemy. If the regional pact is perceived by the domestic conflict parties as self-enforcing and thus sustainable, a condition of nested peace is likely to emerge in which the intergroup divide gradually loses political salience, consolidating inter-ethnic cooperation within the target state.[36] Endogenous stabilization occurred in the Åland Islands in the mid-1930s, when Sweden and Finland recognized that they had a common interest in militarizing the islands. With mutual incentives to establish a joint defense to counter the rising threats of Nazi Germany and Soviet Russia, the two governments formed a bilateral defense pact that resolved outstanding bilateral grievances over the minority. At this point, the ethnic dispute lost all political salience in the public sphere, as there were no outside parties to fan the flames of conflict. Effectively cut out of the deal, the Swedish-speaking Ålanders grudgingly accepted that they were now indelibly tied to Finland, as any chance of Swedish annexation had been effectively nullified.

What does all this mean for soft-power conflict management? The logic of nested security implies that the wider conflict environment should be stabilized before (or at the same time as) peacemakers engage in domestic conflict management. The most surefire, lasting resolutions to civil conflicts begin from the systemic and/or regional levels and work inward toward the domestic level. Although stabilizing the external conflict environment does not by itself guarantee conflict reduction on the ground, the central policy lesson is that third-party mediators are highly *un*likely to contain nascent civil conflicts so long as the regional and systemic conflict dynamics remain unchecked. This, in turn, often requires muscular great-power intervention.

Methods and Research Design

To demonstrate the explanatory power of the theory, I examine cases of cooperative intervention to see if shifts in tensions on the ground are preceded by changes in external conflict dynamics. If this pattern is found, then process tracing is used to isolate the pathways that connect shifts in the independent variable (external conflict dynamics) with shifts in the dependent variable (the level of conflict on the ground). The goal is to identify the sequence of actions and reactions that precede temporal shifts in communal conflict. This will help to determine whether the regional/international conflict environment is associated with the domestic conflict environment and, if so, whether the relationship is causal or spurious.

At the same time, the controlled comparative method is used to explain differential success of third-party mediation in highly similar circumstances—effectively controlling for the strategy used, the historical and geopolitical circumstances surrounding the intervention, and the identity and resources of the mediator. When comparing mediations, the causal pathways are first mapped longitudinally within each case and then compared within each cluster of cases to determine whether nested security is a necessary condition for successful cooperative conflict management.

I assess the explanatory power of nested security against competing theories as follows. I examine each case over time to see whether patterns of tensions on the ground match the evidentiary "signature" of nested security better than those of alternative theories. Nested security predicts that the stabilization of external conflict dynamics ameliorates intercommunal tensions at the domestic level, and vice versa. By contrast, institutional theories expect domestic tensions to diminish once the minority is offered meaningful concessions such as territorial autonomy or power sharing in the central government; we should not see a decrease of tensions in the absence of such concessions. If instead the legitimacy of a mediator matters most, then we should see lower domestic tensions where the third-party mediator has more power, resources, or perceived credibility. If, finally, liberal minority policies are decisive, then domestic tensions should be lowest where the target government is conciliatory or where it implements substantial minority protections.

The Cases

My units of analysis are cases of mediated low-intensity conflict in interwar and post–Cold War Central and Eastern Europe; these interventions are further subdivided by mediator strategy—preventive diplomacy and induced devolution. Under preventive diplomacy, the mediator persuades both sides

	Preventive diplomacy	**Induced devolution**
League of Nations security regime	League minorities regime (German and Hungarian minorities in Central Europe)	League protectorates and territorial autonomy (Danzig; Memel; Åland Islands)
EU/OSCE security regime	EU/OSCE interventions (Russophones in Baltics; Albanians in Balkans)	Territorial autonomy (Montenegro, post-1999 northern Kosovo; post-2001 Macedonia)

Figure 2.2 Cases for analysis

of the conflict to de-escalate tensions while encouraging the government to enact policies that increase minority integration into the state-society. The interwar cases include minority conflicts that were believed to have significant potential for upsetting the peace in Europe: the German minorities in Poland and Czechoslovakia and the Hungarian minorities in Czechoslovakia and Romania. In the post–Cold War period, the most important cases of preventive diplomacy involved the Russophone minorities in Latvia and Estonia and the Albanian minorities in Macedonia and Kosovo during the 1990s. Under the second strategy, induced devolution, the mediator attempts to persuade the government to devolve state powers to a minority region through regional autonomy or federalism. Cases of induced devolution in interwar Central and Eastern Europe include the Åland Islands, Danzig, and Memel for the entire interwar period. The post–Cold War cases include Macedonia, Montenegro, and Kosovo during the 2000s.

Concepts and Measurement

Within each case, I track shifts in regional/international stability, as well as shifts in the level of domestic tensions over time, to determine whether apparent variation in mediation success can be explained by the theory of nested security. I measure these variables qualitatively using an original mixture of primary field data, as well as secondary sources. Regional stabilization occurs when the host state concludes a peace pact or normalizes bilateral relations with external lobby actors (foreign meddlers in the conflict such as kin states or diasporas), when cross-border support for minority rebellion is disrupted, or when conflict spillover from neighboring states is contained. Regional *de*stabilization occurs when any one of these conflict dynamics (re)emerges. I judge stabilization to be *exogenous* when regional conflicts between the host state and lobby actor are suppressed through third-party conditionality, pressure, coercion, or security guarantees; I judge it to be *endogenous* when the peace between regional actors is self-enforcing, such as when the host and lobby states agree that it is in their mutual interest to establish or maintain peaceful bilateral relations. I make the distinction between endogenous and exogenous stabilization by assessing the policies and official statements of the state governments or other lobby actors and by reviewing scholarly accounts of these events. In this way, I determine whether the peace agreement was the outcome of external pressure or, alternatively, the spontaneous recognition of common interests by regional rivals themselves. The level of stabilization can thus be seen to shift over the course of each intervention; I examine these shifts using process tracing to identify causal connections between the external environment and internal conflict while controlling for environmental factors.

The dependent variable *level of conflict* is measured qualitatively using the following indicators: (a) intergroup political coalitions at the local and national levels; (b) public support for extremist or nationalist parties; (c) repressive/nonrepressive minority policies; (d) sectarian violence on the ground; and (e) integration of the minority in educational, employment, and other arenas. Since the model makes predictions concerning *shifts* in internal conflict (that is, conflict reduction versus escalation), the case analysis focuses primarily on whether these indicators increase or decrease over time. If one or more of these indicators increases, the conflict will be judged to have escalated; if one or more of the indicators decreases, the conflict will be judged to have de-escalated. If two or more indicators move in opposite directions, the level of conflict will be judged indeterminate.

In the course of this analysis, careful process tracing is used to establish the causes of conflict (de)escalation in order to rule out alternative explanations. Each case study is divided into periods that represent shifts in the level of domestic conflict. Each shift is then closely examined using field research material (for contemporary cases) and scholarly sources (for both periods) to determine why each shift occurred when it did. Nested security posits that neutralizing external conflict dynamics is a necessary condition for successful cooperative mediation. The theory will be disconfirmed if I find that internal tensions de-escalated in the *absence* of external stabilization. I also pay attention to whether shifts in internal conflict *preceded* or *followed* external stabilization; if domestic conflict de-escalated before the regional environment was stabilized, this would also disconfirm the theory.

By taking the steps outlined above, I assess whether these cases match the evidentiary "signature" of nested security better than those of alternative accounts. To facilitate these assessments, I lay out the predictions or "signatures" of the competing explanations at the outset of each of the four case chapters. The indicators for the independent and dependent variables are measured qualitatively through data triangulation, which is a "method of cross-checking data from multiple sources to search for regularities in the research data."[37] Finally, each chapter contains a concluding section, where I comparatively evaluate each explanation to see which offers the fullest account of the factual pattern in each case.

The Data

The data for the analysis include personal interviews and other field data, as well as historical records, contemporary media reports, and scholarly accounts. To obtain data on interventions in post–Cold War Central and Eastern Europe, I visited the archives of the OSCE, the EU, and the Open Society Institute to review internal reports prepared by the intervenors concerning the impact of mediation on the conflict in question. I also conducted dozens of interviews with OSCE representatives, officials of the High Commissioner on National Minorities, NGO workers, activists, journalists, and local analysts to identify shifts in internal conflict and solicit expert opinions concerning the causes of each shift. I supplemented these data with scholarly accounts, research reports, and news articles concerning the relative success of the mediators and the obstacles they faced in managing the conflict.

For the interwar period, I drew on a mixture of scholarly work, League records, and other materials obtained at the League of Nations archives in Geneva, Switzerland, concerning the effects of League mediation. With respect to archival materials, I relied to a great extent on the minutes of the meetings of the League Council and Assembly, as well as official correspondence and commission reports concerning the impact of mediation; much of this material is contained in the League of Nations official journals. Special attention is paid to the Secretariat's responses to petitions on behalf of the German and Hungarian minorities that were sent to the League in the 1920s and '30s, as well as the outcome of these mediations. In addition to the official journals, I analyzed primary archival materials such as memos, telegrams, and other correspondence between League officials and mediators on the ground. This is especially important for the cases of Memel and Danzig, which featured considerable correspondence between field officials and the League headquarters. I supplemented these analyses using diplomatic records from the British foreign office, as well as scholarly accounts of minority conflict and conflict management in interwar Europe.

Caveats and Methodological Limitations

The ambitious scope of this study presents significant challenges. The first relates to the comparability of cases. Despite considerable similarities in mediator aims and strategies under the two European security regimes, the question remains whether the lessons of the interwar period remain relevant today, given the very different global environment during the two periods. Today's world is far more interconnected, and non-state actors have had a far greater and more instantaneous impact on "high" politics. Moreover, the OSCE, EU, and NATO enjoy far more leverage in CEE countries today than the League did during the interwar period. Finally, although there was a similar division of labor among mediators during both periods, the current European system is far more complex than the League system, with no overarching authority to coordinate the actions of the numerous organizations involved in conflict management. A related question is whether the intervening variables may be adequately "controlled for" when comparing cases of interventions across regimes. It is even questionable whether interventions under the same regime are comparable, given how widely the conflict processes varied from one country to the next. Moreover, an adequate assessment of competing tools requires separating the effects of each intervention from those of other factors that may be intervening simultaneously.

While acknowledging the importance of these concerns, I argue that it is the very diversity of cases that makes this comparative analysis so valuable. Indeed, the primary motivation for this research was to determine whether the nested security model maintains its explanatory leverage across very different mediations undertaken in a variety of subregional and historical settings, conflict participants, strategies of mediation, and geopolitical environments. I demonstrate that nested security is effectively a precondition of success for cooperative conflict management. Using Mill's method of difference, I compare successful mediations with failed mediations, all with similar contextual conditions, to identify the key differences that drive conflict escalation versus de-escalation. In the case studies themselves I use process tracing over time to identify which of these factors might be driving success/failure in a single mediation; this means looking within each intervention to identify factors that predate (and could possibly be causing) shifts in the level of conflict from one point to the next.

A second challenge relates to the problem of measuring "success." Indeed, the quality of this analysis turns on the extent to which my measure can be applied across a wide range of interventions. In some cases, mediation success is extremely difficult to measure. Such is the case with preventive or "quiet" diplomacy, where the third party offers confidential advice to the disputants, facilitating dialogue between two or more sides, thereby de-escalating a brewing conflict. For these reasons, as noted above, I avoid measuring mediation outcomes dichotomously as successes or failures. I instead measure success indirectly—focusing on whether and why tensions increase or decrease once mediation has begun. In so doing, I seek to account for patterns of conflict *over time* rather than a single measure that explains the overall degree of success of each intervention. I find that—in the course of mediations—regional stabilization is a critical facilitator of conflict reduction, whereas regional *de*-stabilization tends to shorten the periods of peace.

The analysis in this book provides not inconsiderable support for an outside-in model of conflict management, where powerful states or international organizations stabilize the external conflict environment as a first step toward containing domestic conflict. This means that domestic conflicts should first be securely nested in a stable regional environment, which in turn should be nested in a stable hegemonic or systemic environment. In the absence of these critical background conditions, third-party mediation efforts are likely to founder. This project speaks directly to key questions in the fields of conflict management, foreign policy and intervention, regional security regimes, and external conditionality. The broad conclusion is that much of the mediation literature understates the importance of external factors and events on the success of civil conflict management.

The findings of this analysis have direct policy relevance as well. By exploring Europe's failures and successes under the League regime, this analysis yields important insights concerning the ways that peace builders can avoid replicating the mistakes of an earlier generation of European leaders. These policy insights are still relevant to Europe today, as the EU struggles to accommodate new member states beset by the problems of conflict spillover, mass migration, ultranationalist movements, minority rebellions, and right-wing attacks on marginalized groups such as the Roma. Further to the east, European governments and institutions have had to confront an armed insurgency in Ukraine and interventions by Russia on behalf of its ethnic kin and other groups in satellite states.

This study has applications well beyond CEE as well, since internal conflicts span the globe and constitute the bulk of militarized conflict today. State governments and international and regional organizations have intensified their search for remedies to conflicts that generate humanitarian disasters and that exacerbate failed and failing states. If strategies of *non*violent mediation can be found that serve to dampen these conflicts—sparing populations incendiary, and often counterproductive, military strikes, economic sanctions, or occupations—then we have come a considerable distance toward fulfilling the dictum of the Hippocratic oath "to do good or to do no harm."

3

Preventive Diplomacy in Interwar Europe

With the German, Habsburg, and Ottoman Empires in ruins at the end of the First World War, the victorious Allied powers set about establishing nation-states in their place. Although the architects of the Versailles peace endeavored to respect the principle of national self-determination in drawing the state borders, several large minorities found themselves stranded outside their homeland countries. Concerned that this would fuel irredentist movements and thereby imperil the fragile peace settlement, the conference powers designed a Minority Protection System (MPS)—an elaborate system of conflict prevention based on monitoring and enforcement of "minority treaties" that the new and enlarged states were to sign with the League of Nations. The treaties mandated that the signatory states implement specific provisions to protect *certain* national minorities. For their part, the new and enlarged states promised to privilege their minority treaties over domestic laws and state constitutions.[1]

Which states were obliged to sign the treaties? According to Sir James Headlam-Morley, the minority treaties were designed for states that "are new, inexperienced and have no established traditions or to which large minority populations were transferred against their will."[2] All newly created Central and Eastern European states were required to sign such treaties, or issue declarations promising to protect national minorities on their territory. It is no accident that these states contained territorially concentrated groups that abutted revisionist homelands, as these were the groups that posed the greatest threat to the postwar settlement. It was hoped that the provisions in the treaties would remove incentives for minority secessionism and encourage assimilation. In a very real sense, the raison d'être of the MPS was cooperative conflict management, not the advancement of universal minority rights.

The League MPS operated through the principles of preventive diplomacy. Individuals, groups, or kin states issued complaints to the Minorities Section of the League that a certain government had violated its minority treaty. If the Secretariat ruled the petition receivable, then a Committee of Three was convened to consider the case, and the offending party was invited to respond. The subsequent mediation most often occurred through backdoor negotiations between League officials and the host government. In nearly all cases, a deal was worked out whereby the offender promised to improve its minority policies, and the matter would end there. If the claimant remained unsatisfied with the deal and had the support of a member of the League Council, the petition could be brought before the Council for a decision. In the final step of appeal, the case could be submitted to the Permanent Court of International Justice for an advisory opinion.

Because of their size, territorial concentration, economic power, and active patronage of revisionist states, the German and Hungarian minorities of Central and Eastern Europe enjoyed far greater leverage than did smaller, unsupported minorities such as the Roma and the Jews (see map 1).[3] Their mobilizational clout is reflected, among other things, in the proportion of complaints submitted on their behalf—fully 104 of the 525 complaints that reached the Minorities Section from 1921 to 1930 concerned German minorities alone.[4] The League responded by devoting a significant portion of its resources to resolving German minority conflicts. Hungarian minorities also received considerable attention as co-ethnics of the second-most-important revisionist state in Central Europe. By examining the German and Hungarian minority disputes over time, I identify factors that optimized the success of League diplomacy in these cases.

The minority protection system has traditionally been viewed as a failure because it did not prevent war, which is the main point of preventive diplomacy. It also failed to ensure the protection of many minorities while serving to justify Nazi Germany's expansionist campaigns. However, I demonstrate that the League system *did* yield success when the conflicts in question were effectively nested in a stable regional environment. To show this, I periodize the mediations of two German and two Hungarian conflicts according to shifts in the level of each conflict on the ground. I then detail the events leading up to each shift to identify the causes of conflict reduction and escalation in each mediation. Careful process tracing demonstrates that mediation success largely hinged on the prevailing degree of "nested security" in each case. The nesting of the minority-majority relations in a stable regional and hegemonic environment ushered in periods of relative ethnic harmony in each of the four cases. By contrast, bilateral struggles or conflict spillover from neighboring states created a condition of "nested *in*security," which led to an escalation of tensions on the ground. I conclude that the stability of the wider conflict environment was a key precondition for effective preventive diplomacy in each case.

The following section lays out nested security predictions for successful League diplomacy, as well as the predictions of competing theories for success. I use the patterns of the German and Hungarian minority conflicts to test the nested security model against the most viable alternative explanations. The final section synthesizes the case evidence to adjudicate between the most plausible accounts of each mediated conflict.

Nested Security versus Alternative Explanations

Nested security makes four broad predictions related to preventive diplomacy. First, the external environment in which a conflict is nested may be *destabilized* at any time as a result of power shifts or events on the regional or systemic level. This condition of nested *in*security sustains domestic conflict and undermines preventive diplomacy efforts. There are two possible variants here. Under Variant A, external factors that generate perceptions of increased *minority* leverage against the state center are likely to produce minority radicalization or rebellion,[5] leading the center to offer the minority concessions or (alternatively) confront the minority through violence. Under Variant B, external conflict processes may produce perceptions of increased *majority/state* leverage, increasing the odds of minority repression so long as the government enjoys the upper hand. Third-party mediation is unlikely to yield success under either variant of nested *in*security.

There are also two variants of nested security, both of which increase the likelihood of successful preventive diplomacy. First, the conflict between the relevant regional actors (in these cases, the host government and minority kin state) may be *exogenously* stabilized. Here, the regional conflict is held in check by outside inducements or sanctions. Under exogenous stabilization, overt conflict on the ground is likely to de-escalate; however, both sides will remain mobilized because the peace has been externally induced and may unravel at any time. In sum, although exogenous pressures may stabilize the internal conflict, the society itself is likely to remain divided in anticipation that these external pressures may change, imperiling the peace deal.

A more profound state of nested security occurs when the wider conflict environment is *endogenously* stabilized. This occurs when the relevant regional actors anticipate significant mutual gains from bilateral cooperation, such as a valuable trade agreement or a bilateral alliance against a common enemy. If the minority and majority perceive regional peace to be self-enforcing, a condition of "nested peace" may emerge in which the sectarian divide gradually loses political salience, permitting extensive interethnic cooperation.

I have chosen to assess League diplomacy in these four cases because the Secretariat devoted the bulk of its resources to managing these conflicts—a task deemed critical to maintaining peace in interwar Europe. The period of analysis extends from 1920 to 1938, which marked the beginning and end of the League's mediations. The cases are examined in pairs in order to assess the importance of the regional environment, particularly the actions of external states, for triggering escalation and reduction of conflict over the course of the mediations. The cases are also segmented over time based on fluctuating levels of conflict on the ground. For both German and Hungarian minorities, the early postwar period was one of minority passivity in the face of discrimination. The second period (late 1920s to early 1930s) is one of concessions and relative domestic peace, while the third period (mid- to late 1930s) was one of kin state intervention and minority rebellion (see table 3.1). This chapter examines each period to identify the critical factor(s) that precipitated the shift from one phase to the next. Is the timing of each shift best explained by domestic-level factors, factors related to the third-party mediator, or the degree of stability of the wider environment in which the minority disputes were embedded?

There are alternative explanations for these cases as well. One could argue that the League's failure to keep the peace was due to its illegitimacy in the eyes of the treaty states. In this view, the MPS was illegitimate because Western governments were exempt from the rigorous standards of minority protections that were forced on the new and defeated states. In the 1930s, a keen observer of European nationalism asserted, "It is natural for any man

Table 3.1 Nested security predictions for League diplomacy

German minorities	Regional environment	Conflict outcome
(1918–1925)	Destabilization (*majorities* have upper hand)	Host governments choose policies based on domestic considerations; minorities moderate
(late 1920s–early '30s)	Exogenous stabilization through hegemonic leveling	Conflict de-escalation, disputes resolved, emergence of interethnic cooperation
(mid-1930s–World War II)	Destabilization (*minorities* have upper hand)	Minority rebellion, internal conflict
Hungarian minorities	**Regional environment**	**Conflict outcome**
(1918–mid-'20s)	Destabilization (*majorities* have upper hand, Little Entente)	Minority moderation, host states choose policies based on domestic considerations
(late 1920s to early 1930s)	Exogenous stabilization through hegemonic leveling	Conflict de-escalation, disputes resolved, emergence of interethnic cooperation
(mid-1930s–Word War II)	Destabilization (*minorities* have upper hand)	Minority rebellion, internal conflict

to resent outside interference in his affairs, however well intentioned. . . . No sensible man can expect a state to enjoy the spectacle of the representatives of fourteen states sitting in judgement, and the press of the world commenting, on her behavior towards certain of her citizens," predicting presciently that such hypocrisy was a "factor making for disharmony in Europe."[6] These views are reflected in contemporary accounts as well. Mark Mazower stated that, fatally, the League MPS gradually lost its legitimacy in the eyes of all parties: "The Great Powers increasingly disliked being required to pass judgment on how Poles, Romanians, or Czechs—their client states—were behaving towards their minorities. . . . The latter for their part felt humiliated by the international obligations they alone had been forced to sign, and blamed their minorities for publicizing their grievances abroad and failing to assimilate."[7]

A second argument holds that the League system itself contained the seeds of both success and failure. For instance, some have faulted the machinery of the League, such as a lengthy petition process involving the League Council, which tended to politicize the conflicts and delay their resolution.[8] Another view is that the League Minorities Section was far too secretive in its dealings and tended to privilege the interests of states over those of beleaguered minorities.[9] Still others attributed both the successes and failures of the system to the personal diplomacy of top officials in the Minorities Section—in particular, Erik Colban—who helped to de-escalate certain conflicts in the 1920s through his personal interventions.[10] Susan Pedersen writes that "for a time, great-power interests and League processes did appear to coincide—or at least some astute politicians of the 1920s tried hard to make them do so. Aristide Briand, Gustav Stresemann, and Austen Chamberlain may not have pored over the Covenant . . . but all three nevertheless found the League 'a much more useful body' than they had anticipated, and made it central to their efforts at rapprochement."[11] In this view, the skills of League diplomats and their staffs may be credited with inducing governments to enact minority protections in some cases, placating rebellious minorities and helping to keep the peace within and between states.

A third set of arguments, most often associated with realist theories, holds that the League failed to keep peace on the Continent because it was unable to offer sizable and credible rewards for peace, nor was it able to impose sanctions for bad behavior.[12] Since the League could not offer adequate incentives for implementing minority protections, target states would often alter the status quo to suit their interests. At the same time, the League had no standing army, no credible backing of the Allies, and thus no enforcement power.[13] These theories expect conflict to emerge when either minorities or target states have the incentives and the capacity to mobilize violently for a greater share of resources.

This leads to a final set of arguments, which hold that the apparent successes of League diplomacy can be largely attributed to domestic-level factors—namely, the presence of moderate elites in the treaty state, which facilitated ethnic compromise. Stephen Krasner writes, "Only in states where there was domestic support [for minority rights] were the minority regimes more successful; invitation was more effective than intervention." Thus, the liberal Czechoslovak state was observant of its minority protections, whereas the antiliberal Yugoslav and Romanian governments were not.[14] A related domestic-politics explanation follows that the minority protections themselves

Map 1 Interwar Central Europe

(for example, pro-minority education and language laws or equal employment opportunities) served to mollify both minority populations and their external kin states, discouraging both ethnic rebellion and kin state intervention in the states that implemented them.

To assess these explanations against the theory of nested security for relative explanatory power, the mediations of conflicts over German and Hungarian minorities are examined over time to see whether periods of relative peace were preceded by a neutralization of wider conflict factors as opposed to changes in these other variables.

Case Evidence

German Minorities in Central Europe

According to the Polish census of 1921, the reunified Polish state contained a little over one million ethnic Germans (3.9 percent of the population), who were concentrated mainly in the western "Polish Corridor." In 1921, Poland also gained control over a part of Upper Silesia, which contained a significant German population.[15] Although the larger Belarusian and Ukrainian minorities in the east were actually subjected to greater repression, the German minority was better educated, more urban, wealthier, and had an active and powerful kin state. With such formidable resources, Germans in Poland were the most avid users of the League MPS and consumed a significant share of the Secretariat's diplomatic resources.[16]

In Czechoslovakia, too, (Sudeten) Germans were the most mobilized minority.[17] Sudeten Germans enjoyed even greater internal leverage than Germans in Poland. Not only were they territorially concentrated, but they also made up a substantial portion of the state—numbering over three million, or 23 percent of the population.[18] Moreover, they enjoyed outsize political and economic advantages due to the legacy of the Germanic Austro-Hungarian Empire: although the working class of the Czech lands had been made up of both Czechs and Germans, Sudeten Germans were overrepresented in the civil service as well as the landholding and capitalist classes.[19] They also dominated the local Diets and the imperial Reichsrat in Vienna. Despite the threat posed by their relative size (or perhaps because of it), Germans received better treatment in Czechoslovakia than in Poland. Still, both minorities chafed under the new Slavic governments that sought to remove their prewar privileges. A comparative exploration of conflicts over these two minorities reveals that fluctuating tensions on the ground were largely driven by conflict dynamics in the wider region.

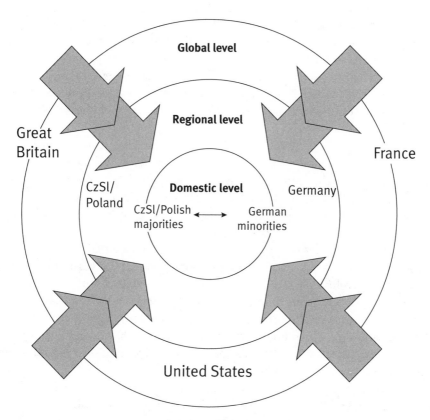

Figure 3.1 Nested security and the German minorities

Destabilization—Host States Enjoy the Upper Hand (1918–1925)

Stranded on the wrong side of the border in new and enlarged Slavic states, the German minorities of postwar Czechoslovakia and Poland called on their external homelands to annex the ethnic German territories. However, Berlin and Vienna—devastated by their defeat in the war—were in no position to come to the aid of their cross-border co-ethnics and therefore ignored these appeals. Berlin underscored its pacific intentions: the undersecretary of defense, Paul Goehre, assured the Polish government that "[Germany] could not wage a war even if we wanted to."[20] To demonstrate its good faith, Berlin dismissed or transferred to the west any German representatives who tried to interfere with Poland's campaign to nationalize the border region.

The German minority of Czechoslovakia fared no better in garnering external support. In response to demands for kin state annexation, Berlin told the Sudeten leadership that "the Sudetendeutschen must satisfy themselves with autonomy" within Czechoslovakia.[21] Although Austrian chancellor Karl Renner had at one time petitioned the Allies for a border adjustment that would give Austria parts of Moravia and Bohemia, his entreaty was categorically rejected. In the end, Renner promised to discontinue all support for Sudeten German irredentism in return for much-needed food and coal shipments, advocating for the more modest goal of "liberation of Deutschböhmen *within* Czechoslovakia."[22]

Roiled by domestic unrest, Austria turned completely inward. Berlin behaved similarly, in reaction to its absolute military defeat and the harsh terms of the armistice. The Versailles Treaty, in fact, explicitly prohibited Germany from intervening directly on behalf of the *Volksdeutsche* (ethnic Germans living abroad).[23] The German government calculated that maintaining ties with its kin abroad would "carr[y] too great a diplomatic risk" because overt support would have been "vetoed by the Allied Powers who exerted strict budgetary controls in order to maximize reparations payments."[24] Berlin thus kept its distance from minority organizations in neighboring countries, cut off support to irredentist organizations within Germany, and strictly limited its cross-border engagement with its co-ethnics. Germany refused to provide any official assistance whatsoever to the Sudeten Germans; the agencies tasked with looking after the *Volksdeutsche* devoted most of their meager resources to the Germans in the Polish Corridor.[25]

It is important to note that, while punishing the minorities' kin states, the peace settlement strongly favored Poland and Czechoslovakia. The two states had been given valuable minority territories at the expense of the defeated powers (Germany and Austria-Hungary); meanwhile, Britain and France had furnished them with direct security guarantees against any invasions by neighboring countries. According to the nested security model, such "hegemonic tipping" should have given the upper hand to the Czechoslovak and Polish governments, creating the conditions of nested *in*security that permitted the host states wide discretion in dealing with their internal conflicts (Variant B). In such a destabilized environment, the model predicts that League diplomacy would accomplish very little in quelling communal tensions in these countries. Since the leveraged states had no external incentives to accommodate minorities, their governments would be expected to choose minority policies according to domestic political considerations alone.

Poland and Czechoslovakia did indeed pursue different approaches to the German minorities, which was a function of divergent domestic political considerations. With its martial leader, Chief of State Józef Piłsudski, and substantial military resources to consolidate control over its newly acquired territories, Warsaw assumed a harder line toward its minorities—particularly in the German-speaking Polish Corridor. Prime Minister Władysław Sikorski articulated the logic of its policy in 1923 in Poznań: "The process of de-germanization . . . [had] to be completed relatively quickly, through expropriation and expulsion of optants, so that German nationalists and officials learn that their vision of the temporary character of the Polish Western border [is] wrong."[26] In national media, Polish opinion leaders promoted an exclusivist, anti-German ideology; Poland was to be a centralized state with assimilated minorities.[27] To "polonize" the strategically valuable corridor, the government enacted a citizenship law that expropriated ethnic Germans who had opted to become German citizens. Poland also denied citizenship to Polish Germans whose residence had been interrupted at any time between 1908 and 1920. Tens of thousands of Germans were thus slated for expulsion under these measures.[28] German nurses, teachers, and government officials lost their jobs almost overnight when the government nationalized the civil service.[29] Many German schools were also closed, and ethnic Germans faced severe job discrimination. In some places, threats or mob violence were used to drive Germans and Jews from their homes.[30] As a result, the number of self-identified Germans in Poland decreased by over 25 percent to 741,000 in under a decade.[31] They flooded over the border, even in the face of Germany's efforts to stanch the influx of immigrants.[32] The newly formed Zentralverband der Deutschtumsbunde united the German minority politically in 1921, but the Polish government dissolved it in 1923 and put its leaders on trial for treason.

By contrast, Czechoslovakia—a binational country founded by liberal intellectuals and depending for its existence on the goodwill of the Allies—assumed a relatively liberal stance toward its minorities.[33] Alone among the minority states,[34] Czechoslovakia established a system of minority protections over and above what was required under its minority treaty. Czechoslovakia permitted minorities to form ethnic parties and associations and to use their language in official business in minority areas. Nonetheless, the Czechoslovak leadership took advantage of its leverage to create an explicitly national state dominated by Slavs. The government closed German-language schools that had relatively few pupils. Land was confiscated from large property holders (nearly all ethnic Germans) and redistributed to peasants (predominantly Czechs and Slovaks).[35] Second, the 1920 language law made "Czechoslovak" the official state language, and German civil servants were ordered to learn Czech within two years or risk losing their jobs. This led to public demonstrations across the Sudeten German region.[36] Largely as a result of this law, *almost half* of all German state employees (excluding teachers) lost their jobs between 1921 and 1930.[37] Moreover, Sudeten Germans were continually depicted as outsiders and enemies of the new state; Czechoslovak president Tomáš Masaryk proclaimed in 1918 that "our Germans who originally entered the country as immigrants [*sic*] and colonists" must "work with us" in building the new state.[38]

German minorities in Czechoslovakia and Poland, recognizing their relative weakness in the new conflict environment, had moderated their demands by the early 1920s. Although they had been hoping for a border adjustment that would unite them with their kin states, the signing of the peace treaties in 1919 had dashed their dreams, leading German minority leaders to ratchet down their demands, acknowledging that "nothing now remained for Germans but to work for autonomy and civic freedom [within the new state]."[39] With the exception of a few renegade bases on the border, the Sudeten Germans put up little resistance as Czech legionnaires moved in to occupy the border regions and dissolve the provisional governments ethnic Germans had formed in hopes of annexation by Austria or Germany.[40] Having boycotted the first national elections in protest, the Sudeten Germans now began to participate in national elections, electing largely moderate leaders. A newly accommodating spirit began to develop within the Sudeten German political elite, with the emergence of German parties ("activists") willing to cooperate with their Czech counterparts in government. Over the 1920s, the activist wing began to garner greater electoral support within the German minority than the rejectionist "negativists."

The Germans in Poland also responded to their de-leveraged position by abandoning their demands to be united with Germany. Prior to the Versailles Treaty, German minority leaders had actively solicited assistance from the Reich to prepare the ground for Berlin to reclaim its "lost territories."[41] By the early 1920s, however, the minority raised little resistance when Warsaw consolidated its control over German territories. One minority leader responded to reports of advancing Polish units by saying, "We won't let ourselves be beat up here. . . . Let them come; we'll gladly surrender the city to them."[42] The most prominent nationalist organization, Deutscher Ostmarkenverein, had largely disappeared after the war, with much of its leadership having emigrated to Germany.[43] While there was some resistance to integrating into the Polish state—most notably the Poznanian Insurrection of December 1918—Warsaw put down most German resistance with minimal bloodshed as would-be irredentists realized that no assistance would be forthcoming from Germany.[44] By the time Germany and Poland began to normalize relations with the 1922 Geneva Convention on Upper Silesia, ethnic Germans in Poland had largely resigned themselves to their minority status and had begun to turn to the League for redress.

As predicted, external leveraging of the Slavic states undermined the effectiveness of preventive diplomacy. Despite the scores of minority petitions they had received, the League mediated the minority conflicts in ways that privileged the host governments. The Committees of Three conducted their "investigations" of ethnic German petitions through secret talks with the Polish and

Czechoslovak governments in ways designed to induce "a minimum of concessions." No accounting of the talks or the outcome was given to the minority complainants. In the rare cases that one of their decisions was appealed to the League Council, the host state (but not the minority petitioner) was allowed to attend, receiving full voting rights. In the proceedings, "debates were prearranged, and resolutions were tailored to the sensitivities of the accused government."[45] The host states were consistently favored over the minorities because "London, Rome, and Paris considered 'a little local suffering' by minorities to be a natural consequence of the new order in Eastern Europe."[46]

Preventive diplomacy was particularly ineffectual in addressing the very real discrimination faced by German optants in the Polish Corridor. Christian Raitz von Frentz estimates that from 1922 to 1930 the League Secretariat received 112 petitions from the German minority in Poland (excluding Silesia); almost all were declared admissible.[47] Minority organizations complained that the new Polish government had limited their rights to Polish citizenship. When the League found in favor of the minority, Poland refused to accept the ruling, and the matter was not resolved until 1923. The petitions also accused the government of expelling and expropriating ethnic Germans who had opted for German citizenship. Although League arbitration found in favor of the optants in this specific case—a decision codified in the Vienna Convention of 1924—the League proved unable to enforce the ruling. Preventive diplomacy thus failed to stem subsequent expulsions, and an additional twenty thousand were slated for removal in 1925. Through it all, the German minority assumed a surprisingly loyal, albeit oppositional, stance toward the Polish government—even participating in the political process. The Deutschtumsbunde helped to establish the Bloc of National Minorities, which ran a list of minority candidates in the 1922 national elections. In response to the constitutional requirement that members of parliament swear an oath of loyalty to "the Polish state as a whole,"[48] the leader of the German members of Parliament, Josef Spickermann, declared to the Sejm that "our Polish state will not need to be ashamed of the citizens of German nationality for whom it cares. . . . [From our behavior] our opponents will be convinced that one should not regard the German minority in Poland as an undesirable element, but should value it as an important and necessary factor in the state organism."[49] This illustrates a remarkable shift from openly hostile to strongly conciliatory minority discourse in the first few years of Polish independence.

League diplomacy also proved ineffectual in calming ethnic tensions in Czechoslovakia. Although not as active as Germans in Poland, the Germans in Czechoslovakia petitioned the League to halt and redress acts of Czech chauvinism. Because Geneva regarded Czechoslovakia as a liberal state, it was less sympathetic to the situation of minorities there. As a result, Sudeten

German leaders tended to lodge fewer complaints than their counterparts in Poland. The first Sudeten German petition in April 1922 was a lengthy a catalog of grievances against the Czechoslovak leadership. The petitioners accused the Prague government of excluding minority input in crafting their state constitution, rendering it invalid. They also contended that the Czechoslovak leaders had designed the land reform act to confiscate property from German landowners and redistribute it to the Slavs. A subsequent series of petitions held that minority compensation for expropriated property was grossly inadequate.[50] Few of these complaints gained traction, as Czechoslovak leaders—particularly the canny foreign minister Edvard Beneš—were able to use their personal connections in Geneva to convince the League that the minority petitions had no real merit given Czechoslovakia's highly liberal regime. League diplomats were largely satisfied with this response and took a consistently soft line on Prague.

The minority conflicts in Czechoslovakia and Poland in the early 1920s are best understood through the prism of nested security. With the Slavic states externally leveraged, this gave the host states wide latitude over the treatment of minorities (Variant B of nested insecurity). Whereas Czechoslovakia followed a relatively liberal path, Poland went down a more assimilationist path—the effects of which the League failed to mitigate through successive diplomatic interventions. Because the treaty states enjoyed the upper hand, League officials found it nearly impossible to enforce the decision in favor of the Polish optants. This explains the failure of preventive diplomacy better than any glitches in the mediation process. Raitz von Frentz writes, "The excessive delays between the receipt of petitions and the redress of legitimate grievances are to be explained by the [League's] *lack of enforcement powers*, rather than the inertia of the League bureaucracy."[51] The supposed failure of League diplomacy—in other words—had less to do with the identity of the mediators, much less the League dispute mechanism, than with the League's inability to impose sanctions on externally leveraged host governments.

Exogenous Stabilization—Nested Security under Locarno (1926 to Early 1930s)

The regional environment shifted dramatically in 1925 once Germany had concluded a treaty with France and Great Britain guaranteeing Germany's western borders in return for Allied withdrawal from the Rhineland. Germany henceforth joined the "Locarno Group" on the League Council, where the Big Three (Britain, France, and Germany) held private negotiations on geopolitically significant issues. The balance of power in Central Europe was gradually equalized as Britain and France withdrew their direct security guarantees for Czechoslovakia and Poland and as Germany regained diplomatic clout. Having secured a permanent seat on the League Council in 1926, Berlin could now lobby on behalf of its co-ethnics in neighboring countries. This meant that the two eastern states could no longer risk discriminating against ethnic Germans on their territory. At the same time, Germany was also constrained. Berlin could not afford to antagonize the West, whose help it needed to demilitarize the Rhineland and revise its punitive reparations payments. Germany therefore limited its interventionism to verbal posturing in League Council meetings and covert funding of minority organizations abroad. As German foreign minister Gustav Stresemann put it, Germany must "[settle] the political problems in the West, in order to be given a free hand in the East."[52] Accordingly, Berlin encouraged the Sudeten Germans to cooperate with Prague to demonstrate its pacific intentions to the West.[53]

The Locarno Accords had thus equalized the power balance between the host and patron states. This exogenous regional stabilization created a condition of nested security at the domestic level. The model therefore predicts de-escalation of sectarian tensions in both states, as neither German minorities nor Slavic majorities stood to gain from radicalizing against the other. As predicted, the Locarno Accords ushered in a period of interethnic cooperation known as the "Locarno spirit."[54]

Indeed, Czechoslovakia held national elections soon after the accords were concluded: German activists obtained the plurality of the minority vote for the first time in the new republic, while the German negativist bloc lost popular support. Rudolf Lodgman, the "father of Sudeten German nationalism," even lost his own seat in the Chamber of Deputies to a vocal advocate of German activism.[55] As the German-Slav cleavage lost political salience, Czechoslovak parties formed a governing coalition with their German counterparts for the first time; the leaders of the two German parties even garnered cabinet positions.[56] The German members of government adopted a resolution in September 1926 pledging to cooperate with the government so that "the German people in Czechoslovakia can acquire their rightful share of power and full equality in national, cultural, and economic affairs."[57]

The late 1920s was marked by a profound degree of Czech-German harmony, with German activists urging their constituents to support the government. At a German Christian Socialist party congress in Liberec, Justice Minister Robert Mayr-Harting stated categorically that the pursuit of irredentism "is just as dangerous as declaring a revolution."[58] The German agrarian party leader and public works minister Franz Spina designed proposals for educational autonomy in minority districts.[59] The minority leaders thus hewed to a policy of accommodation—making demands that could be easily satisfied within the existing state framework. In 1928–29, German and Czechoslovak parties formed alliances from the left to the right.[60] By 1930, even the Sudeten German Nazi Party proclaimed its willingness to collaborate with the Czechs, "given the right conditions."[61] This signified a complete realignment of coalitions in Czechoslovakia from ethnic to economic cleavages.

In Poland, too, the Locarno Accords created a condition of nested security on the ground, ushering in a period of relative interethnic cooperation, despite clear signs of distrust on both sides. Echoing the reaction in Prague, the Polish government reviled the Locarno treaties. According to Marshal Piłsudski, "every good Pole spits with disgust at the name [Locarno]."[62] In Germany, meanwhile, military officers and diplomats declared darkly that Poland was a *Saisonstaat* (a state for a season).[63] Despite their mutual hostility, both Warsaw and Berlin understood that for the time being, Poland's western borders were sacrosanct. The two countries agreed to "a kind of de facto East-Locarno . . . that should provide an adequate basis for good-neighborly relations."[64] In the late 1920s, therefore, "foreign policy decision makers in both Germany and Poland quite consciously and laboriously strove for a modus vivendi in their routine relations."[65] This had an immediate salutary effect on minority-majority relations in Poland. As part of the Locarno Accords, the Great Powers persuaded Warsaw to allow the remaining German optants (about seventeen thousand) to retain their residences in Poland.[66] Berlin and Warsaw also reached an agreement on outstanding reparation payments; the remaining citizenship questions were resolved in 1931.[67]

The two countries also sought to normalize their trade relations in the Locarno era. For Warsaw, a tariff war with Germany was a terrifying prospect, given that 40 percent of the Polish exports were destined for the German market.[68] Because of this, "Polish authorities became more amenable to entering into negotiations."[69] Likewise, "Germany could not afford to wage a tariff war with Poland for the sake of forcing her to her knees" on the border issue.[70] While a degree of economic warfare did ensue, this conflict was primarily due to Germany's industrial and agricultural lobbies; the two governments were engaged in earnest bilateral talks throughout, in a genuine effort to reach a trade deal with a side agreement on German minority rights.[71]

According to nested security, this "eastern Locarno" between Poland and Germany should have paved the way for improved ethnic relations on the ground. Consistent with this expectation, Kazimierz Bartel's government in 1926 (following Piłsudski's coup d'état) made significant improvements in minority rights. A Committee of Experts on the Eastern Provinces and National Minorities was established to debate the initiatives of Interior Minister Kazimierz Młodzianowski, who said that "the real task of the [Polish] state is to include [Germans, Jews, and Lithuanians] in the state system, to integrate them into it."[72] Poland's minority policy thenceforth shifted from national assimilation (*asymilacja narodowa*) to assimilation into state structures (*asymilacja państwowa*). As part of this initiative, the committee of experts recommended that minority activists be included in the workings of consultative bodies on minority issues. While the government did not really follow this advice, the principle of minority integration informed state policy into the 1930s.[73] Also consistent with nested security predictions, there was a concomitant de-escalation of sectarian tensions on the ground. According to one scholar, incidents involving the German minority occurred "somewhat less frequently between 1926 and 1929."[74]

Exogenous regional stabilization also increased the effectiveness of League mediation. German minority leaders in both countries praised the MPS as their best chance for obtaining a fair hearing in cases of official discrimination. At the pan-European Congress of Nationalities, Wilhelm von Medinger, a Sudeten German senator, averred that "we must . . . above all appeal to the League of Nations. Notwithstanding all its weakness, it still remains the most important forum for the expression of our complaints and desires. . . . We must collaborate wholeheartedly in its development."[75] In reality, the Sudeten Germans submitted very few petitions against Czechoslovakia during this time. With bilateral relations normalized, minority disputes were predictably handled at the domestic level, as both minority and majority had incentives to solve their problems internally.

In Poland, the League scored real diplomatic successes in the late 1920s. When the League Council ruled against the minority's right to mother tongue instruction in 1927, German foreign minister Stresemann accepted the judgment, saying that negotiations over the status of the Saar were more important than this "second-rate issue."[76] Indeed, it is largely because of cordial bilateral relations that the League was also able to resolve complaints of election tampering by the Upper Silesia Volksbund in 1931 and anti-German acts of terrorism by the nationalistic Insurgents' Union. Following League arbitration, a compromise was reached whereby the Polish government agreed to investigate cases of minority discrimination, list "compensations awarded for damages to persons and property," and report back to the League.[77] The late 1920s also saw a concomitant moderation of Polish German demands; minority leaders had dialed back their protests as well as the number of petitions they submitted to the League because they feared a backlash in the still-nationalistic state.

The Allied-brokered Locarno Accords had thus leveled the playing field between Germany and the two Slavic states. This created a condition of nested security in Czechoslovakia, yielding a decade of Czech-German political coalitions and compromise. Although less dramatic, this "hegemonic leveling" also led to bilateral negotiations between Poland and Germany, resolving important outstanding disputes over expropriated German optants and improving the treatment of minorities. The League did facilitate the resolution of disputes over the German optants and education issues in Poland, but these efforts bore fruit only after Locarno had rendered both sides open to compromise. In the earlier period, League intervention had little impact in Czechoslovakia and actually provoked a backlash in Poland. It was only when the conflicts were nested in a stable regional environment that League diplomacy yielded success.

Exogenous Destabilization—Minorities Enjoy the Upper Hand (Mid-1930s to World War II)

In the 1930s, Germany regained its geopolitical dominance of Central Europe, upsetting the fragile modus vivendi it had achieved with its eastern neighbors. Meanwhile, the economic crisis and associated rise of extremist groups and parties began to put pressure on moderates in the German Foreign Ministry to harden their stance against the eastern states, particularly Poland. Berlin now submitted a series of complaints to Geneva on behalf of its co-ethnics, accusing Warsaw of disenfranchising ethnic Germans in western Poland. By making stringent demands on the Polish government and threatening to withdraw from the League if Poland did not address its concerns, the German government sought to recapture the support of its radicalized electorate. Raitz von Frentz writes that Berlin's habit of seizing the League Council to deliberate these petitions during this time "was poorly planned and primarily guided by propaganda considerations."[78] By the mid-1930s, Reich agencies also accelerated their financial and logistical support of German minority organizations in Czechoslovakia and Poland, effectively re-creating conditions of nested *in*security in Central Europe.

As expected by the model, Germany's revisionist posturing encouraged the minorities to mobilize against their host governments. Elizabeth Wiskemann writes that despite the many differences in minority leadership between Czechoslovakia and Poland, "the effect of the Nazi régime in Germany was to bring about a parallel *Gleichschaltung* within the German minorities abroad, in preparation for their exploitation as fifth columns in the cold, and then the real, war."[79] Notwithstanding Czechoslovakia's ever-increasing concessions to the Sudeten Germans, Sudeten representatives thus continually rejected a negotiated agreement.[80] In the mid-1930s, Sudeten Germans thence switched their allegiance from moderate German parties to the nationalist Sudeten German Party (SdP) headed by Konrad Henlein.

Formal negotiations between minority and government leaders were initiated in 1936, just as Germany began to challenge its eastern borders. After many failed attempts to broker a compromise, Prime Minister Milan Hodža finally demanded that the German parties in government produce a concrete list of demands. Following monthlong talks between Czech and German ministers, the government issued the Memorandum of 18 February, promising to meet these demands. However, the SdP refused to accept the memorandum and staged demonstrations in protest, claiming that the document was little more than government propaganda.[81]

In Poland, too, the rise of Nazi Germany radicalized the German minority and improved the fortunes of German minority extremists. A national socialist Jungdeutsche Partei in Polen (JdP), created in Bielitz, Poland, in 1931, soon spread to Pomerania and the Posen region. Although formally declaring its loyalty to the Polish state and supporting the country's "independence from foreign powers" (including Germany),[82] the party also proclaimed that the German minority must have "free space to regulate their life in line with German principles and worldview."[83] Older German minority organizations such as Deutsche Volksbund (DV), which competed with the JdP for the German minority vote, also grew more nationalistic. DV chair Otto Ulitz stated that the "Nazi" tag, used by the Poles in relation to his organization, should be regarded as a compliment.[84]

The Polish government initially ignored the threat of minority radicalization—in the eyes of Piłsudski, the Nazis were "nothing but windbags."[85] However, Warsaw soon perceived the growing Nazi threat for what it was and, despite concluding a nonaggression pact with Germany in January 1934,[86] accelerated its assimilationist policies in the border regions to rid the country of German influence once and for all. This meant increased employment discrimination, further minority expropriation, and the closure of numerous religious and cultural associations.[87] The German minority also gradually lost political power. After the 1928 elections, Germans had nineteen members of parliament (4.3 percent of Sejm delegates), but their number fell to five (1.1 percent) after the 1930 elections. By 1938, there were no German minority representatives in parliament whatsoever.[88]

Consistent with the logic of nested security, League diplomacy became utterly ineffectual during this time. While favoring the Slavic states in the early 1920s, the League became ever more deferential toward the revisionist states in the 1930s. Although Germany's threats to withdraw from the League were generally scorned by the international community, League officials never confronted Germany directly. They instead attempted to work *around* Berlin and its kin organizations by inducing Warsaw to redress German minority grievances and thereby forestall Berlin's expansionism. Tellingly, the League Secretariat actually stepped up its investigations of outstanding German minority petitions *after* Germany had exited the League.[89]

Preventive diplomacy also failed to de-escalate ethnic tensions in Czecho-slovakia. As Sudeten German hard-liners effectively radicalized the German minority, Sudeten German moderates appealed to the League and the Great Powers to impose sanctions against Prague and thereby give the moderates a win. To this end, they sent a petition to the League against the Machník Decree that purportedly discriminated against non-Czechs in awarding defense contracts. The hope was that the petition would go before the League Council (presided over by the British) and result in a finding against the Czechoslovak government, demonstrating the ongoing value of ethnic moderation. In the course of this campaign, Heinz Rutha and other Sudeten German moderates actually visited London on multiple occasions to enjoin London to pressure Prague for concessions—all to no avail.

The Czechoslovak government eventually complied with the League's request to "tone down" the decree, but the case became entangled in bureaucracy and was eventually buried.[90] By then, it was too late; the Sudeten radicals had assumed control of the minority movement, and Henlein—reading the writing on the wall—threw in his lot with the hard-liners. From 1937 onward, the Czechs would play a cat-and-mouse game with the Sudeten German Party leadership, offering ever more generous concessions that Henlein continually rejected as inadequate. In August 1938, Britain belatedly sent Lord Runciman as an "independent advisor" to Czechoslovakia to assess Sudeten German grievances and assist in brokering a compromise between the Czechs and Germans. Pressured by London to facilitate a settlement, Runciman lamely concluded that the Czechs should continue to offer concessions to the German minority.[91]

In April 1939, Hitler declined to renew the nonaggression pact with Poland (after Poland refused Nazi foreign minister Joachim Ribbentrop's demands for significant territorial concessions), and Warsaw retaliated by renouncing its 1937 minority declaration—leaving Germans in Poland undefended. With their host and kin states on the brink of war, Poland's Germans fully threw in their lot with Nazi Germany. Fearful of the emergence of a German fifth column in the eventuality of a Nazi invasion, the Polish government responded by closing German schools and newspapers, outlawing the majority of German political organizations, and arresting minority leaders and activists.[92] Authorities rounded up thousands of civilians and marched them to the east to be interned, killing many in the process.[93] Nazi propagandists used this as proof that Warsaw was engaged in a systematic campaign of "Polish atrocities" in order to justify, ex post facto, their subsequent invasion of Poland in September 1939.[94]

In Czechoslovakia, too, the German minority welcomed Nazi German forces who invaded, dismembered, and occupied the country in 1938.

Following the war, millions of Sudeten Germans would be expelled from Czechoslovakia on charges of collective collaboration—as many as several hundred thousand were killed or summarily executed in ethnic cleansing legalized retroactively under the Beneš decrees. As this case narrative makes clear, regional destabilization in the 1930s had tragic (even fatal) consequences for the German minorities, who eventually suffered tragic losses at the hands of vengeful majorities. This should serve as a stark illustration that, under conditions of nested insecurity, preventive diplomacy is all but useless in containing sectarian violence.

Hungarian Minorities in Central Europe
The 1920 Treaty of Trianon reduced the multinational Kingdom of Hungary to an ethnically homogeneous rump, with just one-third of its former territory and two-thirds of its nationals. By far the biggest beneficiaries of the transfer were Romania (Transylvania), Czechoslovakia (Slovakia and Transcarpathian Ruthenia), and the Kingdom of Serbs, Croats, and Slovenes.[95] To head off insurrections by revisionist minorities, the new and enlarged states were required to sign minority treaties with the League in which they pledged to accommodate their sizable Hungarian minorities. In addition to providing for language, educational, and cultural rights, Romania's treaty included an additional proviso that the government confer autonomy upon the territorially concentrated Hungarian and Saxon minorities in Transylvania.

The severity of minority disputes varied considerably across the three successor countries. As with the German minorities, Hungarians fared best in Czechoslovakia—a small country with a relatively liberal leadership and weak military, which needed the support of its large, concentrated minorities (not to mention the Allied powers) to survive. The situation was rather different in Romania, whose non-liberal head of state viewed the country's minorities as enemies rather than potential allies. The least mobilized Hungarian minority was in Yugoslavia, where the royal dictatorship looked askance upon minority protections and was even less enamored of foreign involvement. Variation in the treatment of minorities is reflected in the pattern of petitions submitted to the League and other international forums from 1920 to 1939. Whereas just twenty-one petitions were submitted on behalf of Hungarians in Yugoslavia and twenty-six petitions for Hungarians in Czechoslovakia, fully fifty-five petitions were submitted on behalf of the Hungarian minority in Romania.[96] To assess the influence of regional conflict dynamics on the mediations of minority conflicts, I conduct a comparative longitudinal analysis of the Hungarian minority conflicts in Romania and Czechoslovakia.[97]

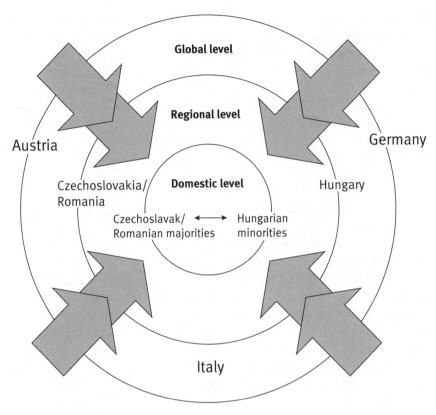

Figure 3.2 Nested security and the Hungarian minorities

Destabilization—Host States Enjoy Upper Hand (1918 to mid-1920s)

In 1921, Romania, Czechoslovakia, and Yugoslavia formed the Little Entente—a regional security pact made up of a series of bilateral alliances. The fact that Yugoslavia and Romania were able to set aside their simmering border dispute to establish a defensive alliance demonstrates the depth of their fear that Hungary would attempt to restore its historical borders and prewar monarchy.[98] At the same time, they understood that they now enjoyed Allied leverage against the defeated power. Czechoslovak foreign minister Beneš commented that "the ratification of the Peace of Trianon, the birth of the Little Entente . . . have convinced the Hungarians that they must submit themselves to our political line."[99] Indeed, Hungary was constitutionally barred from rearming and was encircled by the Little Entente, which enjoyed the backing of Great Powers (in the 1920s France signed security guarantees with Czechoslovakia, Romania, and finally Yugoslavia). Given its unfavorable geopolitical position, Budapest had little choice but to appeal to the Allies for a friendly revision to the punitive peace agreement. Count Albert Apponyi, head of the Hungarian delegation to the League, suggested hopefully that "the composition of the Council of the League of Nations is not unfavourable and it cannot be denied that there is . . . some evidence of good intentions to make improvements."[100]

In its weakened position, Budapest therefore refrained from supporting Hungarians abroad in favor of indirect appeals to the League on their behalf. Apponyi complained to the Council in 1923 that the relative weakness of Hungary as compared to Romania meant that Hungary "can count only upon the League of Nations, [giving it] only one recourse, namely, appeal to an institution which you yourselves established."[101] Hungary's best and only course of action was to work within the system, despite the League's apparent bias against the defeated states. Accordingly, Budapest submitted numerous complaints to the League over the 1920s—mainly to do with the dispossessed Hungarian optants and Székelys in Romania. At the same time, Budapest steadfastly refused appeals from its co-ethnics for direct assistance.

The regional balance of power between Hungary and its neighbors was thus skewed in favor of the neighboring states, creating a condition of nested *inse*curity. The model predicts that the host states would respond to their leverage by pursuing policies driven by domestic political considerations (Variant B). At the same time, minority leaders—recognizing their lack of leverage—should remain relatively passive. As expected, minorities *were* treated differently by each target state. The Czechoslovak government enacted greater minority protections than required under its minority treaty, at least partly to retain the goodwill of its Allied sponsors. As a result, ethnic Hungarians fared best in Czechoslovakia.[102] Nonetheless, the government attempted to remove the privileges the minority had enjoyed in the Slovak region due to centuries of Hungarian suzerainty. Particularly, "in the cities near the Slovak-Hungarian ethnic borderlands," the new Slovak administrators "used the schools as a dike to help stop the advance of Magyarization."[103] Anti-Hungarian sentiment ran high in the region: immediately after the establishment of Czechoslovakia, the Hungarian university in Bratislava was closed and its monuments torn down. Many Hungarian schools were closed or converted into German or Czechoslovak schools. The government dismissed many Hungarians from civil service or teaching positions, and the early postwar period saw an outflow of tens of thousands of ethnic Hungarians to the motherland.[104] Despite these unprecedented losses, minority leaders merely sought to roll back Slavic assimilationism in the areas of education and language policy, as predicted by the model.

The situation for minorities was far worse in Romania—a sizable, powerful country whose government was hostile to both the League and its treaty obligations. One scholar wrote, "In the view of Bucharest, the Hungarians were a potential Trojan Horse because of their presumed allegiance to Hungarian revisionism." The government therefore set out to aggressively "Romanianize" its territorial acquisitions by replacing Hungarian officials with Romanians and imposing Romanian as the official language of the state.[105] Bucharest targeted the Hungarian upper class by violating its pledge to establish autonomy for Hungarians and Saxons in Transylvania; it also used an old agrarian law to strip land from the (predominantly Hungarian) large landholders, redistributing it to the wider population. Finally, the government expropriated its Hungarian optants—ethnic Hungarians in Transylvania who had chosen to apply for Hungarian citizenship. Although Trianon accorded individuals the right "to retain their immovable property in the territory of the other state where they had their place of residence before exercising their right to opt," Bucharest paid no attention to this stricture.[106]

As expected, ethnic Hungarians responded to their de-leveraged position by dialing back their demands. Before the signing of the Trianon Treaty, minority leaders had forcefully demanded independence for Transylvania. In May 1919, a twelve-point memorandum for Transylvanian independence stated that "independent Transylvania considers relationships with Hungary or Romanian [*sic*] as foreign policy issues and seeks solutions which will not violate its independence."[107] After the treaty was signed, however, the same leaders quickly scaled back their demands. Their kin state apparently impotent, the Hungarian minority now attempted to negotiate directly with the Romanian government. Their 1921 political program proclaimed that the Hungarians in Transylvania "want to build autonomy for two million Hungarians *within this framework*, part of which had been promised to us by the sanctioned laws of Romania . . . and the rest of which will be acquired by our will and strength, granted by the sober discretion of Romania."[108] In the years that followed, Romania's campaigns of national assimilation led ethnic Hungarians to moderate their claims still further—in 1927, the leadership called for "universality in culture" and for approaching the majority nation with "moral truths."[109] For the remainder of the decade, minority leaders had little choice but to turn to the League with their hopes for redress.

Allied leveraging of the new states had thus created a condition of nested *in*security in the new states, leading to the prediction that preventive diplomacy would be fairly ineffective in managing Hungarian minority conflicts. As expected, while sympathetic to Hungarian minority grievances, League officials proved reluctant to champion their cause. In a comment to the British representatives on the council, League secretary-general Eric Drummond admitted that the Romanian agrarian law did indeed discriminate against ethnic Hungarians, since it was applied in a far more draconian fashion in

Hungarian minority regions. However, he cautioned against supporting Hungary, noting that "we do not wish to appear as protagonists on behalf of big Magyar landlords."[110] In 1923, Drummond and Erik Colban, head of the Minorities Section, traveled to Romania to assess the minority situation. Once there, however, they met almost exclusively with government officials. Colban later delivered a speech at a Hungarian university in Cluj, averring that the minority conflict could be solved only in direct talks with the Romanian government—signaling that neither the Hungarian minority nor the minority's kin state would have a say in the talks.[111] British foreign secretary Austen Chamberlain likewise observed that "this was not a question between Hungary and the League nor one in which Hungary had any *locus standi*; it was a question between the League and the Romanian government."[112]

Even when the League decided in favor of the Hungarian minorities, it appeared unable to enforce its decisions. In a landmark minority victory in 1927, a Mixed Arbitration Tribunal ruled that Romania's expropriation of land in Transylvania had violated the terms of Trianon. However, Romania rejected the decision and withdrew its judge in protest. The League was forced to acknowledge that it was powerless to ensure compliance with the ruling. The failure of the League to mediate this and other conflicts involving Hungarians in Romania left both parties dissatisfied and may have even exacerbated domestic tensions. Hungarian minority leaders meanwhile concluded that they could do no better outside the League and continued to petition the League for redress. Disgusted by the apparent failure of League diplomacy to manage the conflict, Budapest began to threaten to leave the international body. However, the government later admitted that this was mostly a bluff. In 1927, Hungarian prime minister Count István Bethlen affirmed that "the Hungarian Government [does] not intend to withdraw from the League of Nations, but [will] fight for their rights within the League."[113]

In Czechoslovakia, meanwhile, the League was wholly unresponsive to Hungarian minority claims. In the mid-1920s, Hungarian organizations submitted petitions to the League claiming that Prague had disproportionately expropriated Hungarian landowners, placed restrictions on Hungarian media, dismissed Hungarians from the civil service, and arrested individuals for listening to the Hungarian national anthem on the radio or displaying the Hungarian tricolor. Generally speaking, these petitions never went further than private consultations with Czechoslovak officials, who invariably convinced League officials that they had more than fulfilled their treaty obligations.

The League did little during this period to de-escalate tensions between ethnic Hungarians and the ethnic majorities. Indeed, it may have even legitimized the leverage of the host state governments, creating a permissive environment for their nationalizing policies. In their weakened position, meanwhile, the Hungarian minorities could do little more than petition the League for small measures of redress (such as fair compensation for property expropriation)—petitions that became ever less frequent as the MPS continued to favor the host states.

Exogenous Stabilization—Nested Security and the Danubian Détente (Late 1920s to Early 1930s)

The regional balance of power began to shift in Hungary's favor in the late 1920s. To counter French influence in the Danubian region, Italy had signed a Treaty of Friendship and Cooperation with Hungary in 1927. At the same time, the Allies removed control over Hungary's disarmament from inter-Allied agencies, while controls over Hungary's finances were terminated. In an incident that attracted significant international attention, five carloads of machine guns from Italy to Hungary were intercepted at the Austrian-Hungarian border; the League Council overlooked the incident owing to Italy's status as a permanent member of the Council.[114] Meanwhile, the owner of the London *Daily Mail*, the First Viscount Rothermere (Harold Harmsworth),[115] launched a public relations campaign in the British media to revise Trianon's borders in Hungary's favor, creating a wave of excitement in Hungarian diplomatic circles. Italy eventually joined Austria and Hungary in a tripartite pact under the Rome Protocols of 1934. At the same time, an alliance between Nazi Germany and Hungary began to crystallize following a secret trade agreement between Budapest and Berlin in early 1934.[116] This catapulted Hungary into something resembling geopolitical parity with the Entente states by the 1930s.

Despite these changes, Hungary's territorial aspirations remained constrained until the late 1930s. This is mainly because Germany had encouraged Hungary to broker bilateral pacts with Czechoslovakia and especially Romania. Although he had earlier advocated Hungarian revisionism, Hitler scaled back his support for Greater Hungary after coming to office. Once in power, Hitler informed Hungarian leaders that they would have to satisfy themselves with Slovak territory alone, as they would receive no assistance in reclaiming the regions of Transylvania (in Romania) or Vojvodina (in Yugoslavia)—a tactical move on Hitler's part to cement good relations with Hungary's neighbors. Italy, too, urged Hungary to reach a rapprochement with these countries, particular Romania. At the same time, worsening economic conditions gave Hungary strong incentives to bury the hatchet with Romania in order to break out of its position of diplomatic isolation with the West.

Although he had earlier earned a political reputation as a nationalist revisionist, the new Hungarian premier, Gyula Gömbös, therefore sought to strengthen ties with Bucharest. In 1933, he put forward a ninety-five-point plan declaring himself "prepared to consider any reasonable co-operation of the Danubian States."[117] Thomas Sakmyster notes that Hungary made a decision to shelve its revanchist goals for the time being; Prime Minister Bethlen made neither irredentist demands nor military plans to alter the Trianon borders. Instead, he publicly committed Hungary to a "policy of fulfillment of the Treaty of Trianon" in hopes of improving Hungary's status in the eyes of the Allies. Bethlen recognized that in a time of global recession, the country needed foreign investment, international trade, and Allied assistance to achieve an economic recovery.[118]

In view of Hungary's growing diplomatic leverage, the Romanian diplomat Nicolae Titulescu affirmed that Romania unconditionally desired friendship with Hungary. In an interview published in Hungarian newspapers, he called for bilateral cooperation and the creation of an economic bloc consisting of the members of the Little Entente, Hungary, and Austria. To sweeten the deal, he offered Hungary the use of a Romanian port, better treatment of the Hungarian minority, and the "spiritualization of borders."[119] This led to a series of negotiations the following year, producing two bilateral agreements, on bank-clearing regulations and wood sales.

Hungary's regional patrons had effectively created a situation of nested security in the Danube region by allying with Budapest while encouraging it to exercise restraint toward its neighbors. This promoted bilateral normalization, nesting the minority disputes in a stable regional environment. Under these conditions, the model predicts greater minority integration in both Romania and Czechoslovakia. Consistent with these expectations, Hungarians in Transylvania welcomed Bucharest's newly conciliatory attitude, and support grew within the minority population for a "spiritual" community of ethnic coexistence between the Romanians and Hungarians. Regional stabilization also appears to have influenced the attitudes of Hungarians in Czechoslovakia, who increasingly accepted their minority status in the Slavic state as well as the prospect of integrating into Czechoslovak society. This was reflected in rising rates of Hungarian enrollment in Czechoslovak schools and faculties, which demonstrated "an increasing Hungarian preference for Czechoslovak (over German) education."[120]

Exogenous stabilization by Germany, Italy, and Austria also facilitated successful League diplomacy. The optant case in Romania was finally settled in favor of ethnic Hungarians under the Paris-Hague Agreement of 1930, which set up a fund to compensate Hungarian optants for their expropriated property. In 1932, an international committee of jurists determined that the Székely case should be decided at the international level rather than in Romanian courts, which Bucharest accepted. League officials attempted to arbitrate fairly in that case, traveling to Bucharest as well as the frontier region to get both views. Based on their findings, the Committee of the League adopted a solution that involved returning some of the expropriated land to the Székelys. League officials professed satisfaction with this resolution, citing the absence of new petitions on behalf of the Székelys as evidence that the problems had been solved. Although there were episodic minority attacks in Romania in the early 1930s, Bucharest endeavored to contain ethnic tensions in the country. Titulescu proclaimed that the government was determined to punish any demonstrators who targeted ethnic Hungarians. Following an exceptionally violent protest in Cluj, Titulescu penned a condemnation of the attacks, which appeared in all the Bucharest newspapers.[121] Meanwhile, a combination of Colban's personal diplomacy, credible threats to impose sanctions on Romania at the League Council or the Permanent Court, and fears of provoking the ire of Budapest prevented further minority expropriations.[122]

This demonstrates that preventive diplomacy had become much more effective once Austria, Italy, and Germany stabilized the Danube region, creating a condition of nested security in Czechoslovakia and Romania. As Hungary attracted external allies, and as Hungary's neighbors lost their direct security guarantees from France, bilateral relations between Budapest and its neighbors became exogenously stabilized. In these conditions, both sides welcomed arbitration by the League, permitting successful mediation of decade-long minority disputes.

Regional Destabilization—Kin State Gains Upper Hand (Mid- to Late 1930s)

By the mid-1930s, Hungary had strengthened its ties with Nazi Germany to the point where it no longer looked to the League to redress its grievances concerning Hungarians abroad. Indeed, only *one* of the dozens of League petitions in the mid-1930s was submitted by an organization with ties to Budapest.[123] The increasingly leveraged Hungarian government in turn leveraged ethnic Hungarians in Romania and Czechoslovakia, creating a condition of nested insecurity that made minority radicalization more likely (Variant A). Carlile Macartney, a contemporary observer of Hungarian minorities in the region, wrote that "the old Transylvanian spirit has revived in remarkable fashion. . . . They would like to see a modification of the old Transylvanian system, i.e., the cohabitation of three 'nations'—now the Magyar, the Romanian, and the German—on an equal footing, each enjoying the widest possible self-government."[124] Piroska Balogh confirmed that Hungarian revanchism had a palpable impact on Hungarian minority demands against Romania: "As Hungarian foreign policy changed as chances for revision also changed, advocates of Transylvanianism raised increasingly radical demands."[125] Hungarian minority leaders began to advocate "a policy of self-sufficiency and rejection, and hoped for revisionism. This rejectionism was demonstrated in 1937 with the "It is not possible" debate initiated by Sándor Makkai, in which he stated that the life of a minority was "unworthy of humans."[126] While it is unclear how popular such sentiments were on the ground, there was an obvious connection between Hungary's increasingly revisionist rhetoric, Nazi Germany's expansionist foreign policy, and the radicalized Hungarian minority.

Seeing this, the Romanian government assumed an apparently more conciliatory stance, offering greater concessions to the Hungarian minority in hopes of reaching a bilateral agreement.[127] In 1935, Titulescu made the unprecedented offer of territorial autonomy for the minority Székely lands. Despite these overtures, Hungarian officials eschewed serious negotiations, claiming to distrust their Romanian counterparts. Undeterred, Titulescu made a determined plea for rapprochement, appealing to Budapest to specify the exact conditions under which a bilateral treaty could be concluded.[128] These gestures were roundly rebuffed.

The Hungarians in Czechoslovakia were more moderate than Hungarians in Romania—in large part because Budapest's revisionism was mainly directly toward Transylvania.[129] Macartney noted the striking moderation of Hungarians in Slovakia as late as the mid-1930s: "It is safe to say that active agitation against the Czechoslovak State—even the active resentment against it—is confined to a small fraction of the [Magyar] population."[130] Nonetheless, Budapest's growing leverage led Hungarians in Czechoslovakia to radicalize as well. A survey conducted in the late 1930s suggested that "under normal circumstances, 70 percent of the Magyar population of Slovakia would vote for a return to Hungary."[131] By the time of the 1938 Anschluss, Nazi Germany had formed a wartime alliance with the Hungarian government through a mix of economic pressure, threats of military invasion, and the promised return of Hungary's lost territories. As a reward for Budapest's allegiance, Hungary received the Hungarian region of Slovakia in 1938 and Transylvania in 1940—territories that were again removed from Hungary following the defeat of the Axis powers in the Second World War.

These cases demonstrate that the external environment had a significant influence on the intensity of minority conflicts in Romania and Czechoslovakia. So long as Hungary was constrained by a punitive postwar treaty and hemmed in on all sides by the Allied-backed Little Entente, a condition of nested *in*security prevailed. Allied leveraging of Czechoslovakia and Romania in the 1920s, meanwhile, gave the target states the upper hand in minority affairs. In view of this, Hungary and its minorities limited themselves to passively petitioning the League of Nations. For its part, the League tended to institutionalize this power asymmetry by favoring the target states over Hungary and ethnic Hungarians, whose complaints were generally ignored. It was only in the early 1930s that the region was exogenously stabilized—when the target states lost direct security guarantees from the Allies while Hungary gained the backing of Italy, Austria, and Germany. At this point, the League was able to resolve outstanding minority disputes.

However, once Hungary's power (backed by Nazi Germany) began to exceed that of its neighbors in the mid- to late 1930s, and as it began to intervene more aggressively on behalf of its kin, preventive diplomacy once again became ineffectual. With Germany leveraging Hungary, Budapest no longer had the need to appeal to the League, and its empowered kin no longer had incentives to accept a League-mediated resolution.

What explains the variable effectiveness of League diplomacy in managing Hungarian and German minority conflicts in interwar Europe? One argument is that a cooperative or liberal host government is a critical determinant of mediation success. Indeed, the relatively illiberal Romanian and Polish regimes *did* engender more intractable conflicts (measured in terms of number of minority petitions and seriousness of complaints) than did the relatively liberal Czechoslovak state, whose minorities were far more quiescent and politically integrated. However, even the relatively pro-minority policies of interwar Czechoslovakia did not prevent the radicalization of the Sudeten German minority in the late 1930s. Moreover, the attitudes of the host government cannot easily explain variable conflict *within* the same state. In Czechoslovakia, for instance, the Hungarian minority conflict proved less intense than the German minority conflict, despite the fact that far more concessions had been afforded to the Germans. Finally, although Germans in Poland suffered harsher discrimination than the Germans in Czechoslovakia, both groups ultimately turned against their host states—some even assisting the Nazi government in annexing territories in the late 1930s.

Another explanation for mediation success relates to the credibility and resources of the League. The fact that the MPS was not generalized to minorities in the West might have created resentments in the East, leading target states to adopt an uncooperative stance toward League diplomacy. While there is some truth to this, the unfairness of the system does not explain *fluctuations* in the success of the League. Indeed, defeated powers and minority states alike accepted the League system enough to work within it, even taking into consideration the obstructionism by some minority states and the bitterness of the defeated powers. The fact remains that hundreds of minority petitions—originating with the defeated powers and disgruntled minorities themselves—were submitted to the Minorities Section from the early 1920s to the mid-1930s. The League succeeded in resolving a number of these issues diplomatically—including bilateral trade and banking agreements, as well as the treatment of minority optants.

Perhaps the variable success was due to inadequate funding and inefficiencies in the League system, which led to delays that aggravated ethnic tensions on the ground. While the MPS was indeed grossly underfunded (leading to oversights, inconsistencies, and inadequate resolutions), the resources commanded by the League did not change very much after the early 1920s, and thus cannot explain the episodic successes of preventive diplomacy in the four cases. The qualified successes achieved by the League in the late 1920s and early 1930s, for example, were accomplished with roughly the same resources that had been allotted to the League already by the early 1920s.

This chapter shows that the unique pattern of events in the four mediated conflicts cannot be explained without taking into account the stability of the regional neighborhood. One student of Hungarian politics noted that "the duel [between Budapest and Prague] kept the atmosphere tense, and decreased the likelihood of a rapprochement."[132] Another scholar observed that "without effective external pressure, threat or constraint, an agreement between the two rival countries, Romania and Hungary, based on a mutually acceptable equitable compromise was inconceivable."[133] Hungary had been encircled by the Little Entente states, whose security had in turn been guaranteed by Britain and especially France. Hungary's weakness in the early 1920s largely accounts for the dismissive attitude toward Hungarian minority complaints in Transylvania—not only by League authorities, but also by Britain, which consistently took the side of the Romanian government.

This began to change in the late 1920s, when Hungary entered into an alliance with Italy and sought closer ties with Germany and Austria—producing a kind of Danubian détente. From this point forward, League officials began to broker more meaningful settlements that took into account the concerns of all parties. As the 1930s progressed and Hungary strengthened its ties with a revanchist Germany, the leveraged Budapest government abandoned bilateral negotiations with Romania and exited the League. This had the overall effect of fueling minority radicalization in Transylvania in particular.

The German minority cases offer even stronger support for the theory of nested security. The position of Germans abroad improved significantly once Germany had begun to recover from the First World War, particularly after Germany entered the League with a seat on the Council. At that point, Germany was still too weak to push for border revision, but strong enough to lobby effectively for its minorities. At the same time, Poland and Czechoslovakia

Table 3.2 Summary evaluation of theories

Case pair	Minority protections / liberal government	Credibility of mediator / value of carrots and sticks	Nested security
German minorities in Poland and Czechoslovakia	*Partially confirmed* Greater level of liberal democracy in Czechoslovakia helps account for greater ethnic cooperation in Czechoslovakia than in Poland in the early interwar period, but does not account for similar minority radicalization in the mid- to late 1930s.	*Disconfirmed* The League has the same enforcement powers throughout interwar period. However, these cannot account for fluctuations over time in mediation success.	*Confirmed* Regional destabilization in the early 1920s empowers target states vis-à-vis Germany; they implement minority policies according to domestic preferences. Exogenous stabilization in the late 1920s leads to some mediation success. Regional destabilization in the mid-1930s leads to minority mobilization in both states.
Hungarian minorities in Romania and Czechoslovakia	*Partially confirmed* Greater liberalism of Czechoslovakia accounts for higher Hungarian minority integration in Czechoslovakia than in Romania, but does not account for fluctuations in the success of League diplomacy from the 1920s to the 1930s.	*Disconfirmed* The League has roughly the same resources and credibility through the entire interwar period. Mediator legitimacy and capacity does not explain fluctuations in the success of League diplomacy over time.	*Confirmed* The region is destabilized in the early 1920s, empowering target states to follow domestically driven minority policies. The region is exogenously stabilized in the late 1920s and early '30s, facilitating some mediation success. Later, Nazi leveraging of Hungary leads to minority mobilization in both states.

had lost their direct security guarantees from the Allies, making them vulnerable to German revanchism. Given a regional stalemate—with Germany unable to revise the status quo and Poland and Czechoslovakia no longer able to openly discriminate against German minorities—a condition of nested security emerged at the domestic level. From the late 1920s to the early 1930s, League diplomacy met with greater success. With Hitler's rise to power in the mid-1930s, nested *in*security again prevailed as Reich-supported minority organizations in Czechoslovakia and Poland began to rebel against their respective governments. League officials could do little more than watch helplessly as the opening scenes of the Second World War unfolded.

Could the League have averted the events of the late 1930s? Although it had no enforcement power of its own, it did have a mandate for monitoring and information sharing that could have been used to identify early violations of the Versailles Treaty, such as cross-border interventions on the part of the Reich. Rather than focusing solely on the minority policies of the target governments, League officials could have monitored the status of *bilateral* relationships in troubled regions more systematically in order to identify factors that threatened to destabilize the regional equilibrium. Through continual engagement and monitoring of conflict dynamics throughout the region, the League might have issued earlier warnings of the events that together created a condition of nested *in*security in Central Europe. This might have given major powers more time to prepare a response to Axis policies of territorial expansion.

4

INDUCED DEVOLUTION IN INTERWAR EUROPE

There were a handful of conflicts in Central Europe that presented no easy solution to the architects of the Versailles peace. Most of these cases featured two or more states with competing claims to a uniquely valuable piece of land. The Allies chose to handle conflicts over energy-rich Upper Silesia and the Saarland through direct international administration—similar to the mandates that the League of Nations applied to the former colonies of defeated powers. However, in the cases of Danzig, Memel, and the Åland Islands (see map 1, chapter 3), the League opted to lean on state governments to devolve significant autonomy to the region in question.

Unlike the Saarland—internationally administered for fifteen years until 1935, when the residents were given the choice to join either France or Germany—these regions received extensive territorial self-government in their host states. Of the three, the Åland arrangement is the only one that remains in place today; the autonomy of the other two regions lasted only until the beginning of the Second World War. The three cases offer valuable tests of the nested security model, as each internal dispute was nested in a wider regional conflict, which fluctuated over time. Memel was a port city on the Baltic Sea claimed by Poland, Lithuania, and Germany. Danzig, contested by Germany and Poland, also contained an important outlet to the Baltic Sea. Finally, the Åland Islands—claimed by Finland and Sweden—were a strategically valuable archipelago in the Baltic Sea.

Why did the League succeed in resolving the Åland Island dispute, but not the other two? The most obvious explanation is that the 1921 Åland agreement gave Sweden, Finland, and the Ålanders a higher payoff than conflict or war, facilitating an end to an emerging dispute. In other words, it provided the minority with sufficient autonomy over the policy areas it cared most about, including mother tongue education, language laws, and the like—satisfying the Ålanders and their kin state, Sweden. The arrangement was also good for Finland, as it allowed the government to retain territorial control over the region. Devolution was less successful in Memel and Danzig, according to this logic, because their autonomy arrangements represented an unsatisfactory division of sovereignties relative to what the disputants could expect to gain through violence.

When examined over time, however, it is far from clear that the value of the autonomy arrangements can account for fluctuations in sectarian tensions in the three cases. Consistent with the nested security model, the stability of the regional environment does a better job of explaining mediation success at nearly every stage of conflict. So long as the relevant regional players were locked in conflict, ethnic tensions remained elevated at the grassroots level. By contrast, once deals were reached at the regional level, the disputes on the ground became far more amenable to soft-power conflict management. This suggests that the apparent "failure" of devolution in Danzig and Memel had less to do with the details of their autonomy arrangements than with destabilizing events or regional power imbalances in the wider neighborhood. In other words, autonomous institutions helped to de-escalate tensions on the ground only (or mainly) insofar as they helped to resolve related conflicts at the regional level.

The following section outlines the expectations of nested security versus alternative accounts of the three cases. I then describe the method used to evaluate the nested security model against rival explanations. This is followed by a periodized analysis of the three cases and a summary of the results.

Nested Security versus Alternative Explanations

Under territorial devolution, a state government grants sovereign powers to one or more minority regions so they can exercise a degree of self-governance over "their" territory. Autonomy is most often granted in areas of special interest to ethnic minorities such as education and culture but may also include the right to levy and collect taxes, establish local assemblies, and/or engage in law enforcement. Real-world examples include the UK's devolution of power to Scotland and Wales in the late 1990s, Belgium's devolution to Flanders in the late twentieth century, and Spain's granting of autonomy to Catalonia, Galicia, and the Basque Country under the 1978 constitution. By granting broad autonomy to a restive minority region, the central government hopes to split the difference between a unitary state (its preference) and secession (preferred by the rebelling group). In extreme cases, devolution may result in a confederation, where the minority region enjoys de facto independence. Confederations sometimes serve as a halfway house for seceding entities seeking statehood, which is why many states are reluctant to start down the path of devolution.

Induced devolution occurs when third-party mediators prevail upon an otherwise reluctant state government to give autonomy to a rebellious minority region, either through persuasion or direct economic or political incentives. Although autonomous institutions are sometimes used to resolve civil wars, and are often imposed from the outside through force, this chapter looks at conditions under which third parties can use induced devolution to de-escalate tensions in low-intensity civil conflicts.

The theory of nested security says that when a domestic conflict is embedded in turbulent regional or systemic conflict processes, this wider security environment is likely to undermine any salutary effects of an autonomy arrangement. In Variant A, external events or outside patrons leverage the minority. Even in the presence of a functioning devolution agreement, an externally leveraged minority is then more likely to mobilize around a more radical position to extract concessions from the state. In Variant B, by contrast, external events or interventions leverage the host government, tempting some state leaders to deal with certain troublesome minorities through repression or discrimination. Either way, regional destabilization is prone to exacerbating communal tensions on the ground.

On the other hand, outside actors or events may also *de*-escalate tensions on the ground through *exogenous stabilization*. For example, regional hegemons may put pressure on a neighboring state to disengage from a minority conflict. When this happens, third-party mediation has a greater chance of success. Here, however, the combatants are likely to remain mobilized along sectarian lines in anticipation that external incentives for peace will be removed. Finally, if incentives for peace are *endogenous*, such that both sides expect to gain a dividend from brokering an agreement, then a more consolidated domestic peace becomes possible, as the political salience of the sectarian divide declines in favor of issue-based coalitions. In short, the stability of the wider environment is a necessary (and perhaps sufficient) condition for managing internal tensions—even in the context of extensive autonomy arrangements.

To test these predictions, the three cases are periodized on the basis of the prevailing level of conflict on the ground. The starting point for each case study is the point at which third parties prevailed on the target state to devolve power to the minority. For the Åland and Danzig cases this was 1918; for Memel it was 1923. Each region then experienced a period of conflict reduction in the 1920s, followed by consolidation of peace in the Ålands and conflict escalation in the other two cases. Moving from one conflict phase to the next, the chapter gives an account of the relative effectiveness of induced devolution in the three cases. Focusing on each shift in conflict on the ground, I cast my gaze backward to locate the source of conflict fluctuation. In doing so, I pay close attention to the relationship between shifts in domestic conflict

Table 4.1 Nested security predictions for induced devolution under the League

Åland Islands	Regional environment	Conflict outcome
(1917)	Regional destabilization (Sweden intervenes)	Minority radicalization (Åland separatism)
(1918–1939)	Exogenous stabilization (Britain induces Sweden's withdrawal)	Minority moderation (acceptance of League's Åland agreement)
(1939–)	Regional peace (Swedish-Finnish security alliance)	Minority integration into Finnish state
Memel	**Regional environment**	**Conflict outcome**
(1923)	Regional destabilization (Lithuania intervenes)	Minority radicalization (Klaipėda Revolt)
(1924–1929)	Exogenous stabilization (Allies adjudicate conflict)	Minority moderation with Memel agreement
(1930–1939)	Regional destabilization (Germany intervenes)	Minority radicalization (rebellion of German Memellanders)
Danzig	**Regional environment**	**Conflict outcome**
(1918–1930)	Exogenous stabilization (Allies establish Free City of Danzig)	Minority moderation
(1931–1939)	Regional destabilization (Germany intervenes)	Minority radicalization (revolt of German Danzigers)

on the one hand, and changes in relationships between regional players and League officials on the other. In this way, I ascertain whether shifts in communal tensions on the ground were primarily a function of the wider conflict environment, mediator resources, the government's minority policies, or some combination of these factors.

In addition to nested security, this chapter also evaluates two competing accounts for conflict mediation in the Ålands, Memel, and Danzig. The first is that the devolution agreement itself was critical for containing violence in each case. To test for this possibility, I examine the period surrounding the brokering of the autonomy agreement in each case to see whether the terms of each agreement imperiled or contributed to peace. In making this assessment, I first look to see whether the agreements in question met the group's demands while protecting the group from discrimination. I also investigate whether each agreement was acceptable to the host government. If the institutions themselves were central to the longevity of intra-state peace, then there should be clues in the negotiations surrounding the respective agreements. Any changes in the agreement or its implementation over time should also influence tensions on the ground.

A second possibility is that it was the resources or commitment of the third-party mediator that mattered most. If this is the case, then the policies and stance taken by the mediator should lead to observable shifts in conflict on the ground. To test for this possibility, I look to see whether indications of mediator bias (or lack thereof) altered the trajectory or intensity of the conflict; I also pay attention to whether credible signals of third-party enforcement had a measurable effect on the intensity of conflict at the substate level (see table 4.2).

Adjudicating among these different accounts means looking at whether over-time fluctuations in conflict in the Ålands, Memel, and Danzig were preceded by (1) shifts in the wider security environment as predicted by nested

Table 4.2 Summary evaluation of theories

Case	Minority protections/ liberal government	Credibility of mediator/value of carrots and sticks	Nested security
Åland Islands	*Disconfirmed* Ålanders were no more satisfied with the Åland agreement than with the (substantially similar) Autonomy Act passed by Finland the year before.	*Partially confirmed* Britain (through the League of Nations) was influential in persuading Sweden and Finland to submit to League arbitration, after which tensions permanently subsided.	*Confirmed* Ålanders did not moderate their claims until Sweden withdrew, stabilizing the regional environment; Swedish-Finnish cooperation in World War II cemented peaceful internal relations on the islands.
Memel	*Disconfirmed* Domestic tensions were high but minority demands moderated even as the Lithuanian government violated the terms of the Memel agreement in the 1920s.	*Disconfirmed* League resources and perceived legitimacy did not change throughout the period, although internal tensions in Memel fluctuated considerably.	*Confirmed* Domestic tensions were lower in the 1920s owing to exogenous stabilization by Allies; ethnic tensions increased in the 1930s as Germany began to challenge its eastern borders, destabilizing minority-majority relations.
Danzig	*Disconfirmed* Although German Danzigers enjoyed extensive autonomy throughout interwar period, their leaders mobilized in the 1930s because of Nazi German intervention.	*Disconfirmed* League resources and legitimacy in the eyes of the conflict parties did not change, although internal tensions in Danzig fluctuated considerably.	*Confirmed* Tensions in Danzig were low in the 1920s when the regional environment was stabilized but reemerged in the 1930s when Nazi German revisionism destabilized the region.

security, (2) shifts in the terms and/or implementation of the autonomy agreement as predicted by institutional theories, or (3) shifts in intervenor resources and commitment to enforce the agreement. I now comparatively evaluate these theories using the factual patterns in the three cases.

Case Evidence

Åland Islands

Both Finland and the Åland Islands had belonged the Swedish kingdom for centuries when Russia annexed the territories in 1809. In the 1856 treaty that ended the Crimean War, Western powers ensured that the islands were demilitarized to prevent Russia from using them to launch a campaign against the West. At the end of the First World War, Finland obtained both national independence and control of the islands from Russia. Protesting that their rights to self-determination were being violated, the Ålanders—who spoke Swedish and identified as Swedes—sought to unite with Sweden. The Swedish public, too, was in favor of annexing the islands, and newspaper editorials openly spoke of using force to achieve this goal, if necessary. Finland objected strongly to these claims, arguing that the islands were part of its sovereign territory and that Sweden had no say over its internal affairs.

Regional Destabilization—Sweden Makes Demands on Finnish Territory (1917)

In August 1917, a group of Ålander separatists gathered in the town of Finström, where they resolved to notify the Swedish government and parliament that the "population of Aland deeply desired the reincorporation of its islands with the Kingdom of Sweden."[1] A proclamation to this effect was delivered to the Swedish high command in October, and an embassy was formed to represent the islands in negotiations with Sweden. In December, over seven thousand Ålanders signed a petition calling for a "reunion of the archipelago to Sweden."[2] They introduced the resolution to the king of Sweden, Gustav V, in February of the following year; in a plebiscite held at the end of the year, 95 percent of the population called for reunification. Thus began a low-level separatist movement on the islands. The leaders of the movement warned that newly sovereign Finland would oppress and assimilate the Swedish-speaking Ålanders, depriving them of their cultural and linguistic heritage. Such warnings were given credence by the elevation of the Finnish language under the country's new constitution and by the fact that the Finnish-speaking community on the islands had grown rapidly over the past few decades.

It is unlikely that these grievances would have produced rebellion in the absence of the political opportunity created by the Russian Revolution and the Red-White Civil War. The widening political unrest permitted the Ålanders to campaign for independence against Finland.[3] It was in this context that the king of Sweden received the delegation of Ålanders who communicated their wish for annexation. Pro-annexation sentiment also began to grow in the Swedish public following the publication of articles decrying the oppression of Ålanders by the Finnish government. The Swedish government obligingly sent a contingent of soldiers to secure the liberation of the islands from the re-maining Russian troops, disrupting communication links between the islands and Helsinki in the process. After having invaded the islands without Helsin-ki's permission and compelling the withdrawal of both Russian and Finnish forces, Sweden eventually withdrew as well, but maintained close connections with the islands' irredentist leadership.[4]

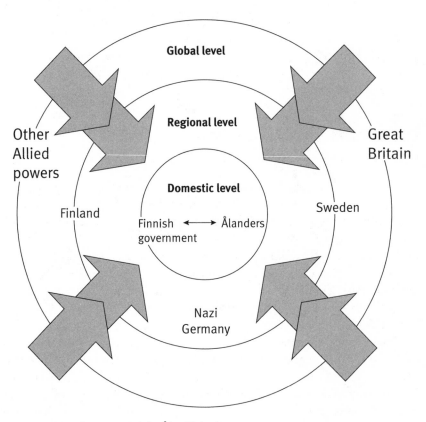

Figure 4.1 Nested security and the Åland Islands

In response, Finnish leaders sent a note to Sweden condemning Stockholm's interference in Finland's domestic affairs in violation of international law; they also accused the irredentist leadership of being disloyal to Finland by negotiating with a foreign government.[5] These events underscored the power advantage of Sweden, the minority's external patron, whose material and diplomatic support greatly fueled the separatist movement. As predicted by the nested security model, Sweden's intervention encouraged the radicalization of the islanders (Variant A), who had been utterly quiescent for the previous sixty years. Regional destabilization had thus created a condition of nested *in*security at the domestic level, leading to minority mobilization.

With the Swedish public and Ålanders in favor of unification, the Swedes urged the islanders to petition the Allies for the right to hold a popular plebiscite to determine their political fate; the results of such a plebiscite would clearly support Swedish annexation. Stockholm also approached Helsinki on behalf of the islanders. On the heels of private negotiations, Stockholm stated in an official demarche that it "desir[ed] that the question of the future regulation of the Åland archipelago be resolved by a plebiscite." Helsinki roundly refused Stockholm's request and demanded that the Paris Peace Conference powers place the "economic and military security of the nation" over the wishes of the minority, as they had in other territorial conflicts.[6]

Exogenous Regional Peace—Regional Stabilization and the Åland Agreement (1918–1939)

As Swedish-Finnish tensions escalated, the United Kingdom intervened to quell the conflict. London had decided against advocating on behalf of either government, reasoning that splitting the difference between the two states was the best means of de-escalating tensions on the ground.[7] Accordingly, London proposed submitting the issue to the nascent League Council for arbitration, with the understanding that both parties would accept its decision. Francis Walters affirmed that "from the moment that the dispute had been laid before the League, it was evident that the danger of war had receded."[8] Finland consented to placing the question before the League, and a special meeting was held in London where the two governments were invited to argue their cases before the Council. Presenting the Swedish side was Socialist prime minister Hjalmar Branting, together with two delegates from the Åland Islands. The Swedish team requested a plebiscite to help determine the fate of the islands; it was understood that they would win the vote. The Finnish representatives countered that the question of the islands was a purely sovereign affair and that Finland had sole jurisdiction over the territory, regardless of its ethnic makeup.[9]

In the course of arbitration, the League Council established an international commission of three jurists to study the conflict and provide the Council with an advisory opinion on the matter. The jurists returned their opinion on September 5, 1920, that the Åland Island question was not simply an internal affair, as it "originated in the separatist movement among the inhabitants, who invoked the principle of national self-determination, and certain military events which accompanied and followed the separation of Finland from the Russian Empire."[10] The commission thus acknowledged the international character of the dispute, concluding that "a solution in the nature of a *compromise*, based on an extensive grant of liberty to minorities, may appear necessary according to international legal conception and may even be dictated by the interests of peace."[11]

In accordance with the outside-in approach to conflict management recommended by nested security, the commission focused first on resolving the territorial conflict *between Sweden and Finland*, rather than between Finland and the Ålanders. The satisfaction of the Ålanders was never a major consideration in these deliberations. It was understood that events on the regional level were the critical drivers of conflict on the ground. The bilateral Swedish-Finnish conflict had escalated separatist tensions, and so the restoration of Swedish-Finnish peace was expected to undermine the separatist movement—even if the Ålanders were not wholly satisfied with the outcome. The League Council accepted the opinion of the jurists and sent an expert commission to the region before issuing its decision. The commission sought to split the difference between the claims of Stockholm and Helsinki by recommending that the islands remain in Finnish hands but be given broad territorial autonomy to protect their Swedish character. It thus recommended broad autonomy with the proviso that the islands could not be fortified militarily—a concern shared by all involved states.

Helsinki continued to object to League interference in what it viewed as a purely domestic matter. Nonetheless, it passed its first Autonomy Act in 1920 to "guarantee Ålanders the possibility to take care of their affairs in as free a manner as is possible for a region that is not an independent state."[12] The act aimed to give the islands greater autonomy than what was provided under the 1919 Finnish constitution. Although it established a local assembly with legislative authority, the Ålanders rejected the act, claiming it did not meet their demands. Undaunted, the League hammered out an agreement between Sweden and Finland with very similar provisions. The most contentious issues in the negotiations were the militarization of the islands, the location of the inter-state boundary, and the extent of the territorial waters, as well as the status of the islands in case of war. Internal questions surrounding territorial autonomy and the status of the islanders in Finland were relegated to secondary importance. Throughout the arbitration, "both the Swedish and the Finnish representatives evidenced a conciliatory attitude toward each other and toward the problem as a whole, thus considerably facilitating the work of the conference."[13] In the end, the Åland agreement resolved the inter-state dispute and was signed by the principals in October 1921 over the objections of the Ålanders, who were compelled to make their peace with the agreement. Consistent with the expectations of nested security, exogenous regional stabilization had thus created a condition of the model, de-escalating the internal conflict and leading the Ålanders to abandon their irredentist demands.

Endogenous Stabilization—Sweden and Finland Find Common Ground (1939–)

By the late 1930s, the region had become endogenously stabilized as the former antagonist states began to view each other as potential allies facing common foes. According to one historian of the interwar period, "Life in the Åland Islands was happy and peaceful until the menace of the Second World War began to throw its ominous shadows over the Baltic."[14] Nonetheless, significant grievances remained among the Ålanders themselves. These mainly revolved around the growing presence of Finns on the islands, as well as land reforms that led to a net land transfer of property from Swedish to Finnish speakers.[15] However, in the context of a stabilized regional environment, separatism among the islanders remained latent, as expected by the model.

In 1939, Sweden and Finland jointly brought an appeal to militarize the Åland Islands before the League Council; their pact had deepened into an alliance as the two governments sought to defend against a resurgent Germany. Over the objections of the Ålanders, who were greatly aggrieved by Helsinki and Stockholm's collusion to militarize their territory, the two governments launched a campaign to abrogate the 1921 settlement in order to fortify the islands. The main concern was that the islands would fall into the hands of an aggressor state such as Germany or Russia, which threatened the industrial and military well-being of both countries. They therefore requested the consent of all original signatories of the 1921 convention to permit joint militarization of the islands. All the signatories save Russia ultimately gave their permission, and Finland went forward with fortification plans.

Endogenous regional stabilization led to yet another shift in relations between Finland and the Ålanders. Recognizing that their erstwhile patron, Sweden, had colluded in militarizing the islands, the Ålanders became further alienated from their kin state, and minority representatives proclaimed that Sweden had betrayed its ethnic kin in pursuit of its sovereign interests. At the same time, a consolidated regional peace ushered in a new phase of peaceful coexistence between Finland and the Ålanders, who, having turned their back on their kin state, now reconciled themselves to integrating fully into the Finnish state. Henceforth, the Ålanders no longer saw themselves as an occupied Finnish possession, but rather as an integral yet autonomous part of Finland. Consolidation of peace at the domestic level followed predictably on the heels of a self-enforcing bilateral contract between Sweden and Finland, as expected by the nested security model.

What was the role of the devolution agreement in achieving this success? Here it is important to note that what the minority received under the agreement did not differ all that much from what they already enjoyed under Finnish law. Thus, what led to successful League mediation was not the autonomy agreement itself, but Great Power pressure on Sweden to withdraw, as well as the agreement reached between Sweden and Finland over the disposition of the islands themselves. James Barros affirmed that "it was power considerations that decided the Aland question, and it is power considerations that decide all questions in the international community, regardless of whether or not they are submitted to an international organ."[16] Nonetheless, the League was instrumental in facilitating a path to peace, as it channeled an escalating international conflict into a peaceful "[conflict] of words and procedure." Induced devolution can deliver on its promises, in other words, but only insofar as power issues at the wider regional level are simultaneously resolved or held in check.

Memel

The interwar Memel region was predominantly Lithuanian in the hinterland, although the port town of Memel, which had been stripped from Germany after the war, was mostly German speaking.[17] At the end of the First World War, the territory was claimed simultaneously by Lithuania and Poland, both of which desired an outlet to the Baltic Sea, and by Germany, which claimed the land on the basis of ethnic composition. With multiple sovereign claims on the territory, the Allies placed Memel under the direct supervision of the League until its final status could be determined. In 1920, the area north of the Neman River was made into the League-protected Memel Territory, to be guarded by a small contingent of French soldiers. The Allies endeavored to ensure that the guarantor force was, so far as possible, acceptable to the Lithuanian government.[18]

After the war, the German Memellanders sought annexation by their kin state.[19] However, post-Versailles Germany was effectively powerless, so the German minority began to rally around an independent Memelland. Ethnic organizations sprouted up, and the German Workers' Association for the Free City of the Memel Region (Arbeitsgemeischaft für den Freistaat Memelland) held a successful popular referendum for independence.[20] In 1922, the organization presented its demands in the so-called Yellow Book, which

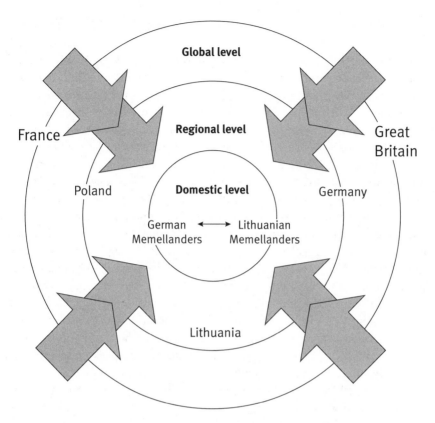

Figure 4.2 Nested security and the Memel case

asserted that Memel was politically, economically, and culturally distinct from the "Russian Lithuanians."[21] According to the 1925 census, 44 percent of the population of Memel was German, 28 percent Lithuanian, and fully 25 percent Memellander/Klaipėdiškiai—suggesting that the population was truly distinct from Lithuania as a whole.[22] Meanwhile, a small countermovement of Lithuanians promulgated the 1918 Act of Tilsit, demanding unification with Lithuania. Ongoing regional competition for the land began to upset ethnic relations in Memel, with ethnic Germans seeking independence for Memel, while ethnic Lithuanians urged annexation by their own kin state.

Regional Destabilization—Lithuanian Occupation and the Klaipėda Revolt (1923)

With the League still stalling over Memel's final status, Lithuania's leaders— believing the territory rightfully belonged to them—decided to "take matters in their own hands" and prepared to invade.[23] In 1922, Lithuania started build-ing up paramilitary organizations in Memel to boost national consciousness among young Lithuanians in the region. Winning the support of the local population was critical, as the government did not want to be held responsible for the takeover. Accordingly, Lithuanian prime minister Ernestas Galvana-uskas sought to create the impression that local Lithuanians had taken the initiative to reunite with their motherland. Lithuanian officers leading the military operation even changed their surnames so as to appear German.[24] In early January 1923, some one thousand Lithuanian soldiers, officers, and marksmen crossed the border, overcame the small French occupation force, and asserted sovereign control over the territory. They justified their invasion on the basis of the Tilsit Act, which called for unification with Lithuania and served as important propaganda for the invasion. Kaunas (the Lithuanian capital since 1919) proclaimed that "for four years the legitimate aspirations of the Lithuanian majority had not been taken into account."[25] Lithuania also used economic pressure to tilt the scales in its favor, placing a moratorium on trade with Memel and tightening its grip on the local economy.[26]

Consistent with the expectations of nested security, the Lithuanian inva-sion destabilized ethnic relations on the ground. Hundreds of minority Lith-uanians joined the rebellion as Lithuanian troops marched over the border to occupy the territory. At the end of the campaign, the Supreme Salvation Committee of Lithuania Minor asserted interim control over the region and established a local assembly. On January 19, 1923, 120 representatives of local "salvation committees" gathered in Heydekrug and voted unanimously for Lithuanian annexation.[27] Among other things, they declared their intention to dissolve the French directory, free the political prisoners, elevate the status of the Lithuanian language, and declare martial law. Although League officials strongly condemned the move by Kaunas, the Allies were far more concerned with the simultaneous French occupation of the Ruhr. The Great Powers were too distracted by other crises to respond to the Lithuanian invasion in a timely manner, and the League was powerless on its own to expel the invading force. Therefore, nothing was done to reverse the Lithuanian annexation of Memel.

Although the Lithuanian takeover was a setback for ethnic Germans in Memel, Berlin accepted it because it was too weak to pursue counterclaims to the region. Moreover, Germany preferred that Lithuania, rather than its historical rival Poland, control the Memel port.[28] While the Allies vigorously protested Lithuania's fait accompli, they were insufficiently motivated to use force and therefore refrained from imposing sanctions on the tiny state. The Conference of Ambassadors[29] tried to persuade Lithuania to accept a joint Polish-Lithuanian administration of Memel. Failing this, it thereafter washed its hands of the dispute and turned the matter over to the League. With

Lithuania unchecked by determined Allied intervention, the regional balance of power tilted decisively in its favor, creating a condition of nested *in*security between Lithuanian and German Memellanders, leading to Lithuanian nationalization of the territory (Variant B).

Exogenous Stabilization—Allied Intervention and the Memel Convention (1924–1929)

Although the Allies had declined to counter the fait accompli by Lithuania, the Conference of Ambassadors did act to ameliorate the consequences of the takeover through devolution. Namely, the Conference induced Kaunas to devolve considerable autonomy to the German Memellanders. In Paris on May 8, 1924, the members of the Conference signed the Klaipėda Convention (or Convention concerning the Territory of Memel), which set out the terms of territorial devolution in the region. The convention also included the Statute of Klaipėda Region, which consisted of thirty-eight articles and served as a constitution for the region. Under the convention and the statute, German and Lithuanian would be made coequal official languages in the territory. Memel would also have its own legislative assembly, tax authority, judicial system, social security, citizenship, and control over natural resources. At the same time, Lithuania would continue to exercise sovereign control over the region and enjoy unlimited access to the port, which would be supervised by a neutral member of the Harbour Board of the League Transit Committee. The terms of the agreement were accepted by Kaunas, which had succeeded in gaining permanent access to seaways. Poland, although decrying the agreement, did not actively oppose it. Warsaw well understood that postwar Poland was essentially a client state of the Allies. Consequently, "the wisest Polish Foreign Ministers . . . showed a patience and moderation which was not usually characteristic of the national temperament."[30]

By constraining Lithuania, the Allies had thus exogenously stabilized the region, creating the conditions of nested security in Memel. We should therefore see a reduction in internal tensions on both sides. Indeed, although Lithuanian leaders periodically attempted to "Lithuanianize" the region to dilute its strongly German character, the international statutes governing the region ensured that the region's inhabitants remained relatively unmolested, even after the authoritarian Lithuanian leader Antanas Smetona came to power in a 1926 coup. As expected, Lithuania largely upheld its promise to allow the German-speaking region broad political autonomy. In line with the Statute of Memel, in force since 1924, the region had a Lithuanian governor who had the right to appoint the president. The members of Memel's government, known as the directory, were appointed directly by the president, and elections to the local Diet were free and universal.[31] Beginning in 1924, ethnic Germans managed to secure at least twenty-four of the twenty-nine seats in the Diet. Following the 1926 general elections in Lithuania, ethnic Germans won all five seats reserved in the country's parliament for the Memel region representatives. Lithuania thus largely respected Memel's right to self-governance, as well as protection of German Memellanders, under its autonomy agreement.[32]

Exogenous Destabilization—the Rise of Nazi Germany and Ethnic German Rebellion (1930–1939)

By the early 1930s, the rise of German power led to a new regional conflict—this time between Lithuania and Germany. Having obtained a permanent seat on the League Council in 1926, Berlin had begun to seize the League Council to deliberate complaints from its co-ethnics, including ethnic Germans in Memel. In these complaints, German Memellanders continually accused Kaunas of discrimination and repression, despite the fact that they enjoyed economic and political advantages relative to other groups in the region. As one scholar put it, "the German Memellanders (they had half the population but all the power) were high-handed and provocative."[33] The escalation of tensions between Lithuanians and Germans on the ground had everything to do with the intervention of the German government. Although the conflict over Memel appeared to have been satisfactorily resolved through League mediation, in September 1930 Germany approached the League with a petition accusing Lithuania of violating the Memel Convention by interfering in the operations of its assembly and financial control bodies, obstructing the freedom of the judiciary, and undermining electoral freedoms. The following year, Germany sent another letter to the Council, stating that Lithuania was "guilty of a denial of justice and the dislocation of the whole judicial system in Memel."[34] Lithuania responded by cracking down on German nationalists and activists in Memel. In February 1932, the Lithuanian governor of the region dismissed the directory's president, Dr. Böttcher, who had met with two German ministers during a recent trip to Berlin. According to Kaunas, the president's actions constituted an "infringement of [Lithuania's] exclusive right to control the foreign policies of Memel."[35] Böttcher refused to resign and was arrested. The entire directory was later dismissed and a Lithuanian president appointed in his place. This was a nonstarter for the German-dominated Diet, which was also dissolved. When Berlin complained to the League, the Permanent Court of International Justice ruled that Lithuania's dismissal was legal and "reminded German Memellanders that a minority has duties as well as rights."[36]

By the mid-1930s, Germany had become deeply involved in Memel's internal affairs. Berlin had already provided financial support to German candidates in the 1930 elections, transferring 10,000 German marks to the candidates through the minority-assistance organization the Deutsche Stiftung. During the elections, radio stations from East Prussia blocked the signal of Radio Kaunas, while boosting the signals of Prussian propaganda programs. Later, the German government helped Memellander cultural associations and the consulate distribute wireless radio sets designed to block Lithuanian national radio. Last but not least, Germany gave support to "patriotically inclined Germans in the Klaipėda [Memel] region"[37] by paying salaries to ethnic German teachers and civil servants—actions that were illegal under the Memel Statute.[38]

Lithuanian-German relations worsened still further after the National Socialists' electoral victory in Germany in 1933. Increased German leverage and increased bilateral tensions placed the Memel conflict in a situation of nested *in*security. Bilateral destabilization having effectively leveraged the German Memellanders (Variant A), the model predicts conflict escalation led by the German minority. As observed by Valentine Gustainis, "when . . . Germany changed her domestic political aspect, she changed also her foreign policy."[39] With Nazi Germany at their back, German Memellanders escalated their demands. In 1934, Ernst Neumann and Theodor von Sass, the leaders of local fascist parties, Sozialistische Volksgemeinschaft (Sovog) and Christlich-Sozialistische Arbeitsgemeinschaft (CSA), were charged with "plotting to use armed force to separate Klaipėda region from the Republic of Lithuania."[40] Indeed, an analysis of correspondence between the Memel activists and the National Socialist German Workers Party (NSDAP) indicates that the alleged coup had been co-plotted, although Hitler and Rudolf Hess officially denied their involvement in the conspiracy.[41] Over one hundred people were arrested and many convicted in a 1935 trial, with sentences ranging from one-year prison terms to the death penalty (this was later replaced with life imprisonment); the Nazi Party was also outlawed in Memel territory.[42] The court verdicts "aroused great indignation" in Germany and led to the intensification of anti-Lithuanian propaganda in the Reich; Germany also closed its markets to Lithuanian products—a major blow to the Lithuanian economy.[43]

Kaunas responded to German intervention by "consolidat[ing] Lithuanization of Memel Territory"—changing the street names into Lithuanian and requiring the city to go by its Lithuanian name; it also placed greater controls over Memel's Protestant Church. Hitler countered by declaring that Germany was "ready to negotiate non-aggression pacts with all our neighbor states" except Lithuania, "because we cannot enter into political treaties with a state which disregards the most primitive laws of human society."[44] The German position was driven by geopolitical rather than humanitarian interests: "The Germans might accuse the Lithuanians of violating their engagements . . . [but] their real purpose was not to ensure that the Statute was respected, but to hasten the day when Memel should once more lie within the frontiers of Germany."[45]

When Nazi Germany invaded Czechoslovakia in 1938, Memel's extremist minority leadership became emboldened still further, proclaiming the "freedom to live as a National Socialist community, owing allegiance to 'the Führer of all Germans.'"[46] Shortly thereafter, "in the autonomous Memel Territory . . . a wholly undisguised National Socialist regime with all its symbols came to power."[47] The "One Reich, One People, One Führer" slogan chanted during mass demonstrations in Memel in late 1938 indicated the extent to which the German Memellanders had been radicalized. On March 21, 1939, Germany issued an ultimatum demanding that Lithuania return Memel to the Reich. With the Allies standing mutely by, Lithuanian officials accepted Germany's demands two days later.[48] On the same day, a triumphant Hitler gave a speech to the Memellanders, celebrating the port's return to "*Heim ins Reich.*"

Case analysis shows that the Memel conflict shifted in intensity over the interwar period not in response to changes in the provisions of the Memel Convention—which was generally accepted by all parties in the 1920s—nor as a function of shifts in the mediator's legitimacy or position toward the conflict, which also did not change considerably over the intervening period. Rather, the conflict escalated primarily in response to conflict processes in the wider region (namely, the Lithuanian occupation of the region in 1923 and German intervention on behalf of German Memellanders in the 1930s). The League succeeded in mediating the crisis in 1924, when the Conference of Ambassadors (made up of the Allied powers) backed the convention and put pressure on the Lithuanian government to implement it. The success of devolution in Memel began to diminish in the 1930s, however, as Germany began to advocate aggressively on behalf of German Memellanders—as expected by the nested security model.

Danzig
Already by the end of World War I, the port city of Danzig (Gdańsk in Polish) had long been invaluable to Poland as its only outlet to the Baltic Sea. Danzig first gained autonomous status in the 1200s and later became a full member of the Hanseatic League. Located close to the boundary dividing Germanic and West Slavic territories, the city had alternated between Polish, German, and fairly extensive self-rule for hundreds of years. Prussian rulers had coveted Danzig and launched military campaigns to capture the city as early as the fourteenth century. That Poland was economically dependent on the city was recognized by Frederick the Great, who famously proclaimed that "whosoever possesses the mouth of the Vistula and the city of Danzig will be more master of Poland than the King who reigns there."[49]

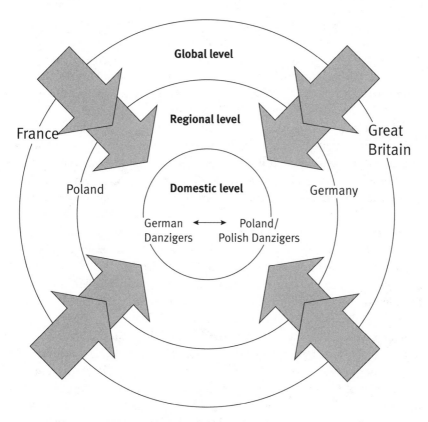

Figure 4.3 Nested security and Danzig

Although Prussia (later Germany) had held Danzig for nearly a century, the postwar settlement would change all of this. Because of the commercial value of the port, the Allied powers originally intended to strip the territory from Germany and cede it to the new Polish state. In his Fourteen Points speech, Woodrow Wilson declared his support for an independent Poland "which should be assured a free and secure access to the sea." A Polish Corridor containing Danzig was therefore carved out of former German territory to give to Warsaw. However, since Danzig was ethnically German (95 percent of the city's population was classified as German, according to the 1923 census), Berlin had a strong competing claim to the territory under the principle of national self-determination. In view of this, the Allies settled on a compromise solution.

Exogenous Stabilization—Establishing the Free City of Danzig

The League awarded Danzig to Poland but induced Warsaw to devolve extensive powers to the region. The Free City of Danzig was established as a quasi-state with a League-appointed external supervisor—an arrangement that covered the city itself, the seaport, and some of the surrounding hinterland. The city itself was given extensive self-government in internal affairs, including a local parliament, executive body, judicial system, and currency; German was declared the city's sole official language. At the same time, Poland enjoyed control over Danzig's external relations with other states as well as unimpeded use of the city's railways, waterways, docks, and other important infrastructure.

The Germans in Danzig were in no position to complain about the arrangement. Poland, too, was predisposed to compromise over Danzig, owing to its heavy reliance on Western security guarantees—Warsaw had strong incentives to curry the favor of the West and sought to accommodate the Allies in League Council meetings. In the Paris Convention of November 1920 and the Warsaw Agreement of October 1921, Poland vowed "to protect the interests of the Free City of Danzig so far as possible" and "promote [Danzig's] competitive possibilities with respect to other harbors."[50]

From the mid-1920s to 1930, an uneasy peace held between Warsaw and the Free City. For the most part, the two sides managed to get along—both within the city and between Danzig and Warsaw. Even so, the city's high commissioner was called upon to settle scores of ethnic disputes. Most consisted of Danziger German complaints that Warsaw was attempting to subvert their autonomy. For their part, the Polish minority argued that Germans were seeking to control Danzig and restrict Warsaw's sovereignty over the region. Although the high commissioner's mediations were sometimes successful, the majority of his decisions were appealed to the Permanent Court of International Justice by one side or the other.

Ethnic relations in Danzig improved somewhat after the 1927 elections, which yielded a victory for the Social Democrats in the Free City's Volkstag. The new government declared its readiness to cooperate with Poland and settled a number of outstanding conflicts. The emerging détente was also visible in Polish prime minister Kazimierz Bartel's visit to the port town in early 1929, earning him "a warm welcome" from Danziger officials.[51] According to Francis Walters, this period coincided with a general climate of cooperation: "The Free City usually reflected in miniature the political complexion of the Reich. [From 1927 to 1930] a left-centre coalition had been in power; and, in spite of the unchangeable dislike and suspicion which Poles and Danzigers cherished for one another, their official differences had been dealt with in a reasonably accommodating temper."[52] Germany thus accepted Polish suzerainty over Danzig and was helpless to change the situation in any case; Poland too had an interest in honoring the League's devolution agreement so as to maintain good relations with the Allies. This de facto détente at the regional level effectively nested ethnic relations in Danzig so that disputes between the two groups were somewhat less likely to escalate, consistent with the nested security model.

Regional Destabilization—the Rise of Nazi Germany and Mobilization of German Danzigers

By the 1930s, the global economic downturn, together with the rise of Germany, began to destabilize ethnic relations in Danzig. Economic dislocation was a catalyst for radicalization as unemployment in the city soared. In light of intensifying hardships, German Danzigers looked increasingly askance at Warsaw's habit of staffing customs, railways, and other public services with Polish nationals—particularly since the overwhelming majority of Danzigers were ethnically German.[53] Danzig authorities likewise complained that Poland had significantly decreased the amount of cargo shipments to and from the city in favor of the port of Gdingen (Gdynia), which had been constructed following the refusal of Danzig's dockworkers in 1920 to unload Allied military shipments to Poland during the Polish-Soviet war—a betrayal that was "never forgotten in Poland."[54] By 1932, commercial transportation through ethnically Polish Gdynia began to outpace that of Danzig, leading to accusations of discrimination by Danzig officials. With its permanent seat on the League Council, Berlin became increasingly active in supporting the grievances of the minority, effectively leveraging the ethnic Germans. The League intervened to mediate the dispute, and after protracted negotiations, Poland agreed to make full use of the Danzig port. However, Germans in Danzig were unhappy with the solution, as it "did not affect in any way [Warsaw's] right to open other ports on the same coast."[55]

A second dispute emerged over Poland's *use* of the Danzig port. When the agreement giving Poland access to the harbor expired in 1931, a new system was introduced requiring Poland to obtain special permission before it could steer its military vessels into the harbor. Warsaw responded with a "threatening military gesture." During a friendly visit of British warships to the Danzig harbor in June 1932, Warsaw dispatched a destroyer to greet the British vessels in contravention of the new regulations. Marshal Piłsudski had given the order directly, with the aim of "forc[ing] a showdown with the Danzig authorities and to make them more receptive to the necessity of coming in terms with Poland."[56] Despite vociferous protests by Danzig officials and League representatives, the combative move had its intended effect. In late 1932, Danzig signed a new agreement with Warsaw granting Polish military vessels free access to the harbor. Poland's actions had the effect of polarizing ethnic politics in the city. Meanwhile, the German government deepened its ties with German minority leaders in Danzig.

The nested security model predicts that Germany's leveraging of German Memellanders should escalate tensions on the ground through minority mobilization (Variant A). Whereas Danziger Germans had by and large voted for moderates in the past, the 1930 municipal elections handed a victory to the nationalist, conservative forces. The Nazis, with 16.4 percent of the vote, became the second-strongest political faction in the Volkstag. With the city's nationalist government now hitched to the fate of the Nazi Party in Germany, right-wing German unionists began to call openly for German annexation. Observing this, the Polish minority responded by calling on Warsaw to annex the Free City. This led to pitched street battles between the Germans and the Poles. Tensions escalated to the point where the Polish diplomatic representative in Danzig resigned on the grounds that he could no longer guarantee the safety of the Polish minority. The Danzig high commissioner Count Manfredi Gravina, meanwhile, decided not to invite intervention by the Polish army for fear that this would provoke further violence; he instead sent a report to the League Council requesting League intervention.

In the midst of growing regional destabilization, ongoing League involvement—backed by the Allies—helped to maintain an uneasy peace in Danzig. The fact that the League's rapporteur for Danzig affairs was British "had a restraining influence upon the disputing parties," as neither Germany nor Poland could afford to alienate the Great Powers at this point. Indeed, the nationalist president of Danzig, Hermann Rauschning, shrank from persecuting the city's intellectuals and Jews largely because Danzig still relied on the League Council's guarantee of regional autonomy against Polish assimilationism. Danzig's authorities grudgingly continued to honor the terms of their agreement "so long as they still had that minimum of defense which the League could afford them."[57] For its part, Poland refrained from violating the status of the Free City in order to ensure continued Allied protection against an increasingly bellicose Germany and Soviet Union.

At the same time, the Reich was working with Danzig's Nazis behind the scenes to engineer a coup in the city's Volkstag. In 1930, Reich official Hermann Göring visited Danzig to show his support for the local Nazi activists; upon his return, he advised Hitler to appoint Albert Forster as the gauleiter of the city's NSDAP cell. Forster breathed new life into the local Nazi organization, and in 1933, just months after Hitler had assumed power, the Nazis won a majority of seats in the local legislature.

Nonetheless, bilateral relations were still solid enough to keep the Danzig conflict more or less in check. The 1934 Non-Aggression Pact between Germany and Poland committed both sides to cooperative diplomatic relations, and the Danziger Nazis were ordered to fall into line. Hitler personally warned the Nazi government in Danzig to refrain from persecuting the Polish minority in the city—an order it felt compelled to follow. Danzig officials also embarked on the "policy of reconciliation towards Poland."⁵⁸ For its part, Warsaw discouraged anti-Nazi campaigns by the Polish minority in Danzig. The Polish ambassador to Germany even told Göring in a meeting, "A National Socialist [Nazi] Senate in Danzig is also most desirable from our point of view, since it brought about a rapprochement between the Free City and Poland." Göring responded, "The Chancellor is taking a firm stand that the Danzig problem should under no circumstances create difficulties in Polish-German relations."⁵⁹ This formal regional détente between Germany and Poland helped to induce a mini-détente between Danziger Germans and Poles on the ground.

By the late 1930s, however, Hitler's expansionist campaigns in neighboring territories had finally destabilized bilateral relations between Warsaw and Danzig. The Danzig conflict was now insecurely nested in an unstable regional environment, undermining the League's soft-power conflict management. Despite the League's efforts to keep the peace, Danzig's Nazi leaders began to systematically dismantle democratic institutions in the city—disbanding opposition parties, arresting leaders of the democratic opposition, and abolishing the opposition press. Danzig's opposition parties even filed a petition protesting the *Gleichschaltung* policies of the Nazi-dominated Senate, but the League of Nations failed to respond decisively.⁶⁰ When Sean Lester, the League high commissioner for Danzig, accused the Nazi-controlled Senate of having "behaved unconstitutionally," Senate president Arthur Greiser delivered a vivid speech before the League Council. The humiliated commissioner stepped down and was replaced by a Swiss national, Carl Burckhardt.⁶¹ Burckhardt was known for being "not a strong anti-Hitlerite," considering himself "a slowly dying organ of a decadent institution."⁶² Soon enough, Danzig's constitution had become a dead letter, and the high commissioner's status a fiction. At this point, League mediation went underground, as the commissioner began to communicate secretly with the Allies over ongoing developments in Danzig. The Allies attempted to work through back channels in Berlin to encourage the Reich to sever its ties with Danzig's Nazi Party.

Danzig's Nazis now began to serve openly as a tool of the Reich—persecuting opposition figures and Jews while pursuing German revisionism. In October 1938, Germany demanded an extraterritorial road and railway via the Polish Corridor, as well as sovereignty over the city.⁶³ In March 1939, Foreign Minister Joachim von Ribbentrop reiterated Germany's calls for annexation, although the request was firmly rejected by Warsaw. One month later, Hitler stated, "Danzig is a German city and wishes to belong to Germany."⁶⁴ When an article denouncing these statements was published in the Polish paper *Czas*, Forster organized a mass anti-Polish rally in August, at which he declared, "the hour of liberation is coming."⁶⁵ The British consul to Danzig confirmed that the city was indeed "fully mobilized in preparation for military action," estimating the number of armed and trained men in the Free City to be around three thousand.[66]

On the very day the Molotov-Ribbentrop Treaty was signed—implicitly promising that Poland would be divided between the Soviet Union and Germany—Danzig's constitution was dissolved, and Forster was declared direct ruler of the city. At the same time, the high commissioner was summarily relieved of his duties. Following Germany's invasion and Poland's defeat, Forster was made the governor of the province Danzig–West Prussia, a position he held until the end of the war. In this role, he helped organize a series of brutal ethnic cleansing and Germanization campaigns, under which tens of thousands of ethnic Poles and Jews were exterminated to create a "blossoming, pure German" province.[67] This sequence of events demonstrates once again that unchecked conflicts at the regional level tend to fuel or escalate local conflicts. Further, cooperative conflict management is likely to prove grossly ineffectual for insecurely nested conflicts.

This chapter has examined the variable success of induced devolution in three mediated intra-state conflicts in interwar Europe—the Åland Islands, Memel, and Danzig—revealing that events in the wider neighborhood provide the best account for fluctuating tensions on the ground (see table 4.2). Longitudinal comparative analysis of three interwar cases largely confirms the nested security predictions. While all three regions enjoyed extensive self-government under their respective autonomy agreements, neither the degree nor the timing of devolution explains the most important shifts in tensions on the ground.

In the case of the Åland Islands, the devolution agreement brokered by the League offered little over Finland's Autonomy Act a year earlier, which had already been dismissed by the islanders as inadequate. Despite marked similarities between the two agreements, the islanders grudgingly accepted the League-brokered deal—largely because their lobby state of Sweden had speedily approved the agreement and withdrawn its support for Ålander separatists. Over the course of this period, growing rapprochement between Finland and Sweden—and the perceived need to join forces to counter a common security threat from Nazi Germany and Soviet Russia—had the effect of consolidating peaceful relations between the Ålanders and the Finnish government. The Danzig and Memel mediations came to a far less auspicious end. The autonomy arrangement that German Memellanders had gratefully accepted in the 1920s was no longer satisfactory to the group by the 1930s. Observing Stresemann's active complaints on their behalf in the League Council, the German Memellanders increasingly lodged complaints against the Lithuanian government—demanding ever more self-government. By the late 1930s, Nazi expansionist rhetoric effectively mobilized the German Memellanders around demands for annexation.

In Danzig, too, the institutional structures that had regulated ethnic relations peacefully in the 1920s were no longer tolerable to the German Danzigers by the mid- to late 1930s in view of the rise of Nazi Germany and the growing specter of Nazi expansion. Nested security effectively explains the sharp fluctuations in conflict in the Free City over the course of the decade. The 1934 Non-Aggression Pact securely nested the Danzig conflict in a stable bilateral alliance, ushering in a brief honeymoon on the ground as both sides sought to respect the rapprochement of their outside sponsors. Once the pact was nullified, however, Danzig authorities wasted little time in stepping up their attacks against the Poles, Jews, and other minorities. At this point, Danzig's leadership began to take direct orders from the Reich, paving the way for Nazi German invasion and occupation, despite strenuous efforts by the League to prevent it. Although the city's high commissioner was able to persuade Danzig authorities to postpone their plans to ethnically cleanse the city of its Jews, Danzig was eventually absorbed by Germany, and the genocidal plans ultimately carried out. In the face of growing regional conflict, the League minority system had become utterly impotent.

While nested security trumped the salutary effects of the devolution agreements in Memel and Danzig, it is probably safe to say that the agreements did not *increase* the likelihood of conflict. Although all three regions boasted autonomy agreements, only two experienced violent conflict, and this had little to do with the agreements themselves. Autonomy in the Åland Islands was quite extensive, yet the separatist movement was quickly subverted and later died out completely. In Memel and Danzig, too, autonomous institutions failed to generate secessionist impulses around a Memel or Danzig national identity, instead yielding a long period of non-mobilization, followed by movements for *annexation* by the mother countries rather than independence for the regions themselves. Had these autonomies been in place longer, they might have generated national identities that later gave rise to secessionist movements. However, the Åland autonomy arrangement is by now over ninety years old and shows little sign of generating secessionist impulses. The reason seems clear: although the Ålanders have nursed grievances against the Finnish government over the past century (mainly regarding land reform and the in-migration of Finnish speakers), the wider environment provided neither the opportunity nor the catalyst for such a movement.

In fact, longitudinal analysis of these three cases shows that conflict on the ground was mostly driven by wider conflicts between the host and lobby states on the regional or bilateral level. The separatist movement in the Åland Islands extended from 1917 to 1921—exactly the period of conflict between the war-weary Finnish state and the irredentist Swedish government. The intervention of Stockholm destabilized internal relations between the Ålanders and Finns, laying the groundwork for a low-level irredentist movement. The conflict quickly died down once both governments agreed to submit their dispute to the League for third-party mediation. When Sweden and Finland deepened their alliance in the late 1930s, endogenous regional stabilization cemented relations between the Ålanders and Finnish government. In this state of consolidated bilateral peace, the islanders no longer thought seriously of a separate existence outside Finland.

Lithuania's conquest of the Memel region in 1923 led to regional destabilization, creating a state of nested *in*security on the ground. The Lithuanian invasion transformed the once tiny Greater Lithuania movement into an indigenous revolt against the French administration and in favor of Lithuanian annexation. Under the Memel Convention of 1924, the Allies induced Kaunas to implement an autonomy arrangement. The arrangement securely nested ethnic relations at the grassroots level, ushering in a period of calm. However, domestic relations were again destabilized in the 1930s when the newly empowered Reich set its sights on the eastern lands. The German Memellanders ultimately rebelled with the direct support and encouragement of the German government. Likewise, Danzig's autonomy arrangements helped to resolve domestic disputes, but only insofar as relations between Poland and Germany remained relatively stable. When the Allies failed to check the rise of Nazi Germany, ethnic relations in Danzig once again became destabilized, paving the way for ethnic German rebellion.

This analysis is not meant to suggest that devolution plays *no* useful role in conflict management. To the contrary, autonomous arrangements in contested territories are often needed not just to regulate ethnic relations on the ground, but also to reach a pact on the regional level. The cases of Danzig and Memel are good illustrations of this, as their devolution arrangements split the difference between competing claims of regional actors—leading them to resolve their differences, at least temporarily. This suggests that resolving or containing conflict dynamics in the wider neighborhood should be a principal priority for peacemakers. In nested conflicts, devolution arrangements mostly succeed in de-escalating tensions on the ground if they also satisfy the relevant *regional* players. Once regional conflicts are effectively brokered, domestic spoilers can be managed far more effectively with modest concessions.

Finally, it should be recognized that the management of nested conflicts is an ongoing process, particularly if the wider neighborhood is itself inherently unstable. In such environments, wider geopolitical pressures or other events at the domestic, regional, or systemic levels are highly liable to upset the ethnic equilibrium and can reignite an internal conflict once thought resolved. Exploiting these insights means committing to *ongoing rather than one-off* mediations in conflict-prone regions. These interventions must in turn be continually recalibrated to respond to geopolitical shifts in the wider neighborhood.

5

PREVENTIVE DIPLOMACY IN POST–COLD WAR EUROPE

At the end of the Cold War, ethnic conflicts threatened to break out in Yugoslavia, Moldova, Romania, the Baltic countries, and elsewhere in postcommunist Europe. Hoping to head off mass violence across the region, West European governments began to formulate a system of conflict prevention in the early 1990s. Thinking to prevent future civil wars like those in Bosnia and Croatia, they established the Office of the High Commissioner on National Minorities (HCNM) under the aegis of the OSCE to monitor hot spots that threatened bloodshed.[1] This mandate gave the high commissioner the authority to engage in confidential interventions in distressed states, provide an impartial evaluation of emerging conflicts, and issue recommendations for resolving them.[2] The high commissioner was to "give priority to those [conflicts] with the worst and most immediate international consequences." Minorities of particular concern were those with national homelands or potentially revisionist kin states that could provoke inter-state war.[3] Like the League of Nations regime before it, the contemporary European regime is made up of both monitors (the Organization for Security and Co-operation in Europe, or OSCE) and enforcers (the EU and NATO). Also similar to the earlier regime, the post–Cold War regime is short on military power and long on political ambition. Therefore, also like the League regime before it, the post–Cold War regime has been forced to rely on soft-power conflict management.

Preventive diplomacy has been a central strategy of the post–Cold War regime. The HCNM takes a self-consciously neutral position in emerging communal conflicts, favoring integrationist policies such as expanded access to citizenship or language rights for beleaguered minorities (eschewing territorial solutions such as federalism or territorial autonomy). Former high commissioner Knut Vollebaek stated, "I believe that integration in its proper form, with respect for diversity and without forced assimilation, is the best solution to the challenges we are facing."[4] Tasked with conflict prevention, the commissioner's mandate ends when violence begins,[5] at which point the mediation can be judged to have failed and a different set of international actors step in to take over the tasks of conflict management. The OSCE and

HCNM have been authorized to intervene in troubled states only with the explicit consent of the target governments.[6] Although they have neither the carrots nor the sticks to induce the target states to comply,[7] they have indirect access to such inducements through NATO and the EU, which sometimes offer membership to target states conditional upon the government's compliance with OSCE/HCNM recommendations.

Preventive diplomacy has met with variable success across Central and Eastern Europe. In the 1990s and 2000s, the HCNM and the OSCE intervened to contain escalating conflicts on dozens of occasions—with uneven results. Of the HCNM's many mediations, the high commissioner judged its interventions in Macedonia and the Baltics most successful, whereas others (namely, Kosovo) were viewed as significant failures. To investigate the causes of variable success, I periodize the four most important preventive diplomacy mediations of the post–Cold War period (the Russian minority conflicts in the Baltics and the Albanian minority conflicts in the Balkans during the 1990s) according to shifts in the level of conflict on the ground. Careful process tracing of each mediation reveals that variation in success was driven largely by the stability of the wider neighborhood. I show that a stable neighborhood promotes mediation success, whereas regional instability—a function of conflict spillover from neighboring states or kin state intervention—tends to fuel communal tensions on the ground.

The section below lays out core nested security predictions for successful preventive diplomacy in these cases and describes a plan for testing the predictions against alternative explanations of third-party mediation. The remainder of the chapter explores two paired case studies of preventive diplomacy. I use the pattern of events in these cases to adjudicate between the different accounts of mediation success. This is followed by a comparative evaluation of theories in light of the evidence, and finally policy conclusions.

Nested Security versus Alternative Hypotheses

Nested security holds that regional stability is critical to successful conflict mediation. When there is conflict spillover from civil war in a neighboring country, or when a homeland state intervenes to tip the power balance on either side of the conflict, the region may become destabilized, creating conditions of nested insecurity on the ground that can intensify communal conflict. If external instability empowers the minority, this can lead to rebellion or secessionism (Variant A). If the instability instead empowers the target government, then its leaders may choose to suppress or ethnically cleanse the troublesome minority (Variant B). Similarly, conflict spillover from a neighboring state can trigger conflict in the target state, even when third-party mediation and conditions on the ground favor resolution. In the Baltics, intervention by the Russian government threatened to destabilize ethnic relations on the ground, while in the Balkans, Serbian repression and conflict spillover upset the ethnic equilibrium in Kosovo and Macedonia, respectively.

Given the importance of the regional conflict environment, great-power involvement is often critical to successful preventive diplomacy. Major powers can intervene to *exogenously stabilize* bilateral relations between the minority's host and kin states, increasing the chances of successful mediation. They do this by forestalling kin state interventions and/or creating incentives for the two sides to reach a deal. In the cases considered here, the United States and other Western governments occasionally induced regional peace deals through selective incentives such as loan guarantees or threats of economic sanctions or military force. Over the long run, minority-majority relations may be *endogenously* stabilized, but only if the relevant regional players arrive at self-enforcing peace deals, causing intergroup cleavages to lose their salience over time and generating more permanent solutions to minority disputes. This might be accomplished in the Baltics by incorporating Russia into a tighter pan-Eurasian security regime; the Albanian minority conflicts could be more durably managed once Albania, Macedonia, Kosovo, and Serbia are admitted to both the European Union and NATO.[8]

I have chosen the Russian-speaking minorities in Latvia and Estonia and the Albanian minorities in Kosovo and Macedonia for paired comparative longitudinal analysis because the HCNM and the OSCE viewed these as particularly high-risk cases. The high commissioner therefore focused the bulk of his preventive diplomacy efforts on these four cases—particularly during the turbulent period of the 1990s. Consistent with the HCNM mandate, all four groups are territorially concentrated, and all have bellicose national homelands with a history of violent intervention on behalf of their ethnic kin. Although the HCNM mandate extends to the countries of the former Soviet Union, which are also OSCE member countries, I confine my analysis to Central and Eastern Europe in the 1990s and 2000s in order to make the study more tractable and ensure greater comparability of cases. The four mediations extended from 1993, when the HCNM became operational, to the early 2000s (when the OSCE was ejected from Serbia, conflict began in Macedonia, and the OSCE missions were closed in the Baltics). I divide these cases into phases of greater and lesser communal conflict and look to see whether (1) mediator skills and/or resources (here, conditionality), (2) the policies of the host state, or (3) the stability of the external conflict environment best accounts for variable tensions across cases and over time.

Table 5.1 Nested security predictions

Russian-speaking minorities	Regional environment	Conflict outcome
(early 1990s)	Regional destabilization (Russia intervenes)	Minority radicalization; calls for regional autonomy
(1994–2003)	Exogenous stabilization (U.S. induces Russia to withdraw)	Minority moderation; minority accommodation in Estonia and Latvia
(2004–)	(Tentative) endogenous regional stabilization (Russia and Baltics reach modus vivendi)	Modest minority integration; increased intergroup cooperation
Albanian minorities	**Regional environment**	**Conflict outcome**
(early 1990s)	Regional destabilization (host states have upper hand)	Host states choose minority policies based on domestic considerations
(mid-1990s)	Exogenous stabilization (NATO/UN/U.S. attempt to induce intergroup settlements)	Reduction of tensions at domestic level; tenuous intergroup settlements
(Kosovo, late 1990s; Macedonia, 2001)	Regional destabilization (minorities have upper hand)	Minority rebellion, radicalization of minority demands

In addition to testing the predictions of nested security, I also assess whether alternative explanations do a better job of accounting for mediation success in the region. Many scholars have focused on the role of EU and NATO membership conditionality in stabilizing ethnic relations in Central and Eastern Europe. The European Commission conducted regular assessments of candidate member countries using a general set of standards known as "the Copenhagen criteria" and the *acquis communautaire*.[9] In the course of accession talks, NATO and the EU systematically evaluate each candidate country's compliance with these requirements, including (among other things) domestic stability and minority protection. In countries where the HCNM was involved in this process (mostly in the late 1990s), its evaluations sometimes figured into EU and NATO decisions as to whether to admit the country for membership. In this way, the high commissioner could sometimes "punch above his weight," particularly when dealing with a target state engaged in accession negotiations. Dimitrina Petrova of the European Roma Rights Center observed that "EU accession is *the* instrument for change—that's what governments pay attention to."[10] As HCNM senior adviser Marcin Czapliński put it, "[the] EU and NATO are the teeth of the OSCE."[11] For membership conditionality to work its magic, the EU and NATO not only had to make credible offers of membership, but membership privileges had to be highly valued by both state governments and their populations.[12] Finally, membership prospects had to be seen as imminent by the target government, otherwise it would be unwilling to push through the necessary concessions, and the population would be unwilling to accept them.[13] As noted by Schimmelfennig and Sedelmeier, the "size and speed of rewards," as well as the "credibility" of the promised rewards, have proved critical for securing target state compliance.[14]

Many observers are skeptical of the conflict management potential of NATO/EU conditionality because of the vagueness of accession criteria, the presence of nationalistic domestic elites, and the occasional mismatch between European and domestic norms.[15] One problem is that these factors address only the government side of the equation. The assumption is that liberal policies will automatically reduce intercommunal tensions because minorities, thus appeased, will respond by de-escalating their demands against their host governments. However, there are many cases where minorities challenged their governments even after receiving extensive concessions. Nonetheless, "conditionality" models *do* generate a clear prediction with respect to mediation success, which is that third parties can facilitate conflict reduction if they persuade the target governments to enact liberal reforms.

A second set of arguments focuses on the substate level, namely whether domestic political elites are committed to liberalism and minority integration. Zsuzsa Csergő argues that external mediation or conditionality did little to calm tensions over Hungarian minorities in Slovakia or Romania until political moderates ascended to power and enacted a more liberal agenda. The emergence of more liberal governments was due to growing popular pressures for reform on the domestic level, rather than outside pressures.[16] Gwendolyn Sasse likewise posited that Latvia's domestic political setting was a critical factor in the success of external conflict management.[17] Indeed, the status of Hungarian minorities improved drastically once the nationalist administrations of Romania, Slovakia, and Serbia gave way to liberal, reform-minded governments in the late 1990s and early 2000s. If domestic liberalism is crucial to mediation success, then minority conflicts in the region should be driven primarily by host state policies, with liberalization leading to conflict reduction.

A final set of arguments focuses on the third-party mediator and its legitimacy in the eyes of the conflict parties. Some argue that much of the credit for the success of the HCNM goes to the diplomatic skills and gravitas of the high commissioner. Walter Kemp, a scholar and participant in the 1990s HCNM mediations, notes that First High Commissioner Max van der Stoel was held in extremely high regard by states in the region. Recognizing his stellar record of diplomacy, the target states in the region took his evaluations and interventions more seriously than they otherwise would. His considerable tact and empathy meant that the commissioner was sensitive to the situation faced by these governments, helping him to devise solutions to the conflict through confidential negotiations. At the same time, the office boasted a crack team of technical and legal experts skilled at resolving technical problems and drafting pro-minority legislation that would be acceptable to veto players and nationalists in the respective parliaments. A key prediction here is that the high commissioner's personal interventions would reduce communal tensions following (and because of) his personal interactions with the conflict parties. I seek evidence for the high commissioner's personal impact through interviews with key participants as well as a step-by-step analysis of the actual HCNM interventions. In the pages that follow, I review the details of these four mediations to assess the relative explanatory power of nested security against alternative arguments outlined above.

Case Evidence

Russian Minorities in the Baltics

The Baltic republics were the first to secede from the increasingly fragile Soviet Union in the late 1980s. As a result of internal colonization, they inherited large Russian-speaking minorities, which quickly became targets for discrimination in the newly independent states. Latvia and Estonia had the most fraught conflicts, because of their sizable Russian minorities and their shared borders with Russia; Lithuania had a much smaller Russian minority and no shared border with the Russian mainland (see map 2). In view of this, the CSCE flagged the region (particularly Latvia and Estonia) as a potential flashpoint that would require external mediation.

Regional Destabilization: Moscow Provokes Co-ethnics in the Baltics

The newly independent Baltic states had a uniquely fraught relationship with Moscow, which was widely seen as an existential threat. These views were informed by their history of Soviet suzerainty, large Russian minorities, and sizable Soviet military bases—containing approximately 120,000 soldiers as late as 1992.[18] The Baltics also relied on Moscow to meet their energy needs; Latvia was especially dependent, importing fully 91 percent of the energy it consumed.[19] Moscow thus enjoyed the upper hand in cross-border relations and was quick to exploit this advantage for short-term financial and political gain. According to one longtime observer of the region, the Russian

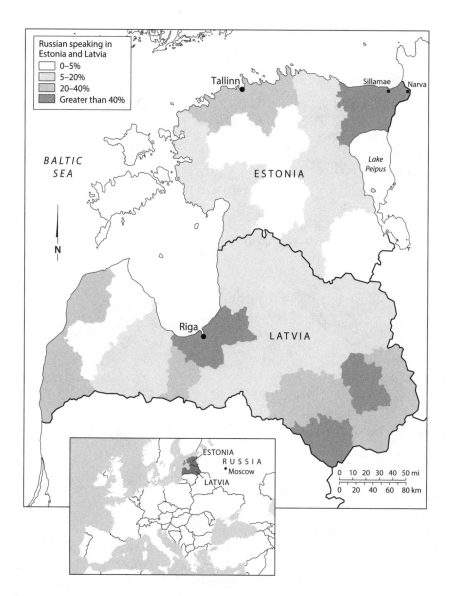

Map 2 Post–Cold War Baltics

Foreign Ministry "undoubtedly used the diaspora issue [in the Baltics] as a bargaining chip in the international arena in return for gains on other issues or to deflect attention from Russian policies elsewhere [such as Chechnya]."[20] Moscow had domestic political reasons for flexing its muscles in the Baltics. Russian president Boris Yeltsin faced a significant electoral challenge from the

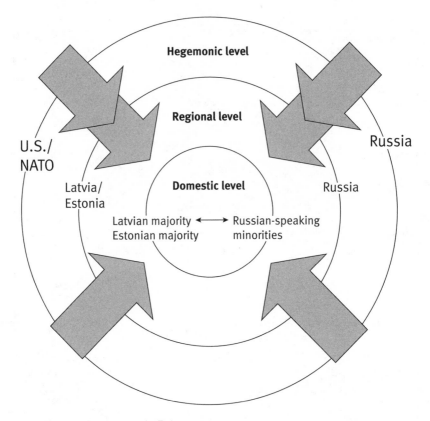

Figure 5.1 Nested security in the Baltic states

nationalist Right and feared the planned troop withdrawal from the Baltics would not go as smoothly as hoped.

In the newly independent states, meanwhile, hard-core nationalist parties won resounding electoral victories—largely because of the perceived threat of Moscow. In Estonia, the nationalist Pro Patria Union won the parliamentary elections on an anti-Soviet platform. Estonian president H.E. Lennart Meri gave a speech in Brussels in which he castigated the West for allowing the Soviet occupation, which led to the "deportation of Estonians to Siberia" and the "settlement of Russian colonists to Estonia."[21] It was in this atmosphere of fear that the new nationalist governments of Latvia and Estonia crafted citizenship laws that effectively denied citizenship to their Russian-speaking minorities. Seeing this, Yeltsin discerned an opportunity to leverage Russia's position for political gain—scoring points with the Russian military as well as the public.[22] Although Moscow had not previously linked the issue of troop withdrawal to the status of the Russian minorities, it did so now. Declaring his commitment to protect the Russian speakers from discrimination, Yeltsin halted the scheduled withdrawal of Russian troops from the Baltic bases. Russia's negotiator, Sergei Zotov, threatened that if Latvia did not end its "apartheid policy" against ethnic Russians, Moscow would shut off its gas pipeline to Latvia and restrict its shipments of industrial raw materials.[23] Meanwhile, Russian officials predicted "Yugoslavia-type chaos" in Estonia if its leaders enacted a discriminatory citizenship law there.[24] With Russia all but threatening war against the Baltic countries, the region was effectively destabilized. The nested security model predicts cooperative conflict management to fail under such circumstances, even when undertaken by skilled negotiators.

The international community lost little time in responding to the crisis. As soon as he took office, High Commissioner Max van der Stoel sought to mediate the emerging conflicts in the Baltic countries using preventive diplomacy. In January 1993, van der Stoel traveled to Riga and Tallinn to urge the governments not to enact their discriminatory citizenship laws, warning darkly that they might have serious international consequences.[25] Van der Stoel wrote a letter to Foreign Minister Georg Andrejevs later that year, stating in the strongest possible terms that the new citizenship law would effectively strip hundreds of thousands of Russian speakers of their "political rights" and "endanger the stability of your country."[26] With the help of his advisers, the commissioner devised a number of specific recommendations for how to liberalize the laws. Despite the fact that the Baltic governments were under the watchful gaze of the international community and keenly desired NATO and EU membership, the high commissioner's warnings were largely ignored. With the international community looking on, the Estonian parliament passed a "Law on Aliens" in June 1993 that formalized the statelessness of Russian speakers. Moscow responded to Estonia's law by making angry threats against the Estonian government. The Russian foreign minister compared Estonia's law to apartheid in South Africa and accused Tallinn of quiet ethnic cleansing. Yeltsin himself warned that Tallinn had overestimated Russia's goodwill, observing that the Estonian government had "forgotten about certain geopolitical and demographic realities" and that Russia had the "means at its disposal to remind Estonia about these [realities]."[27] As if to drive this point home, Moscow abruptly cut off the flow of gas to Estonia for four days. The Supreme Soviet passed a resolution calling for sanctions against Estonia as well as the complete suspension of troop withdrawal from the Baltics.[28] Hanging over it all was the possibility that Russia would intervene militarily—a possibility that was all too real, given the presence of tens of thousands of Russian troops still stationed on Baltic soil.[29]

The available evidence indicates that Moscow's threats had insecurely nested the minority disputes in an unstable regional environment by tipping the internal balance of power in favor of minorities (Variant A). As Moscow escalated its rhetoric, ethnic Russians in Estonia and Latvia responded by radicalizing their own demands—exacerbating domestic tensions in both countries. With Russian officials threatening economic sanctions against Latvia in late 1992, Soviet veterans and Russian military personnel in Latvia demanded the unconditional restoration of their voting rights and privileges in that country, threatening that otherwise they would establish autonomous Russian-speaking regions in Latvia.[30] In Estonia, too, Russian separatists organized strikes in protest of the new law, culminating in demands for referenda on "national-territorial autonomy" for Russian regions.[31] Leaders in Narva and Sillamäe, Russian-speaking cities near Estonia's border with Russia, declared the referenda on autonomy to be their best protection from a nationalist central government. The international community feared these conflicts would invite Russian military intervention, with Moscow seeking to "rescue" its beleaguered co-ethnics.

It was not until NATO and the United States began to negotiate a Russian withdrawal from Latvia and Estonia that a resolution to the crisis was reached, and the restrictive citizenship laws began a slow rollback.

Exogenous Stabilization—U.S., NATO Induce Russian Withdrawal from the Baltics

Western leaders used muscular diplomacy to induce Moscow to step back from the brink. U.S. diplomats in particular pressured the cash-strapped Russian Federation to withdraw its troops from the Baltics quickly and to tone down its interventionist rhetoric. According to a local expert on Russian-Baltic relations, Russia was eager to make a deal with the West over the Baltics, as Moscow was "in retreat" due to internal chaos and the need to maintain productive ties with Western countries. Nonetheless, "no one had any doubt it was the Americans who did it."[32] U.S. president Bill Clinton's growing commitment to NATO expansion moved the process forward, as he declared that the "Baltic litmus test" would demonstrate NATO's continued relevance in European security affairs.[33] In 1996, Washington issued a "Baltic Action Plan" that gave the new states a security guarantee and opened the door for their eventual membership in NATO.

In the context of muscular intervention by the United States and NATO, van der Stoel was able to execute successful shuttle diplomacy between Tallinn and Narva and Sillamäe. He persuaded Estonian president Lennart Meri to submit the new citizenship legislation to the CoE and the CSCE for an impartial evaluation before signing it into law. Van der Stoel later pointed out certain clauses that conflicted with international standards on the treatment of noncitizens. Based on the recommendation of the high commissioner, the president decided not to sign the discriminatory law. In so doing, he was able to claim that he was responding to "objective" and "disinterested" technical and legal advisers rather than political pressure from the West, Russia, or the Russian-speaking minority.[34]

The high commissioner simultaneously engaged in parallel talks with Russophone separatists near the Russian border. He brokered an agreement whereby Tallinn would not interfere with the balloting of the autonomy referenda; in return, the separatist leaders agreed to allow the Constitutional Review Chamber of the Supreme Court to assess the constitutionality of these referenda. Van der Stoel secured this agreement by shuttling back and forth between Tallinn and the Russophone cities to facilitate a dialogue between the two parties. Throughout the crisis, the commissioner maintained constant contact with Moscow. Early on in the negotiations, he met with Russian foreign minister Andrey Kozyrev, who stated that Russia was "keeping all doors open," indicating that Russia was open to—and perhaps grateful for—the involvement of disinterested mediators.[35] In the end, Estonia's Constitutional Court invalidated the referenda results because of obvious procedural irregularities in the elections.

In Latvia, meanwhile, bilateral tensions heated up in 1994 over a restrictive citizenship law that placed quotas on the number of naturalized citizens. Van der Stoel protested that the naturalization quotas would limit the number of people that could be naturalized each year, rendering thousands of Russians stateless and undermining their ability to integrate into society.[36] The high commissioner ultimately prevailed upon Latvian president Guntis Ulmanis to return the law to parliament, where he urged legislators to redraft the law in accordance with the recommendations set forth by the Council of Europe and the high commissioner. In the end, the parliament omitted the quota system from the final legislation that passed in July 1994. As in Estonia, the high commissioner kept in close contact with Moscow throughout the crisis to minimize Russia's potentially destabilizing influence on the outcome. As talks on Latvian accession to the EU approached, the HCNM became increasingly influential in shaping the laws and procedures regarding citizenship. U.S. intervention may have prevented Russia from intervening more aggressively in response to the passage of the law. President Clinton signaled American commitment to Latvian security by visiting Riga in July 1994 and delivering a speech in front of the Monument of Freedom: "We will help you restore your land. And we will rejoice with you when the last of the foreign troops vanish from your homelands. We will be partners so that your nation can forever be free."[37] Judith Kelley concluded that "the United States' and the international community's pressure on Russia to withdraw [from Baltic soil] greatly constrained Russia's ability to leverage change [in the Baltics] using the security threat."[38] Perhaps most important, the United States made much-needed financial aid contingent upon Russian troop withdrawals from Baltic soil. In these ways, "foreign, especially American, assistance played an enormous role in the negotiations between Latvia and Russia."[39] Of getting Moscow to withdraw from the Baltics, analyst Aleksei Semjenov confirmed, "No one had any doubt it was the Americans who did it."[40]

Western governments kept up their pressure on Russia throughout the remainder of the decade. Beginning in 1996, Clinton administration officials initiated bilateral talks with President Yeltsin and Foreign Minister Yevgeny Primakov over NATO expansion. At the Helsinki Summit in March 1997, Yeltsin attempted to strike a deal that would allow NATO to expand to Central Europe but exclude the Baltic countries. However, Washington refused to scale back NATO expansion, and Yeltsin finally gave in, sighing: "Well, I tried."[41] A few months later, Primakov tried and failed to place conditions on NATO enlargement; to his chagrin, U.S. secretary of state Madeleine Albright "made" Moscow accept unconditional NATO expansion, which was "key to Russia's early admission into the WTO, Paris Club, etc. . . . . Russia has to pay for Western economic aid—the only question being the size of the price."[42] By placing barriers on Russian intervention in the Baltic states, the United States and the EU used substantial carrots and sticks to stabilize the region.

In early 1999, international attention turned to Latvia's controversial new language law. The high commissioner objected strongly to various parts of the law, arguing (among other things) that it permitted unacceptable government interference in the private sphere. However, the parliament refused to budge. The high commissioner warned the Foreign Ministry that failure to comply with these recommendations could lead to domestic instability—discouraging foreign investment and diminishing Latvia's chances of EU membership.[43] Despite this strongly worded protest, the government (now in the midst of an election campaign) refused to send the legislation back to parliament, and the new president, Vaira Vīķe-Freiberga, refused to budge on the issue. Post-election meetings with the commissioner's senior legal adviser, however, ultimately persuaded the president to return the law to parliament for revisions. The bill was amended with the help of a team of legal experts sent by the high commissioner's office in late 1999. Falk Lange, a member of the OSCE mission to Latvia, recalled, "the work of the High Commissioner and his mandate in these countries was so intrusive that . . . draft legislation would be on our table before it [appeared] on the table of the ministry."[44] A critical precondition for success was EU influence, as "it was only in tandem with EU [pressure] that changes were made."[45]

The facts of this case show that HCNM preventive diplomacy may have helped to calm internal tensions in Latvia and Estonia. However, any success that the high commissioner enjoyed was predicated on U.S. constraints on Russian intervention, as well as EU and NATO pressures on the Baltic countries to reform their domestic legislation. Latvia's Cabinet of Ministers adopted a newly liberalized language law in 2000, which van der Stoel judged to be in full conformity with Latvia's international commitments concerning human and minority rights. In 2001, the OSCE missions in the Baltics were declared a success and closed down.[46] U.S. president Clinton declared that NATO had passed its Baltic litmus test for overcoming Cold War divisions.[47]

What this case narrative shows is that the United States and the EU facilitated successful conflict mediation by providing critical backing to the high commissioner's diplomatic interventions. Indeed, it was largely due to these background conditions that the senior adviser of the high commissioner, Neil Melvin, could claim Latvia and Estonia as their greatest successes in conflict prevention.[48]

(Tentative) Endogenous Stabilization—Russia and the Baltics Reach a Modus Vivendi

Since Latvia and Estonia gained accession to the EU in 2004, bilateral relations with Russia have gradually moved toward a stable equilibrium. When NATO officials announced the accession of Latvia and Estonia to the alliance in 2002, Russian political discourse was muted, even in nationalist papers such as *Nezavisimaya gazeta*. In marked contrast to the hyperbolic rhetoric of the 1990s, Russian commentators struck a "balanced, business-like" tone toward the Baltics, even on "such potentially hot issues" as the installation of radars in Latvia and Estonia. There was even talk of future Russian-Baltic military cooperation.[49]

Galbreath and Lašas write that "the rhetorical 'heat' of the Baltic-Russian relation[s] over the minority issue sharply declined as the accession process continued." The issue of Russian speakers ("in contrast to the pre-enlargement phase") was gradually sidelined in bilateral relations as time went on.[50] The reasons for this are clear when one considers the importance Russia increasingly gave to commercial ties to the EU (and by extension the Baltic states), as the principal market for Russian gas and oil.[51] The value of stable bilateral relations has only grown with the construction of the Baltic Pipeline System (through which Russia transports gas and oil to Western Europe), the Baltics forming a critical "point of immediate contact" between Russia and the EU energy market.[52]

With the Baltic states now in the EU, bilateral conflicts with Russia are treated as a community issue: all outstanding border conflicts—including migration, security, and trade—also involve the EU and NATO. The Baltics have proven their commitment to NATO, having contributed troops to the missions in Iraq and Afghanistan (including the violent Helmand Province in the south). Estonia is home to NATO's Cooperative Cyber Defense Center of Excellence, and Latvia now hosts NATO's Strategic Communication Center of Excellence.[53] Their membership in EU and NATO has completely changed Baltic-Russian relations: "being part of a larger alliance meant that power relations between Latvia and the Russian Federation became less asymmetrical, and bilateral relations were de-emphasized in favour of a larger multilateral field of interactions."[54] Russia's ambassador to Latvia affirmed that 2004 was a game changer, declaring that "the time of ultimatums drew to an end when Latvia joined the EU and NATO."[55]

Estonia and Latvia have had their own geopolitical interests in improving relations with Russia. The Baltics are still connected to the Russian electricity transmission system, making them "energy islands" "largely cut off from EU energy networks."[56] Common commercial interests also promote bilateral cooperation. Russia was Latvia's fifth-largest foreign investor and fifth-most-important trading partner by the early 2000s.[57] In Estonia, the percentage of tourists from Russia increased sevenfold, from 28,000 in 2002 to 208,000 in 2011 (an increase from 3 to 11 percent of Estonian tourism overall).[58] There are, then, strong mutual interests in achieving a self-enforcing bilateral partnership, which help to securely nest the minority conflicts in a stable regional environment. In line with this prediction, the contemporary Russian-Baltic disputes appear to be self-limiting. Even as Russian president Vladimir Putin ratcheted up his nationalist rhetoric in response to rising energy prices in the late 2000s and early 2010s, Moscow has proven loath to intervene on behalf of its co-ethnics in the Baltics—Russian leaders proclaim their interest in protecting Russians abroad but have avoided any concrete policy that would significantly antagonize Tallinn or Riga.

With the region thus (tentatively) endogenously stabilized, the nested security model predicts that the ethnic cleavage would gradually lose political salience in both countries. In line with these predictions, the Baltic governments embarked on large-scale projects to integrate their Russian speakers in the 2000s. A follow-up study on ethnic relations in Latvia reported that the proportion of Russian speakers claiming no knowledge of Latvian declined from 22 percent in 1996 to just 7 percent in 2008. At the same time, 95 percent of respondents in a survey claimed intergroup relations were satisfactory, good, or very good.[59] In Estonia, the percentage of the population with "undetermined citizenship" [presumably stateless Russian speakers] declined from 32 percent in 1992 (nearly all Russian speakers) to 8.5 percent in 2007.[60] Interethnic integration has also increased markedly, with data suggesting that two-thirds of Estonians and Russians have a friend or close acquaintance from the other group, while two-thirds of Russians under thirty-nine are fluent in Estonian.[61] Political cooperation has also deepened over time. Although the early to mid-2000s saw minority demonstrations over language and education laws, political protests of recent years have included *both* Latvian and Russian participants; individuals appear to have forged political alliances along common economic interests.[62]

Parallel trends can also be found in the formal political sphere. Whereas the 1990s saw segregated voting for Russian parties by Russian voters in both Baltic countries, individuals have increasingly begun to vote across ethnic lines. By 2003, most ethnic Russians had abandoned the minority parties, switching their votes to mainstream nonethnic parties such as the Reform Party and (especially) the Estonian Centre Party, a left-wing populist party modeled after a traditional Social Democratic party of Western Europe.[63] Rather than rallying around minority parties that promote Russian interests in language, education, and the workplace, Russian voters are increasingly supporting centrist parties, which now dominate Estonian politics and which appeal to Russian speakers by running ethnic Russian candidates. At the same time, very little of the Centre Party platform relates to minority issues. The party succeeded by styling itself as the "only Estonian party with a genuinely civic approach, cutting across ethnic lines, as opposed to the divisive 'us versus them' approach employed by the ruling [majority parties]."[64] In this way the Centre Party managed to gain as much as 75 percent of the ethnic Russian vote while maintaining its status as the second-most-powerful party in parliament.[65] Particularly since the recent economic crisis, economic issues have overridden ethnic loyalties in Estonian politics, and Russian speakers have proven willing to vote for majority parties "if they [think the party] would consider the interests of Russian speakers."[66]

In Latvia, too, ethnic Russians have begun to vote in greater numbers for a nonethnic party. In the 1990s, Russians predominantly voted for ethnic Russian parties, which began to run in coalition by the late 1990s. In 2002, however, the most popular of these (Harmony Centre) left the Russian minority coalition to run solo, eventually attracting the majority of Russian voters. Although it is still a Russian party, the left-wing Harmony Centre has called for reconciliation between ethnic Latvians and Russian speakers, improved relations with Russia, increased social spending, and challenging the Latvian "oligarchs." Demobilization from ethnic to economic issues has permitted the party to position itself as both pro-Russian and pro–working class. When Harmony Centre won the largest number of votes in the 2011 parliamentary elections (29 percent of the vote and one-third of the seats), Jānis Urbanovičs, the head of the party's faction in parliament, said, "We must end the escalation of disputes between Russians and Latvians. . . . We need to understand that we have good neighbors with whom we need to develop mutually beneficial relations."[67]

Altogether, the case evidence suggests that endogenous stabilization of Riga-Moscow relations in the 2000s permitted the ethnic cleavage to gradually lose salience at the domestic level. Nonetheless, regional destabilization or certain domestic factors—such as increased incentives to discriminate during economic downturns—can reignite communal tensions in the future. In other words, this trend could still reverse.

The picture has not been wholly peaceful in the post-accession period. The Bronze Soldier statue conflict in Estonia in 2007 powerfully demonstrates that ethnic tensions can reignite after long stretches of apparent harmony. The backstory is that the government decided to move a Soviet war memorial from the city center—ostensibly because it served as a touchstone for sporadic riots by Russian youth in years past. This triggered a bloody incident in which a twenty-year-old Russian man was killed and others injured. Moscow lodged vociferous protests in the media and encouraged pro-Putin activists to attack the Estonian embassy in Moscow; it also shut down cross-border traffic in Narva. Although several of my informants were convinced that Moscow was behind a subsequent cyber-attack on Estonian banking and government websites, the weight of evidence suggests that unaffiliated "hacktivists" were acting on their own accord. In any event, Russia's reaction to these events served to "escalate tensions between Estonia and Russia, as well as between ethnic communities in Estonia."[68]

Despite the poisoning of intergroup relations on the ground, both sides appeared determined to contain the conflict. At its nadir, Estonian president Toomas Hendrik Ilves insisted that bilateral relations between the two countries "can only get better." Russian and Estonian officials have been quick to enter a dialogue to discuss ways to improve cross-border cooperation in the areas of trade and tourism.[69] Nonetheless, this incident presents a stark warning that internal conflicts can still reemerge well after the threat of violence appears to have receded. Nested security holds that the external conflict environment can destabilize intergroup relations on the ground, even in the presence of determined mediators. This means that domestic peace is never fully guaranteed, even with Latvia's and Estonia's membership in the EU. Although few believe that a Ukrainian-style conflict could happen in the Baltics today, Russian intervention in Georgia in 2008 and Ukraine in 2014 raised acute concerns of similar Russian provocation in Latvia and Estonia. To ensure that Russian minority conflicts are securely nested in a stable regional environment, bilateral relations between the Baltics and Russia should therefore be monitored and managed by major powers on an ongoing basis.

Albanian Minorities in the Balkans

Western mediators were most concerned about the conflict potential of Yugoslavia (see map 3). Having failed to forestall the Serbo-Croatian and Bosnian wars, the international community resolved to monitor potential *future* sites of conflict in order to prevent further violence in postcommunist Europe. The newly created HCNM therefore identified the following "zones of potential conflict": the Vojvodina, Sandžak, and Kosovo regions in the Federal Republic

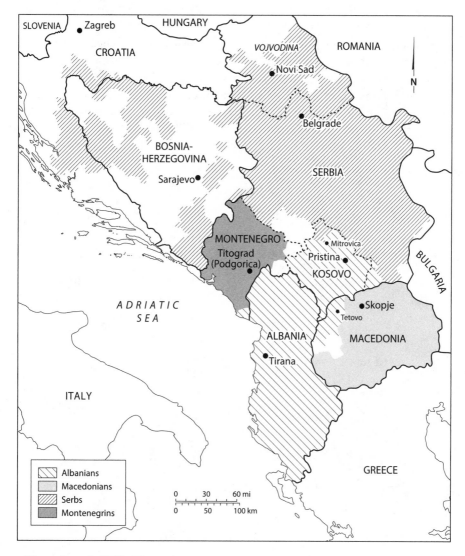

Map 3 Post–Cold War Western Balkans

of Yugoslavia, as well as newly independent Macedonia.[70] The CSCE also sent monitoring missions to Serbia in an effort to de-escalate simmering communal tensions before they led to bloodshed.

Most worrisome from a security standpoint was Kosovo, a province within Serbia that had enjoyed de facto republic status in Yugoslavia. According to the 1991 census (estimated), ethnic Serbs made up 10 percent of the population of Kosovo. The international community feared that the tiny province was a veritable tinderbox. Kosovo had a high concentration of Albanians with an unusually high birthrate; Serbs were emigrating to Serbia proper because of poor economic conditions. The province's changing demographics made Kosovo a compelling target for Serb nationalists. More important, whereas the Hungarian minority in Vojvodina (the other Serbian province) had a relatively calm homeland state that was well on its way toward liberalization and integration into Euro-Atlantic structures, Kosovo had a revisionist homeland state that was prone to violent breakdown. It was feared that Albanian foreign policy or domestic politics could easily radicalize Kosovo Albanians.

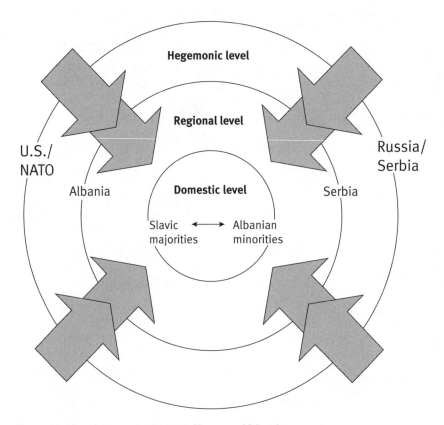

Figure 5.2 Nested security in the 1990s Kosovo and Macedonia

Macedonia was the second hot spot of concern to European conflict managers.[71] The country contained a large proportion of Albanians concentrated along its border with Albania and Kosovo, a situation that appeared to threaten cross-border conflict. As Croatia and Slovenia prepared for independence, Macedonia's leader, Kiro Gligorov, resolved to organize a referendum on statehood to avoid remaining in a truncated Yugoslavia dominated by Serbs. The desire for statehood was affirmed by an overwhelming majority of ethnic Macedonians voting in the referendum (although the Albanian minority boycotted it), and the country's leaders declared independence in 1992.[72] Western governments now feared that the weak, ethnically divided state could easily descend into civil war.

Regional Destabilization—Target States Have the Upper Hand

The international community paid scant attention to events in Kosovo and Macedonia in the early 1990s, as the focus remained on resolving the civil war in Bosnia and other conflicts farther afield. The Kosovo and Macedonian conflicts were in effect handed off to the resource-poor OSCE and the HCNM. Consequently, Belgrade and Skopje enjoyed considerable discretion over their minority policies. Absent exogenous stabilization by Western governments, minority-majority relations quickly succumbed to nested *in*security in both places (Variant B), where the government is leveraged relative to the minority. In the late 1980s, Slobodan Milošević (then head of the League of Communists of Serbia) mobilized support around the cause of Serbs in Kosovo, declaring that they were "oppressed and humiliated" by Albanians. The government passed laws in 1989–90 designed to change the ethnic balance in Kosovo by restricting the sale of property to Albanians, encouraging family planning and the out-migration of ethnic Albanians as well as the in-migration of Serbs. Belgrade also revoked Kosovo's autonomy, dissolved the provincial assembly, shut down minority media, changed the educational system to favor the Serbian language, and changed the street signs to Serbian. The Albanian minority, lacking outside leverage, could do little more than protest Belgrade's actions. Hundreds of thousands of Albanians turned out in a series of strikes and mass protests; at the same time, Kosovo Albanian leaders organized a shadow Kosovo Assembly, which held a referendum on independence in September 1991—gaining near universal support.

European conflict managers resolved to address the brewing conflict in Kosovo. OSCE "missions of long duration" were established in Vojvodina, Sandžak, and Kosovo and tasked with monitoring ethnic conflicts in the region and containing any grassroots tensions that might emerge. Meanwhile, the high commissioner prepared to personally mediate the Kosovo conflict.

Serbian president Milošević was, unsurprisingly, unhappy about what he viewed as a clear violation of Serbian sovereignty and the message that it sent about the Serbian state. He was particularly displeased about the presence of an OSCE mission on Serbian soil because it signified (at least to Belgrade) that Serbia was, in a very real sense, an illiberal state prone to minority repression. Van der Stoel was therefore forced to mediate the Kosovo conflict from afar. In 1993, the high commissioner visited the head of the Democratic League of Kosovo, Ibrahim Rugova, in Tirana, where he ran up against similar obstacles. The Kosovo Albanian leader told him that he would not negotiate with him in his official capacity as the high commissioner because the Albanians were not a Yugoslav minority but rather an oppressed "nation."[73]

Lacking outside pressure to reach an agreement, the Kosovo conflict remained insecurely nested in an unstable regional environment. Under these conditions, the nested security model would expect cooperative mediation to fail. As predicted, neither Belgrade nor the Kosovo Albanians could agree on the terms of mediation (the government rejected the notion of external interference in sovereign affairs, while the Kosovo Albanian leadership rejected the very premise that they were a constituent minority in Serbian state). Realizing that the missions were only subjecting him to unfavorable international scrutiny (and with no immediate prospects of joining either the EU or NATO), Milošević continuously stonewalled the high commissioner and finally ejected the OSCE mission in Kosovo after only one year on the ground.

In the early 1990s, the Macedonian government also enjoyed considerable discretion over its minority policies, which threatened to escalate communal tensions on the ground (Variant B). Macedonian leaders had a strongly radicalizing nationalist flank that threatened to eject them from power. The ruling party therefore enacted a constitution that declared ethnic Macedonians the constituent "people" of the state in a bid to position themselves as champions of the Macedonian majority.[74] The wording of the constitution infuriated the Albanian minority, and the government tried to undo some of the damage by inviting the largest Albanian party, the Party of Democratic Prosperity, into the governing coalition.[75] With this gesture of conciliation, the leadership faced further blowback from Macedonian nationalists, who by then were gaining popularity with the Slavic majority. The government again attempted to prove its nationalist bona fides by enacting language and education laws that were in turn deemed discriminatory by ethnic Albanians. This set the stage for conflict in the mid-1990s.

European conflict managers viewed these events with alarm and redoubled their efforts to de-escalate conflict in Macedonia. As it turned out, Macedonia was easier to manage than Kosovo because Skopje was in a particularly vulnerable domestic and international position. Macedonian leaders believed that the Albanian minority might radicalize violently against the state. They therefore welcomed the high commissioner's mediation. They also welcomed international engagement in order to gain membership in NATO and the EU, which they believed would protect them from Albanian revisionism, Greek hostility, Serbian intervention, and conflict spillover from wars in neighboring states. Finally, Macedonia faced the formidable task of creating a strong nation-state with a large separatist Albanian minority concentrated in its border regions. Macedonian leaders believed that Albanian separatism would challenge the state's very existence and were therefore quite open to international scrutiny and conflict management.

Exogenous Regional Stabilization—U.S., NATO Induce Ethnic Settlements

Although Milošević had been given a relatively free hand in Kosovo, Western diplomats attempted to induce the Serbian leader to reach a negotiated settlement with the Kosovo leadership. According to the nested security model, Western pressure on both sides should have nested ethnic relations in a stabilized regional environment, increasing the likelihood of successful mediation. Consistent with this expectation, Rugova and Milošević met in 1996 to sign an agreement on minority education in Kosovo. Sensing his opportunity to negotiate an agreement, van der Stoel volunteered to facilitate further meetings between the two leaders. Milošević was quite happy to negotiate through the offices of the high commissioner, for doing so affirmed the Albanians' minority status within Yugoslavia. However, the Kosovo Albanian leadership refused to have any dealings with van der Stoel in his official capacity, because they disliked the premise that Albanians were a minority in a Serbian state. To overcome Albanian objections, van der Stoel was appointed the "Personal Representative of the Chairman-in-Office for Kosovo." However, Belgrade rejected the move, arguing that his new title implied that Kosovo was a quasi-international protectorate.[76] In 1997, van der Stoel was finally denied a travel visa to Yugoslavia, forcing him to continue his mediation efforts from abroad. The failure to achieve a meaningful breakthrough was probably due to insufficient Western pressures on the two sides to reach an agreement.

Western efforts to induce an ethnic settlement in Macedonia met with greater success. Fearing that Macedonia's nationalizing policies might eventually trigger a minority insurgency—possibly drawing in neighboring Albania or Serbia—the international community moved quickly to quell intercommunal tensions. Macedonian president Gligorov requested international protection in 1992 as Yugoslavia began to devolve into violence. UN secretary-general Boutros Boutros-Ghali conveyed this request to the Security Council president; the cochairmen of the International Conference on the Former Yugoslavia (ICFY), Cyrus Vance and Lord Owen, had urged the secretary-general to move quickly to prevent violence from spreading to Macedonia.[77] Gligorov described his motives for seeking international protection as follows: "When the first incidents started in Croatia, and before that in Slovenia, after which in Bosnia, it became obvious to us that there could be a spillover in the southern part of the Balkans as well. That was a signal to us, and made us think of how we could prevent it. We had no army to speak of. . . . We didn't have any neighbors that would help defend our country. That's when we decided to put forward a proposal before the U.N. Secretary-General Mr. Boutros Boutros-Ghali."[78]

Accordingly, the United Nations implemented its first preventive action mission on Macedonia's borders to prevent conflict spillover from Albania and Kosovo. The first UN mission in Macedonia was officially part of the UN peacekeeping mission in Croatia (the United Nations Protection Force, or UNPROFOR). The UN mission to Macedonia was rechristened the United Nations Preventive Deployment Force (UNPREDEP) in 1995. UNPREDEP, which had a mandate for preventive action, was "to monitor and report any developments in the border areas which could undermine confidence and stability in the former Yugoslav Republic of Macedonia and threaten its territory."[79] According to Henryk Sokalski, the mission consisted of three pillars: troop deployment, mainly along the borders; good offices and political action to manage emerging disputes between the two largest ethnic communities; and the human dimension, aimed at building civil society organizations and promoting development and peace building.[80] The overall aim of the mission was to prevent both domestic tensions and regional instability from fomenting ethnic violence in Macedonia (which could result in inter-state war). The UNPREDEP mission was tiny, but it sent a powerful message that the major powers would defend Macedonia if its borders came under threat. A Macedonian government official described the deterrent value of the mission as follows:

[UNPREDEP] was lightly armed, never bigger than 1500, but it was a clear message to Milošević: do not touch Macedonia. In 1994, Serbian armed units had occupied one peak in the region; although this was in Macedonian territory, [it was occupied] because it was a strategic location. We deployed our own army units and were quite close to Serbian units. [Macedonian president] Gligorov asked the guy in charge of UNPREDEP to go to Belgrade and talk to the Serbian units there. According to him, he told them: "you shouldn't be here." He showed them some maps, and within 24 hours they withdrew—because the U.S. told them to.[81]

In this way, Macedonia's ethnic relations became securely nested in a stable regional environment. The UN mission enjoyed significant U.S. backing and provided a critical backstop to the high commissioner's diplomatic efforts. Sokalski observed: "The [OSCE and UNPREDEP] did not follow redundant programs of action; in fact, their missions were mutually reinforcing rather than overlapping, greatly facilitating cooperative [intervention]." For instance, UNPREDEP had a mandate to prevent cross-border spillover as well as deter neighboring state intervention, whereas the OSCE and the high commissioner had a mandate to arbitrate thorny conflicts over language and education laws at the domestic level. The high commissioner thus sought to solve "long-term [minority] problems" that fueled the latent ethnic tensions.[82]

Even under these conditions of exogenous stabilization, van der Stoel made slow and uneven progress in Macedonia. Following an initial fact-finding trip to the country in 1993, van der Stoel issued a number of recommendations, including improved Albanian language education, expanded local self-government, and relaxed residency requirements for citizenship.[83] The high commissioner returned to Macedonia later that year to find ethnic relations little changed, with tensions still hovering at a high level.

In the mid-1990s, crisis diplomacy was really put to the test. Intergroup tensions escalated in Tetovo—an important Albanian stronghold—where minority leaders attempted to establish an "Albanian University" without official permission from Skopje. Macedonian nationalists accused Albanian leaders of trying to create a state within a state. Riots broke out at the official opening of the university, killing one Albanian and wounding several other people. Van der Stoel immediately flew to Skopje to urge the government to reach an accommodation with Albanians on the issue of minority education. At this point, Tirana entered the fray, making veiled irredentist threats toward Macedonia. The high commissioner responded by traveling to Tirana to deal with this inter-state conflict separately. In doing so, "van der Stoel was instrumental in temporarily easing the tensions."[84]

Ethnic relations in Macedonia hit another low point in 1997, when Macedonian students and professors held demonstrations in Skopje against a law expanding Albanian teacher training. The municipal authorities of Tetovo and Gostivar began to fly the Albanian flag next to the Macedonian flag at public buildings. Although the constitutional court ordered the flags taken down, the municipalities resisted, and police were sent to enforce the order. This led to further riots, in which two Albanians were killed and several civilians and one police officer wounded. The high commissioner arrived in Macedonia within days, calling for a "constructive and continuous dialogue" while criticizing the Albanian townships for defying the constitutional court. At the same time, he negotiated a parliamentary investigation into Albanian accusations of police violence.[85] Van der Stoel visited Macedonia continually throughout the late 1990s. Sokalski concluded that van der Stoel's diplomacy demonstrated that "genuine dialogue and dignified compromise could ultimately prevent rising ethnic tensions from developing into an ongoing conflagration."[86] According to one former government official, "A key mover behind the scenes was van der Stoel . . . he was respected by both sides. We had big problems . . . with education, and van der Stoel helped to lessen the pressures. At the time we didn't have the carrots, carrots came later with EU."[87]

The biggest test of preventive action in Macedonia came during the 1999 Kosovo War. When hundreds of thousands of Albanian refugees poured over the Macedonian border, van der Stoel issued an early warning of conflict to the Permanent Council of the OSCE in May 1999. At the same time, he called for increased donor support of the UNHCR missions in Albania and Macedonia to help them deal with the refugee crisis. Most analysts believe that the UN and NATO played a critical role in preventing conflict spillover from Kosovo, facilitating successful cooperative engagement. NATO official Dennis Blease observed: "Why do you think that NATO set up the camps in Macedonia and in Albania and started organizing sanitation and tents? NATO needed to . . . get in quickly and give any assistance they could and take the pressure off the host nations instantly. . . . So it was trying to stabilize [Macedonia], and this really is one of the first times they started to use this term stabilization. [NATO humanitarian support for refugees] was a stabilization mission."[88]

By July, the danger appeared to have receded, as nearly all the refugees returned to their homes in Kosovo. In the context of exogenous stabilization, van der Stoel was able to continue his work of brokering ethnic compromise in Macedonia—using the (relatively new) carrot of EU accession. Owing in no small part to these efforts, the years of 1999–2000 were, in a very real sense, a honeymoon period for Macedonia—a time of relative ethnic harmony and accommodation.[89] At the urging of the high commissioner, a Law on Higher Education was passed, allowing for university instruction in Albanian. This did much to assuage Albanian grievances over education. The compromises were facilitated by the active involvement of the main Albanian party, the Democratic Party of Albanians, which was the junior partner in government. Significant credit also goes to the high commissioner, who was praised by observers and participants alike for having guided the country through successive crises.

Altogether, van der Stoel made roughly fifty visits to Macedonia as high commissioner through the 1990s and early 2000s; the success of his interventions has been largely attributed to UN and NATO efforts to stabilize the regional environment. These conditions were suddenly removed in 1999 when the Macedonian government extended diplomatic recognition to Taiwan in return for Taiwanese promises of aid and investment. In retaliation, Beijing took the unusual step of vetoing the continuation of the UN mission in Macedonia in the UN Security Council. With the UN mission discontinued, minority-majority relations in Macedonia were no longer nested in a stabilizing border mission. The likelihood of conflict escalation suddenly loomed larger.

Regional Destabilization—Minorities Gain the Upper Hand (Late 1990s to Early 2000s)

Diaspora support and Western intervention on the side of Kosovo Albanian separatists effectively destabilized the region in the late 1990s, empowering the Albanian minority and escalating tensions on the ground (Variant A). In 1998, the Kosovo Liberation Army (KLA) began to operate openly in Kosovo, accelerating its attacks against Serbian forces and challenging Rugova's pacifist leadership in Kosovo. The Serb military retaliated by targeting civilians in the Albanian population. By the summer of 1998, roughly fifteen hundred Kosovo Albanians had died, and several hundred thousand more had fled the province. There was a lull in the violence in October, when Balkan special envoy Richard Holbrooke and NATO Joint Force Air Component commander Michael C. Short flew to Belgrade to conduct negotiations with Milošević, impressing upon him the devastating consequences of Allied bombing attacks. The result was a tentative peace agreement, with four thousand Serbian special forces withdrawn from Pristina, while two thousand OSCE monitors were sent to the region.[90]

Alarmed by the escalating violence in Kosovo, van der Stoel obtained a visa to travel to Belgrade and Pristina in a "private capacity" to hold talks with both sides. However, Serbia had commenced to ethnically cleanse the Kosovo province in view of imminent Allied bombing, sending hundreds of thousands of Albanian refugees over the border into Macedonia. Consequently, the high commissioner submitted an early warning of conflict to the OSCE Permanent Council. As the Kosovo insurgency gained momentum and casualties began to mount, preventive diplomacy was declared a failure, and the mandate in Yugoslavia officially terminated as the conflict turned to full-blown civil war.[91] Karsten Friis, senior political officer to the OSCE mission in Serbia and Montenegro, acknowledged that preventive diplomacy in Kosovo had failed in the face of Serbian military intervention but insisted "there was nothing the OSCE could have done to stop hostilities in Kosovo. What could you do with a man like Milošević?"[92]

Regional destabilization had similar effects on interethnic tensions in Macedonia. Two years after the Kosovo War, remnants of the Kosovo Liberation Army crossed the border to instigate ethnic violence in Macedonia, leveraging and mobilizing the Albanian minority (Variant A). Despite the unprecedented degree of ethnic harmony that characterized Macedonia in 1999 and 2000, there was no longer a UN mission to prevent violence from breaking out in the hills of northern Macedonia in February 2001. Fighting quickly spread to other villages and towns across northwest Macedonia, even reaching a suburb of Skopje. Minority elites responded by adopting an intransigent position with respect to minority issues.[93] Their demands radicalized to calls for independence, which were decried by Macedonian leaders as "extremist." This sudden minority radicalization can be explained only by conflict spillover from Kosovo caused by the deliberate infiltration of Albanian fighters over the Macedonian border. The rebels, calling themselves the National Liberation Army, attempted to establish a base of operations in western Macedonia, which served to mobilize the local Albanian population. The crisis was now out of the hands of the high commissioner and could be resolved only through coercive intervention.

Macedonia's brief civil war nicely illustrates the central tenet of nested security: cooperative interventions such as preventive diplomacy are highly unlikely to succeed so long as the regional environment remains unstable. Indeed, the failures of the high commissioner in the Balkans shows that major powers and international organizations are often needed to backstop cooperative mediations, particularly if the regional players are actively or passively fueling sectarian violence. Preventive diplomacy failed to prevent the escalation of violence in the face of cross-border infiltration of guerrilla fighters from the Kosovo War, showing that conflict contagion in the neighborhood can easily undermine the best mediation efforts. This case demonstrates that "porous borders, diasporic networks, and the availability of young men and weapons are the key ingredients of ethnic war-making."[94] As the next chapter shows, quick intervention by the United States helped to turn this around, demonstrating the role of major powers in securely nesting communal conflicts in a stable environment. According to the national security adviser to the Macedonian president, the United States played a particularly critical role in this process:

There is not a single thing that has not been fixed by U.S. Before we were a member of the UN in 1992, the U.S. State Department granted Macedonia Most Favored Nation trade status. They told Serbia not to touch Macedonia—"the territorial integrity of Macedonia is of importance to us." In 1995, we became FYROM [the Former Yugoslav Republic of

Macedonia] also because of U.S. . . . In 2001, [the United States] forged
the end of hostilities in Macedonia, and even in 2005, they got us candidate status in NATO. Without having boost from U.S., we would [not be
where we are] today.[95]

In the end, major-power involvement was necessary to contain the Macedonian conflict, with the United States and NATO intervening to halt the
escalation of bloodshed in 2001. These events are detailed in the following
chapter on induced devolution in the Western Balkans.

Preventive diplomacy functions differently in contemporary Europe from
how it did in interwar Europe—in many ways for the better. To begin with,
the post–Cold War system works *proactively* at the discretion of the OSCE
and the HCNM rather than reactively (and overly legalistically) by responding to minority complaints over treaty violations. The current system is thus
less prone to capture by revisionist minorities and their kin states (such as
Nazi Germany). Second, the current European regime is more regularized,
with at-risk states closely monitored for escalating minority-majority tensions. Third, the carrots and sticks available to enforcers are more substantial
in the post–Cold War period. This is because EU and NATO membership
conditionality is valued highly by candidate countries for their associated material advantages and security guarantees; the League of Nations had nothing of comparable value to offer as a reward for compliance with mediator
recommendations.

Nonetheless, the cases in this chapter demonstrate that regional stability
is critical to successful preventive diplomacy. A stable neighborhood helps to
ameliorate internal tensions, assisting mediators in nudging conflict parties
down the path toward ethnic compromise. The HCNM was able to de-escalate
conflicts over the Russian-speaking minorities in the Baltics primarily because
Moscow acquiesced to NATO and ultimately to EU expansion to the Baltics,
signaling that the Baltic states were no longer within the Russian sphere of influence. Meanwhile, U.S. pressure on the weakened Yeltsin government helped
to keep Russian intervention in check in the 1990s. Although there is currently no indication that Moscow intends to play a similarly destabilizing role
in Latvia and Estonia as it has in Georgia and Ukraine, successful preventive
diplomacy in the Baltics necessitates that Russian influence is kept in check.

In the Western Balkans, Kosovo presents a textbook case of how an unstable regional environment can spoil mediation efforts. From their position
of weakness in the early 1990s, Kosovo leaders were generally amenable to
compromise with the Serbian leadership. Xhemil Shahu, protection officer
of the Emergency Management Group in Albania, observed, "The Kosovars

didn't go for independence earlier than 1998 because Albania was unstable until then and couldn't provide support."[96] Increased diaspora and NATO leverage of the Kosovo resistance in the late 1990s led to a changeover in leadership from the moderate Ibrahim Rugova to the more radical Hashim Thaçi, as the Kosovo Albanians became ever less interested in ethnic compromise. Their claims escalated correspondingly from republican autonomy to outright independence. Because of regional destabilization, the high commissioner was unable to use preventive diplomacy to effectively mediate the conflict.

A textbook illustration of the limits of preventive diplomacy is given by Macedonia in 2001. The high commissioner made conflict prevention in Macedonia a top priority throughout his tenure, and until 2001, everything appeared to be going well. Keen to gain recognition and accession to the EU and NATO, the Macedonian government followed van der Stoel's recommendations, readily implementing minority concessions. By the late 1990s, Macedonia was a study in ethnic peace: even the influx of refugees from the Kosovo War failed to upset the ethnic equilibrium. Despite the confluence of domestic factors pointing to peace, the movement of KLA irregulars over the border disrupted domestic tranquillity in the space of a few short months, leading key Albanian political leaders to radicalize their position against the government. This demonstrates that preventive diplomacy can do little to halt or prevent violence so long as the regional environment is dangerously unstable.

The evidence in this chapter also reveals problems with alternative arguments for mediation success. *Conditionality* by itself only partially accounts for the outcomes in these cases. The linkage between HCNM directives and EU/NATO accession goes a considerable distance toward explaining the willingness of Latvia, Estonia, and Macedonia to implement more generous minority protections in the 1990s. However, this is only half the story. The case of Macedonia demonstrates that even generous minority concessions and a liberal government are insufficient for ensuring peace so long as the wider conflict environment is leveraging the minority, thereby encouraging rebellion.

Nor do the *skills of the mediator* account for variable success of conflict management in these cases. The same office (HCNM) and even the same diplomat (van der Stoel) was active in all four cases. Despite the fact that the third party had similar legitimacy and resources across the cases considered here, his interventions in the Baltics were far more successful than in the Western Balkans, even though the high commissioner had also invested considerable time and resources in negotiating solutions to the Balkan conflicts. Variable *credibility of the mediator* in the eyes of the conflict parties might go some distance toward explaining variation in success, as the high commissioner enjoyed far greater credibility in the Baltics and Macedonia than he did in Serbia/Kosovo. Still, this does not explain the over-time variation in mediation success in these cases, with the intervention in Macedonia initially successful but ultimately unable to prevent civil war, while interventions in the Baltics were initially marginalized but grew more effective as the 1990s wore on. If, however, one takes into account the variable stability of the regional environment, the outcomes of these cases become far more explicable.

This comparative analysis yields several lessons concerning the utility of preventive diplomacy for containing nascent civil disputes. Two stand out in particular. The most important is that the benefits of compliance with the mediators' recommendations must be substantial and tangible—that is, the public and elites of the target country (on both sides of the conflict) should stand to gain significant rewards for following the mediators' recommendations. As noted by scholars of conditionality, target states are most responsive where NATO and the EU have credibly signaled their intent to expand membership and where compliance with HCNM and/or OSCE directives are directly linked to NATO/EU membership.

Second, regional stability has an outsize influence on mediation success. OSCE efforts to mediate the Kosovo conflict were virtually hopeless in the late 1990s, given the unstable regional and systemic environments in which the conflict was nested. As soon as either Belgrade or the Kosovo leadership perceived a bargaining advantage, it escalated its demands, making a compromise solution highly improbable. Implicit Western support for the KLA insurgency also leveraged the Kosovo Albanian side, making a deal at Rambouillet highly improbable. In Macedonia, meanwhile, no amount of domestic confidence-building on the ground could prevent conflict from emerging in 2001 once KLA fighters had infiltrated the border (see also the next chapter). By contrast, when the regional environment *was* stabilized (as in the Baltic cases in the mid- to late 1990s and Macedonia in the mid-1990s), the high commissioner was able to resolve successive crises on the ground.

For all these reasons, preventive diplomacy has had very little influence in managing most conflicts in the Commonwealth of Independent States (CIS) region. The OSCE and HCNM have attempted to contain numerous internal conflicts in the CIS, including Georgia, Moldova, Ukraine, Kyrgyzstan, and Kazakhstan. These interventions have yielded far less success than those in Central and Eastern Europe. As HCNM political adviser Mihai Gribincea observed, "[the outcome of preventive diplomacy] depends on Russian actions. If Russia doesn't want [the intervention to go forward], everything stops."[97] The Russian government believes that the United States and other Western powers have used these interventions as a means of gaining a strategic foothold in the region. Because Moscow believes the region to be squarely within its own sphere of influence, it has stymied all efforts by European organizations to effect peace in the CIS. Moreover, since the prospects of NATO

Table 5.2 Comparative evaluation of theories

Case	Minority protections / liberal government	Credibility of mediator / value of carrots and sticks	Nested security
Russophones in Estonia	*Partially confirmed* More liberal minority laws paved the way for greater ethnic harmony between Estonians and Russian speakers; however, this does not explain the reemergence of tensions in the late 2000s when the laws were most liberal.	*Disconfirmed* The high commissioner enjoyed far more success in the late 1990s than in the early 1990s, although there was no increase in the HCNM's resources or credibility.	*Confirmed* Minority conflicts in Latvia and Estonia did not subside until NATO and the United States pressured the Russian government to curb its cross-border interference; endogenous stabilization of bilateral relations in the 2000s helped de-escalate the conflicts, reducing the political salience of ethnic cleavages in both countries.
Russophones in Latvia	*Confirmed* More liberal minority laws paved the way for greater ethnic harmony between Latvians and Russian speakers in the 2000s.		
Albanians in Kosovo	*Partially confirmed* Kosovo Albanians mobilized in response to revocation of autonomy in the late 1980s; however, they moderated their position in the mid-1990s even as Belgrade's repressive policies accelerated. Radicalization came only in the late 1990s with external leverage.	*Indeterminate* The lack of HCNM legitimacy in the eyes of both parties (particularly Serbia) undermined van der Stoel's ability to operate in Kosovo; however, it is unlikely that preventive diplomacy would have succeeded had he been given greater scope to maneuver.	*Confirmed* In the early 1990s, the Kosovo conflict increased owing to an unstable Yugoslav environment; in 1999, Western intervention on the side of Albanian rebels served to escalate the conflict.
Albanians in Macedonia	*Disconfirmed* Albanians in Macedonia made significant demands even in the face of extensive concessions in the 1990s; they radicalized in 2001 despite newly enacted minority protections.	*Disconfirmed* Through the 1990s, the HCNM enjoyed a high level of legitimacy in the eyes of both parties; however, this did not prevent armed conflict in 2001.	*Confirmed* In the early 1990s, a UN preventive action mission stabilized the regional environment, facilitating preventive diplomacy by the HCNM; in 2001, with the UN mission recently removed, conflict spillover from Kosovo destabilized the region, leading to violence.

(and especially EU) membership are dim to nonexistent for many of these countries, it is harder to pressure the target states to comply with the OSCE or the high commissioner's recommendations on minority protections. Until the dual problems of Russian intervention and the absence of incentives for the target states can be sorted out, preventive diplomacy in the CIS has very poor prospects indeed.

6

INDUCED DEVOLUTION IN
POST–COLD WAR EUROPE

Since World War II, states have increasingly used devolution to resolve their internal territorial conflicts, in the belief that granting autonomy to restive minorities will undermine their secessionist impulses. Examples abound in Western Europe. Spain's 1978 constitution established a "system of autonomies" for its national regions of Catalonia, Barcelona, and the Basque Country, yielding an arrangement "remarkable . . . for the extent of the powers peacefully devolved over the past 30 years."[1] The British government also handed off significant state powers to its internal regions in the late 1990s, setting up a Scottish Parliament, a Welsh National Assembly, and a Northern Ireland Assembly through popular referenda. Belgium, too, devolved considerable governmental power to the constituent federal units of Wallonia, Flanders, and its capital of Brussels, beginning in the 1970s and '80s.[2]

Scholars continue to debate whether autonomous institutions have the overall effect of dampening or exacerbating secessionist movements. Although some assert that territorial self-determination remains the best way of securing the loyalty of separatist regions, others forcefully disagree—noting that autonomy can serve as a stepping-stone to independence, as seen in cases ranging from the former socialist federations to South Sudan and Iraqi Kurdistan. State governments usually choose the path of devolution of their own accord. In other cases, however, devolution is *externally* induced by third-party mediators. This chapter evaluates whether and how third parties have successfully used induced devolution to defuse ethnic tensions in postcommunist Europe.

The EU and NATO employed devolution at least three times to manage low-intensity conflicts in post–Cold War Europe—all in the Western Balkans (see map 3, chapter 5). Perhaps the greatest success was the NATO-brokered Ohrid Framework Agreement under which Macedonia devolved significant state power to the regions, effectively giving autonomy to its Albanian minority. Although the agreement helped contain the Albanian insurgency in 2001, it failed to prevent the resurgence of communal tensions in later years. Also in the early 2000s, the EU persuaded Belgrade to devolve power to Montenegro in order to preserve what remained of the Yugoslav federation; this, however, failed to forestall secession, as Montenegro opted for independence in 2006. Finally, the EU prevailed upon Serbia to withdraw its territorial claims from Kosovo in return for promises of autonomy for Serb enclaves. This bargain, initially known as the Ahtisaari Plan (after the Finnish diplomat Martti Ahtisaari, who designed it), was incorporated into the 2008 constitution of independent Kosovo. However, significant tensions remain between the communities.

The analysis in this chapter suggests that induced devolution is most likely to reduce conflict when powerful players stanch the flow of militants or arms across the border (Macedonia) and/or dissuade kin states from intervening on one side or both sides of an ethnic dispute (northern Kosovo). However, nested security by itself may fail to de-escalate internal tensions so long as there is a viable and attractive exit option for the minority region (Montenegro). In short, regional stabilization appears to be a *necessary* condition for successful induced devolution, but it may not be sufficient.

In the following section, I outline the nested security predictions for successful induced devolution in cases of separatist minorities. I then conduct a periodized analysis of conflict fluctuations in postcommunist Macedonia, Montenegro, and northern Kosovo and conclude by evaluating nested security predictions against the most promising alternative accounts of mediation success in the Western Balkans.

Nested Security versus Alternative Explanations

For centuries, state governments have devolved state powers to minority regions through territorial autonomy, federalism, or power-sharing arrangements in a bid to undermine separatist movements. Advocates of devolution believe that the only way to prevent violent civil war and secession in deeply divided societies is to offer the rebelling minority a degree of territorial self-government—splitting the difference between a unitary state (preferred by the government) and secession (preferred by the rebelling minority).[3]

Nested security holds that the wider conflict environment must be stabilized before induced devolution can succeed in defusing communal tensions. If true, this means that a destabilized regional environment is likely to lead to conflict escalation, even in the presence of a resourceful mediator and well-designed devolution institutions. Under Variant A, regional instability empowers the minority, which can escalate tensions by mobilizing around more radical separatist demands. Under Variant B, regional instability empowers the government, which can escalate communal tensions through minority repression. However, when outside actors or pressures intervene to *stabilize* the regional or systemic conflict environments, this can de-escalate communal tensions, although individuals are likely to remain mobilized in anticipation that these outside pressures will eventually disappear or change. The conflict is most likely to achieve a permanent de-escalation when the regional players have *endogenous* incentives to broker and keep the peace. At this point, the salience of the communal cleavage on the ground is likely to decline relative to alternative political cleavages.

To test the model's predictions, I examine three cases of induced devolution in the Western Balkans to determine whether the level of conflict escalated or de-escalated following their respective devolution agreements. In doing so, I pay close attention to the ways in which shifts in the wider regional environment altered minority-majority relations on the ground over the course of a given mediation. If the theory of nested security is correct, then the neutralization of conflict dynamics on the regional and systemic levels should *precede conflict reduction* at the domestic level, rather than vice versa. Conversely, the (re)instigation of conflict in the wider neighborhood should *precede an escalation of tensions* on the ground. In general, induced devolution should fail to reduce tensions on the ground so long as the wider regional environment remains unstable.

I evaluate the pattern of conflict in the cases as follows. As I did in the chapter on induced devolution in interwar Europe, I look at cases where third-party mediators persuaded the target government to grant significant territorial autonomy to restive minority regions as a means of reducing communal tensions. To explain why conflict varied in intensity over the course of a single mediation, I divide each of the three mediations into time segments that correspond with changes in intergroup tensions on the ground. I begin each case study with an overview of the history of relations between the respective state center and minority prior to the application of induced devolution. In doing so, I begin the analysis with the period just prior to the devolution agreement—2001 for Macedonia, 2003 for Montenegro, and 2008 for Kosovo (although attempts to induce devolution in Kosovo began earlier)—and end the analysis at the point where the arrangement was dissolved (2006 in Montenegro) or the present day for arrangements that are still in place (Kosovo and Macedonia).

The main alternative accounts for these cases come down to the devolution agreement itself. The first possibility is that the institutions were not properly designed or implemented, so that the agreement amounted to little more than window dressing. This means that the aggrieved minority was not offered any real degree of self-government or share in state power—the agreement was effectively a dead letter and did nothing to head off minority mobilization

Table 6.1 Nested security predictions

Montenegro	Regional environment	Conflict outcome
(1998–2000)	Regional destabilization (U.S., EU intervene on side of Montenegro)	Growing split in Montenegrin leadership, rising support for state independence
(2000–2006)	Exogenous stabilization (Western governments push for confederation)	Concessions to Montenegrin leadership; creation of confederation, followed by successful independence referendum
Macedonia	**Regional environment**	**Conflict outcome**
(mid- to late 2001)	Regional destabilization (Kosovo Albanian irregulars cross border)	Minority radicalizes, engages in violence, demands extensive autonomy
(late 2001–)	Exogenous stabilization (NATO/U.S. intervention)	Broad decentralization agreement; minority moderates, joins government
Kosovo	**Regional environment**	**Conflict outcome**
(1999–2007)	Regional destabilization (NATO intervention followed by Serbian involvement)	Kosovo Albanians achieve de facto independence, Kosovo Serbs face discrimination
(2008–)	Gradual exogenous stabilization (EU pushes Serbia to recognize Kosovo as a condition of accession)	Gradual minority moderation and integration follow the withdrawal of Serbian parallel structures first in the south and later in the north

or conflict. Perhaps, too, the agreement broke down over time, leading to a re-escalation of tensions. In this case, we should see conflict on the ground escalate in the wake of disputes over the terms or enforcement of these agreements. In either case, if the deal itself is central to the conflict, then the struggle should center on the details and enforcement of the devolution agreement.

A more unsettling possibility is that devolution *did* give the minority substantial autonomy, but this perversely served to *fuel* tensions rather than defuse them. Indeed, there are plenty of cases where autonomous institutions ultimately gave rise to the very separatist movements they had been designed to prevent. The Soviet successor states, for example, mobilized around the very borders, parliaments, flags, and languages that had been given to them generations earlier to encourage minority integration. Likewise, the governments of Czechoslovakia and Yugoslavia devolved substantial authority to powerful minority regions, which later used these institutions to achieve statehood. Scholars suggest that devolution can escalate conflict not only by creating institutions of minority self-government around which separatist movements mobilize, but also by inculcating popular preferences for national independence.[4] Indeed, data analysis has shown that minorities are *more* likely to pursue secession if they had a history of territorial autonomy than if they did not.[5] Nationalizing elites play a key role in this process, but their ability to mobilize national movements is crucially limited by the resources and identities conferred upon them by the institutional environment. If this explanation holds water, then we should see minority leaders mobilize separatist challenges using the very institutions provided by the devolution agreement.

This analysis has important policy ramifications for conflict management. If devolution helps to heal divided societies rather than impel them to violence, then we should study how to design and implement these institutions more effectively. If, instead, devolution provides stepping-stones (or way stations) to full independence, then the leaders of divided states are best advised to avoid autonomous solutions to conflict. This chapter reveals that devolution itself cannot account for the ebb and flow of conflict in any of the three cases. This is because the effects of national institutions are *crucially mitigated by the domestic and international context in which the conflict is nested.* This implies that the details of devolution are less important to mediation success than the wider conflict environment in which the communal struggle is embedded.

Each of the three cases presented unique challenges to European conflict managers. Montenegro already had a federal status in the former Yugoslav state. As violence coursed through Yugoslavia in the 1990s, Montenegro (with U.S. backing) gradually gained de facto political independence from Belgrade—leading to demands for de jure independence. In the post-Milošević era, the United States and the EU attempted to save the Yugoslav federation by inducing Belgrade to agree to a loose confederation between Serbia and Montenegro. The result was a stillbirth—a dysfunctional federation that quickly dissolved once Montenegro's leaders secured the right to hold an independence referendum.

By contrast, the Albanians in Macedonia and Serbs in Kosovo had no prior history of autonomy. In Macedonia, Albanians concentrated in the northwestern regions mobilized violently against the government in 2001; in Kosovo, ethnic Serbs, isolated in the north or in enclaves in the south, rejected de facto (and later de jure) territorial sovereignty of the Kosovo Albanian government. In both cases, third-party conflict managers (Western governments and the EU and NATO) induced the governments to decentralize state powers to districts or municipalities, granting the minorities de facto territorial autonomy in minority regions.[6] I consider these cases devolution in the sense that the explicit aim of decentralization was to devolve power to restive minority regions in order to head off violence.

Case Evidence

Post-2001 Macedonia

Throughout the 1990s, Macedonia retained its status as the "oasis of peace" in the Balkans, having peacefully seceded from the Serb-controlled Yugoslav federation (see chapter 5). The ruling party had heeded the advice of the international community to build an inclusive state through a mix of policy concessions and governmental co-optation (nearly every post-independence government has included the biggest Albanian party). In so doing, Macedonia's leaders hoped the country would be fast-tracked into the EU and NATO, which they viewed as vital to the country's security and prosperity in the post–Cold War era. The 1999 Kosovo War provided a litmus test of Macedonian stability when half a million Albanian refugees poured over the border, dramatically upsetting the ethnic balance and eliciting an "early

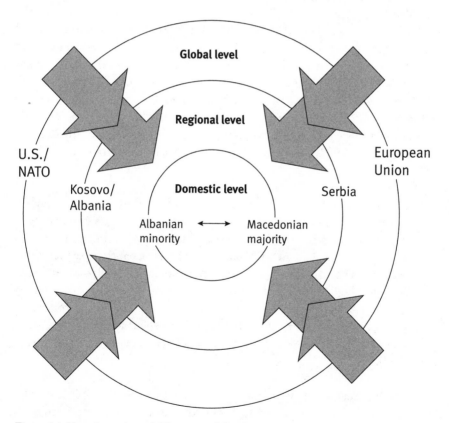

Figure 6.1 Nested security and Albanians in Macedonia

warning" of conflict from the high commissioner. Owing in part to effective international crisis management, Macedonia maintained its ethnic calm throughout the war.

Regional Destabilization: Spillover of Albanian Militants from Kosovo

Ethnic relations took a dramatic turn for the worse in early 2001 when the self-proclaimed National Liberation Army (NLA) infiltrated Macedonia's borders and launched attacks on Macedonian police and other state institutions, condemning the government for subjugating the Albanian minority. There was broad support for the NLA among Macedonian Albanians, many of whom joined the insurgency. Responding to the apparent radicalization of the minority population, the Albanian party in government began to escalate its demands in line with those of NLA leaders. The conflict lasted for the better part of a year and displaced more than 170,000 persons from their homes as Albanians fled Macedonian areas and vice versa.[7]

What had happened? Had the grievances of Albanians mounted to the point that violence seemed their only option?[8] Had their demands for autonomy been frustrated for so long that they resolved to take up arms against the state at the first real opportunity (the infiltration of the NLA)? The intergroup climate at the time of violence suggests otherwise. Although minority discrimination was still a problem in Macedonia, it was a problem shared by all minorities, not just Albanians. Despite this, Albanians were the *only* minority to mobilize. Moreover, interethnic relations had been steadily improving in the late 1990s. The Macedonian filmmaker Milcho Manchevski put it this way:

> The [Macedonian] government and the people were repeatedly applauded by the international community for their efforts in creating and maintaining a multi-ethnic society. Parties representing ethnic minorities sat in parliament. Albanian parties were coalition partners in all governments. Today six out of 17 government ministers are ethnic Albanians, the parliamentary vice-president is Albanian and so are several ambassadors. There are primary and secondary schools and colleges teaching in Albanian; an Albanian university is about to open. There are Albanian TV stations, theatres, newspapers. Why then the recent ethnic violence?[9]

It is possible that the slow pace of reform facilitated conflict spillover from Kosovo. John Phillips reported that Macedonian militants associated with the KLA starting making plans for an insurgency "when reforms promised by the Democratic Party of Albanians [the main Albanian party in parliament] . . . were slow to materialize."[10] As noted by the editor-in-chief of the biggest Albanian television station in Macedonia, "There has always been an Albanian party in government, but because of their inability to improve the rights of Albanians, we had [the violence in] 2001. In the 1990s, there was a lack of readiness on part of government to provide rights to Albanians, and a lack of a capable Albanian party to get the job done."[11]

Nonetheless, it is unlikely that minority grievances would have produced rebellion in the absence of regional destabilization. In January 2001, a band of ex-KLA militants crossed over the border into Macedonia and began staging confrontations with Macedonian police. One NGO noted that "without exception, all the rebellions in Macedonia have broken out on the border with Kosovo and in close proximity to NATO bases or logistical centres in Tetovo, Petrovec and Kumanovo."[12] NLA fighters not only originated from the KLA, but they had also obtained access to Western military matériel. A Canadian journalist reporting from behind Albanian front lines in Tetovo noted that NLA fighters had sniper rifles, grenade launchers, and sophisticated night-vision goggles—all bearing the label "made in the U.S.A." One NLA commander bragged, "Thanks to Uncle Sam, the Macedonians are no match for us."[13] The Kosovo Protection Force (KFOR), a NATO-led international peacekeeping force authorized to secure the peace in post-conflict Kosovo, seemed to know the exact location and activities of NLA forces in Macedonia; when Macedonian forces came close to defeating NLA fighters in a battle in the village of Aračinovo, eighty-one U.S. soldiers and sixteen armed Humvees escorted twenty busloads of NLA militants from the scene of the battle.[14] This provoked an anti-U.S./NATO street demonstration of over ten thousand ethnic Macedonians in Skopje. The rebel fighters had, at least inadvertently, obtained invaluable assistance from international actors in pursuing their rebellion. Regional destabilization had upset the fragile ethnic peace in Macedonia, as expected by nested security.

Exogenous Stabilization: NATO Reins In the Militants, Brokers Peace Agreement

NATO moved quickly to quell the crisis, putting considerable pressure on both the NLA leaders and the Macedonian government to reach a peace agreement. Through a series of parallel negotiations, Western mediators persuaded the Macedonian government to agree to a series of reforms that amounted to devolution for ethnic Albanians and amnesty for the rebels; they also pressured the NLA leadership to disarm and end the rebellion. According to Stojan Andov, Speaker of the Macedonian parliament:

[NLA fighters] said their goal was to banish Slavs from historically Albanian areas. . . . Then the internationals got involved. They pressured the NLA to give up those goals. . . . [They also created] the impression that the Albanians' responsibility was to give their weapons to NATO, and that not to do this was to oppose NATO. . . . The Framework Agreement ended the conflict—they were shooting before the Framework Agreement and not after. . . . Peter Feith, the envoy of NATO, had the responsibility to pressure or calm down [NLA leader Ali] Ahmeti. In his view, Albanians would not go into this without international pressure, if they are told directly to stop, they would stop. . . . For us in [the government], what was important was not having more casualties and political instability.[15]

Consistent with this account, the conflict finally ended when, after much arm-twisting by NATO and U.S. officials, the Macedonian leadership and rebel forces signed separate cease-fire agreements with NATO. NATO officials ultimately induced both sides to conclude the Ohrid Framework Agreement on August 13, 2001, under which Albanian insurgents agreed to disarm in return for political concessions from the Macedonian government. Former NLA leader Ahmeti recalled, "Without the engagement of NATO, Macedonia would have been a second Bosnia. But the international community . . . reacted in time [to forestall significant bloodshed] in Macedonia. And we managed to start the negotiations sooner. But if NATO had not been engaged, then we would have had another Balkan war. . . . I think [NATO and the EU] played a very important role in all of this."[16]

As political talks moved forward, NATO forces quickly stanched the violence. In August, thirty-five hundred NATO peacekeepers were deployed to implement the agreement and collect weapons from the rebels under Operation Essential Harvest. Although rebel disarmament was widely derided as ineffective (failing to collect many weapons), it signaled NATO's commitment to contain the insurgency and prevent its resurgence. This had an immediate effect on the ethnic relations on the ground. One government official seemed stunned by the sudden change in the political climate: "[The Albanian leaders] are surprisingly cooperative given that they [had been] pressing with everything, even using violence. [Now,] without any obvious improvement, they are working for better relations between Albanians and Macedonians."[17] This turning point was the result of exogenous stabilization rather than devolution, which had yet to be implemented under the Ohrid agreement.

Ahmeti now announced that the NLA was officially dissolved. Although a faction of the NLA (the Albanian National Army or ANA) vowed to continue the national struggle, Ahmeti commanded the loyalties of the bulk of Albanian militants, effectively ending the insurgency. In the September elections, Ahmeti and his new party, Democratic Union for Integration (DUI), were elected to parliament with thirty seats, edging out the main Albanian party (the DPA), which had won only two seats. Ahmeti thus became the de facto political representative of the Albanian community in Macedonia. The Albanians on the ground moderated in line with the apparent end of the insurgency. According to Macedonian government official Ljupcho Ristovski, "after NATO came, the Albanians calmed down; they had confidence that once [the forces] were here, what happened in Bosnia would not happen here."[18]

The Ohrid Framework Agreement (OFA) gave amnesty to most rebel leaders (provided that the rebels surrendered their weapons to NATO); mandated greater proportions of ethnic Albanians (along with other minorities) in the courts, government administration, and law enforcement; and made Albanian the second official language in communities with a significant Albanian minority—a key demand of minority leaders. There is little doubt that the government agreed to the OFA because of NATO; Macedonian leaders hoped that by doing so, they could hasten the country's accession to Euro-Atlantic organizations. The EU also put pressure on the government to enact conciliatory policies. The government had already signed a Stabilization and Association Agreement (a precursor to EU membership negotiations) in early 2001; EU officials now emphasized that further integration into Europe was contingent upon implementation of the OFA. In a personal interview, one Macedonian official confirmed that membership in the EU was a key motivation for agreeing to these concessions: "Every reform is now being [justified] in terms of economic development and integration. . . . The best solution is to implement the Framework Agreement and get Macedonia into the EU and NATO."[19]

As expected by nested security, exogenous stabilization facilitated conflict reduction in Macedonia. According to the International Crisis Group (ICG), there were "significant improvements in inter-ethnic relations since the OFA was signed." Rapid implementation of parts of the agreement signaled that the majority government was conciliatory. The government expanded the use of Albanian in official business (particularly in areas with large Albanian minorities), created a voting mechanism to prevent the majority government from enacting provisions that harmed minority interests, eliminated nationalist passages in the preamble of the constitution, and established new rules to ensure higher numbers of Albanians in the civil service.[20]

Nonetheless, the OFA did not guarantee a permanent end to hostilities. Remnants of the NLA have claimed responsibility for at least a dozen incidents of violence over the years, including attacks on the former Macedonian interior minister, the national transportation network, and courts.[21] Like the sudden emergence of the NLA that radicalized interethnic relations in 2001 and the subsequent containment of the NLA by outside parties, the sporadic violence in Macedonia since Ohrid maps perfectly onto the periodic shifts in the regional conflict environment.

In fact, ethnic tensions have increased markedly in recent years—largely owing to the ongoing name dispute with Greece. Paula Pickering writes that "unstable neighbours, and a long EU accession process combine to create conditions ripe for instability in Macedonia."[22] At the NATO summit in Bucharest in early 2008, Greece blocked NATO's invitation to Macedonia because Skopje continues to use the name Macedonia, which Greece claims as its own. This has come as a bitter disappointment to Macedonian citizens, given that the country had obtained candidate status in NATO four years earlier. The dispute has also stalled Macedonia's accession to the EU. Although the country obtained EU candidate status in 2005, the EU chose not to begin accession negotiations with Macedonia, presumably because of Greece's objections. These rejections came as a veritable body blow to the country's leaders, who felt they had done everything asked of them by the international community. As expected by Milada Vachudova,[23] stalled accession to the EU and NATO undermined Macedonia's moderate leaders, who had staked their political careers on Euro-Atlantic integration. These events also empowered nationalist elements within Macedonia, serving to escalate tensions between the two groups.

The name dispute began to divide the country along ethnic lines, with Macedonians opposed to a compromise, and Albanians increasingly in favor. Before 2008, *both* groups had been opposed to compromising on the name. The divide on the name came on the heels of the 2008 NATO summit in Bucharest, which frustrated Macedonia's ambitions for speedy accession to NATO and set off a wave of nationalist protests.[24] In the wake of the 2008 summit, the government of Prime Minister Nicola Gruevski, assumed a more nationalist character, launching an expensive and provocative nationalist urban renewal project, titled "Skopje 2014"—ironically dubbed the "antiquization" of Macedonia. The project erected Slavic nationalist symbols in the center of Skopje and other cities and galvanized strong reactions by Albanians, who were symbolically excluded from these "mono-ethnic" expressions of Macedonian nationhood.[25] This, together with the widespread Albanian perception that the government had not honored the Ohrid agreement, fueled communal conflict between Albanians and Macedonians.[26]

The gradual escalation of ethnic tensions took a more violent turn in 2012, fueled by an uptick of Albanian nationalism across the border. The immediate trigger was Albania's one-hundred-year anniversary of independence from Ottoman rule, which was commemorated in Skopje with one thousand ethnic

Albanians marching on the capital and Albanian prime minister Sali Berisha and Kosovo prime minister Hashim Thaçi in attendance. There were also scattered interethnic skirmishes and flag burnings, set off by the murder of two Albanians by a Macedonian police officer.[27] Minority leaders in Macedonia radicalized their stance in tandem with these events. While some opposition politicians demanded revisions to the Ohrid Framework Agreement to allow for increased minority autonomy, others have called for a more extreme canton-based or federal system.[28] The Albanian minority also appears to have radicalized on the issue of separatism, with 53 percent of ethnic Albanians in Macedonia supporting the creation of a Greater Albanian state, according to a 2010 Gallup Balkan Monitor report.[29] The tiny country continues to suffer sporadic episodes of armed violence.

Despite these difficulties, Macedonia remains an excellent candidate for successful cooperative mediation because the Macedonian leadership is determined to achieve Euro-Atlantic integration, and Albanian leaders are equally committed to preserving a multiethnic state. There appears to be little danger of a return to widespread ethnic violence. Ahmeti is now the leader of DUI in the ruling coalition and has renounced separatism: "Albanians are interested in full implementation of [the] Ohrid agreement; they are interested in a stable country, a state that is loyal to all of its citizens, equal treatment for all. Albanians in Macedonia want Macedonia to have good relations with its neighbors, that their country becomes part of NATO as well as the EU. These are the main goals of Albanians in Macedonia, and they do not want to go back. The past should serve for us all as a painful reminder that we don't want to repeat it."[30]

If the EU and NATO were to induce Greece to set aside its objections to Macedonia's name, it would clear the way for the country to continue down the path of Euro-Atlantic integration. If the international community also worked to contain radicalizing factors on the Albanian side while managing the borders, this would lay the foundation for ethnic peace within Macedonia. The U.S. ambassador to Albania, for instance, counseled Albanian politicians to refrain from using veiled irredentist rhetoric in their public addresses.[31] Such warnings from Albania's most important great-power patron are clearly helpful for stabilizing the region—a precondition for consolidating ethnic peace at the domestic level. The EU, too, has demonstrated its awareness of the importance of exogenous stabilization for containing the conflict in Macedonia: "We must provide incentives for Albania and its people. However, the EU must take a strict stance against nationalistic statements such as the recent ones by the Albanian prime minister. All those concerned must refrain from any actions which could trigger regional tensions."[32]

It seems clear that the stability of the regional environment, rather than the devolution agreement itself, has been the key to ethnic peace in Macedonia. The periodic upticks of conflict are better explained by the level of nested security in the region than by perceptions of the Ohrid agreement or the extent to which it has been implemented. Conflict spillover accounts for the original insurgency in 2001, and NATO and U.S. intervention accounts for its prompt resolution. The prospect of EU/NATO integration has kept ethnic relations relatively peaceful in the years that followed. Nonetheless, stalled integration into these bodies after the 2008 NATO summit was a key factor in the reemergence of communal tensions and Macedonian nationalism. The international community's inability to overcome Greece's opposition to resolving the crisis "risks derailing the strategies of the EU and NATO to stabilise Macedonia . . . through integration and enlargement," and "contributes to a slowdown in inter-ethnic reconciliation."[33] If, on the other hand, Western organizations were to resume the process of integration, then both sides might begin to perceive the net benefits of keeping a liberal peace. Over time, this could serve to demobilize ethnic divisions in Macedonia on a more permanent basis.

Northern Kosovo

In the aftermath of the 1999 NATO war, Kosovo became ethnically partitioned along the Ibar River. Serbs fled to the northern region (which bordered on Serbia), while the area south of the Ibar became mostly Albanian, except for a handful of Serb enclaves.[34] The city of Mitrovica, which straddles the Ibar River, was also split into two mono-ethnic cantons—with Serbs in the north and Albanians in the south.[35] For the better part of a decade, Kosovo was an international protectorate run by the UN Mission in Kosovo (UNMIK) and enforced by the U.S. Kosovo Force (KFOR). A transitional Kosovo government (PISG, the Provisional Institutions of Self-Government) was set up with reserved seats for Serbs in order to encourage ethnic integration. Many years after Kosovo independence, ethnic tensions continue to mar the new country.

Bilateral tensions between Kosovo and Serbia are largely responsible for shifts in communal tensions on the ground. In recognition of this fact, the international community sought to persuade Belgrade to withdraw support for a Serbian shadow state in northern Kosovo while inducing Pristina to devolve a significant degree of autonomy to the Kosovo Serb communities along the lines of the so-called Ahtisaari Plan, to meet Kosovo Serb demands for maintaining a connection with their kin state of Serbia. The facts of this case demonstrate that the timing and location of conflict in Kosovo can be largely attributed to the wider bilateral struggles between Belgrade and Pristina.

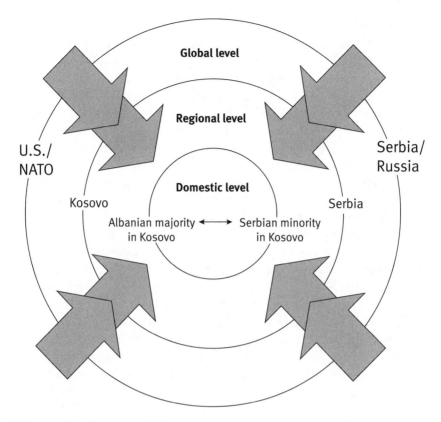

Figure 6.2 Nested security and Kosovo

Regional Destabilization: Serbian Intervention and Minority Intransigence

When Yugoslav president Vojislav Koštunica came to office in 2000, he assumed an accommodating stance—pledging that Serbia would negotiate a resolution on Kosovo with an eye toward joining the EU and NATO. However, he faced growing unpopularity at home due to his compromising position toward the West, so he soon hardened his position. In May 2001, the deputy prime minister of Serbia and head of the Kosovo Coordination Center Nebojša Čović reiterated that Kosovo was an integral part of Serbia following UN Resolution 1244. Accordingly, Belgrade reinforced its control over state institutions in Serb-dominated northern Kosovo and sought to extend its reach to Serb enclaves in the south.

Serbian intervention in 2001 quickly exacerbated tensions in Kosovo, particularly north of the Ibar River where KFOR/UNMIK's authority ended and Belgrade's authority began. As expected by the nested security model, the empowered Serb minority adopted a position of intransigence toward Pristina, UNMIK, and KFOR (Variant A). Mitrovica, straddling the river, was the site of numerous flashpoints between Serbs and Albanians, including attacks on French KFOR troops, a campaign of terror against UNMIK officers, and a firefight between UNMIK police and the Serbian "Bridgewatchers" (a paramilitary group established to defend northern Kosovo autonomy). These incidents had repercussions beyond northern Kosovo, triggering copycat violence in Serbian minority enclaves in the south. Nonetheless, UNMIK and KFOR avoided cracking down on the Bridgewatchers or directly severing ties between Belgrade and the northern enclave, for fear that this would provoke further mass violence and ethnic cleansing.

One journalist wrote, "The neighborhood, together with the adjoining Knjaz Milos area, is a staging ground for Serbian paramilitaries, police and other self-proclaimed 'guardsmen' of northern Kosovo." Oliver Ivanović, head of the Kosovo Serbian National Council, boasted that they had "enough guns and equipment to start World War III." The U.S. State Department confirmed that Belgrade was providing direct surveillance assistance to Serb paramilitaries in Mitrovica.[36] In fact, Ivanović's Bridgewatchers—which had been created for the purpose of patrolling the bridge to prevent Albanians from entering northern Mitrovica—enjoyed critical backing from the Serbian Interior Ministry.[37]

At the same time, Belgrade consolidated control over northern Kosovo through "parallel structures." Serbian law enforcement operated within the region, sometimes bringing suspects into Serbia proper for prosecution.[38] Education and health ministries in Belgrade paid the salaries of teachers and health workers; the region's cellular network was disconnected from Kosovo Telecom and integrated into Serbian Telecom. Salaries and pensions were paid, and taxes collected, by Belgrade.[39] One scholar estimated that, as late as 2013, 62 percent of the people in northern Kosovo "are living from Belgrade, they are afraid of being cut off."[40]

So long as Serbia actively supported a state within a state in Kosovo, providing financial inducements to minority Serbs to boycott Kosovo institutions, the Serb minority maintained its separatist stance. This began to change when the EU used membership conditionality to win Belgrade's commitment to withdraw from Kosovo. At the same time, the international community induced Pristina to devolve state powers to the Serb minority in its 2008 constitution as the price of Kosovo independence.

Exogenous Regional Stabilization: The EU and the Ahtisaari Plan

Beginning in 2006, the international community attempted to contain separatist tensions in Kosovo by settling the bilateral conflict between Pristina and Belgrade at the regional level. The first UN-mediated negotiations over Kosovo's status were held in Vienna and mediated by UN special envoy Martti Ahtisaari, former president of Finland. In early 2007, Ahtisaari presented a draft settlement to both sides that amounted to Kosovo statehood—permitting the protectorate to join international organizations and establish a national security force. It also contained a plan for devolution that would give extensive autonomy to Serb-majority municipalities, including local control over finances, higher education, and health care, and the right to establish liaisons across borders with actors and interests in Serbia.[41] Belgrade rejected these openings, vowing to maintain para-statal institutions in Kosovo—particularly in the north, a region that neither Kosovo authorities nor the international community dared to penetrate.

A major turning point came in 2008, when Pristina declared statehood with the backing of the United States—obtaining recognition from numerous countries. Belgrade reacted by announcing the establishment of a system of "parallel municipalities" throughout Kosovo. Belgrade called on Kosovo Serbs to boycott the Kosovo state, refuse salaries and benefits from Kosovo, and cleave to parallel Serbian municipalities that would be run out of Belgrade. This proposition proved far more attractive to Serbs in the north, where Belgrade provided good salaries, pensions, and other services. By contrast, Serbs in the south had a far more tenuous connection with Serbia. Cut off from Serbia geographically, Serbs in the southern enclaves proved far more amenable to cooperating with the Kosovo state and soon began participating in Kosovo elections, using Kosovo services, and receiving benefits from the state at a far higher rate than Serbs in the north.[42]

Kosovo independence precipitated the collapse of the Serbian government, paving the way for the landslide victory of the moderate pro-EU coalition, For a European Serbia, headed by Boris Tadić. Although nationalist sentiment was still riding high, the election was "widely perceived as a referendum on Serbian membership in the EU" and as a mandate for Serbian leaders to continue negotiations over EU integration. The EU also initialed a Stabilization and Association Agreement (SAA) with Serbia to empower reformist elements in that country.[43] This concession was designed "not only to strengthen reformist forces [in Belgrade] but specifically to pressure the Serbian government to recognize Kosovo."[44] At the same time, the international community leaned on Pristina to secure the rights of Kosovo Serbs, insisting that devolution and minority-majority power sharing be included in the Kosovo constitution. Under the terms of the agreement, ethnic Serbs and other minorities would have 20 guaranteed seats in the 120-seat Kosovo Assembly, a minority veto in the assembly, and a minority quota in the state police and courts.

Regional stabilization achieved much greater success in southern Kosovo. Belgrade's control over local administration in northern Kosovo was nearly total; however, its reach in the south had progressively weakened over the 2000s. Parallel Serbian municipalities in the south were "overstaffed, lacking capacity, riddled with corruption and illegal[;] they [had] given up trying to exercise authority and now function[ed] as liaison offices to Serbia." Most were expected to close once their election mandate expired.[45] According to the ICG, "seeing that Belgrade cannot adequately meet their needs, many Serbs south of the Ibar are already seeking their own ways of reaching an accommodation with Kosovo."[46] In contrast to Serbs in the north, "the southern Kosovo Serbs mostly accept [Pristina's] sovereignty. . . . In a remarkable reversal since 2009, many [southern Serbs] vote in Kosovo elections."[47] Isak Vorgučić, a journalist at KIM (Kosovo Serb) Radio and resident of a Serb enclave in the south, recalled, "The best point [in ethnic relations] was 2010–11 because we got the municipality [status], which made things easier for everyday life. The government rebuilt the infrastructure [through Kosovo funds], and Serbs settled after [the Kosovo] proclamation of independence. We thought it would be fatal for us, but we saw it wasn't, so many people started to rebuild, settle, renew, and that's when I started to build my house."[48]

In the north, however, continuing support from Belgrade for parallel structures led Serbs to maintain a hostile, noncooperative stance toward Kosovo state authorities (Variant A). Consistent with these expectations, Kosovo independence in 2008 triggered a wave of protests and even violence on the part of Kosovo Serbs, some of whom commandeered public institutions. The most violent incident occurred when Serb militants attempted to seize a UN courthouse in Mitrovica, an action that was opposed by the UN and NATO. In the ensuing melee, one UN police officer was killed, and over one hundred people were wounded.[49]

Since 2008, negotiations over Kosovo's final status continued apace. At the same time, the EU made its SAA agreement with Serbia conditional upon Belgrade's *complete* withdrawal from Kosovo. Nested security would predict a comprehensive bilateral deal to securely nest ethnic relations *throughout* Kosovo, yielding minority integration in the north as well as the south and setting the stage for a more consolidated peace on the ground. The EU used similar tactics (membership conditionality) with Pristina to push the nascent state toward bilateral normalization with Serbia. Following muscular diplomacy on the part of the EU (spearheaded by Germany), Belgrade relented by implicitly recognizing Kosovo sovereignty. The final agreement provided for the integration of northern Kosovo into the Kosovo state. According to one disgruntled Serbian lawyer involved in these negotiations, "[bilateral rapprochement] is happening now because of pressure from the EU. They saw [that they could integrate the ethnic communities in Kosovo] because the

Serbian position is very weak at the moment. Serbia is very determined to join the EU, and the political elite saw no alternative. It is either the EU or nothing, and the EU saw an opportunity to use pressure and blackmail to reach an agreement on Northern Kosovo before Serbia's accession talks."[50]

Despite Belgrade's withdrawal of support in the north, Kosovo Serb radicals continued to resist Pristina's attempts to establish sovereignty over the region. When Kosovo authorities seized the customs and border patrols on the Serbian border in 2011, Serb militants responded by placing over a dozen roadblocks in the region to prevent transit through northern Kosovo. This led to a sharp uptick in violence in 2011–12 as Kosovo authorities set about dismantling the barricades. The international community expected Belgrade to assist in conflict reduction, partly by persuading the northern separatists to give up the fight. According to a local OSCE representative, "Belgrade has to inform [minority leaders in the north] what they want from all of this, because [the minority leaders] will not follow Pristina authorities. I do believe that Belgrade really wants to have this done and have this done now. At this stage, [Belgrade is not playing any games]. Kosovo is not valuable for them anymore, it's just costing them money."[51]

Bilateral conflict between Pristina and Belgrade over northern Kosovo has meant greater ethnic tensions in the north. Domestic-level explanations such as fears or grievances cannot readily explain the geographical variation in ethnic tensions. To illustrate, *nearly all* Serbs in Kosovo harbor ethnic grievances from the war, fears of discrimination, and desires for self-determination. However, the Serbs in the north were far more radical than those in the south. This difference is best explained by the fact that ethnic relations in the south were nested in a more stable bilateral relationship, allowing the Serbs there to take advantage of benefits of devolution provided by the Kosovo constitution. By contrast, the north remained conflict-prone because Serbia maintained its support for parallel structures there. Over the past few years, the EU has sought to stabilize ethnic relations in the north as well, by signing an SAA with Belgrade in which Serbia promised to dismantle *all* para-statal institutions in Kosovo as a condition of EU membership.

Echoing the principles of nested security, one ICG report said that "many Serbian actions and policies inside of Kosovo proper, and Mitrovica in particular . . . mirror or are a result of the disagreements and political squabbles within Belgrade itself. Belgrade's influence has thus been a crucial factor in determining the political behavior of Kosovo's remaining Serbs." What was true in 2002 remains true today. It also attests to the asymmetrical influence of outside actors on internal conflicts, as well as the key role played by major powers (first the United States and NATO, and later the EU) in creating preconditions for peace on the ground.

The Kosovo conflict has ebbed and flowed over the course of mediation; these fluctuations can be explained neither by the terms nor the timing of the devolution agreement. Instead, the health of bilateral relations between Pristina and Belgrade appears the most important driver of the level of conflict on the ground. Where Belgrade offered significant support to separatist authorities in the north, the minority leadership refused to integrate into Kosovo. By contrast, the southern enclaves became gradually (if reluctantly) integrated in the Kosovo state as their ties with Belgrade weakened. This led to a bifurcation of minority attitudes and behavior in the north versus those in the south. With the EU pressuring Belgrade to dismantle the parallel structures as a condition of EU membership, the stage was now set for the integration of Serbs in the north as well as the de-escalation of communal tensions in the region. The pattern and timing of conflict in Kosovo demonstrate that the effectiveness of induced devolution depends to a great extent on the stability of the wider neighborhood, as expected by the theory of nested security.

Montenegro

Montenegrins are close ethnic cousins to the Serbs—they share the same Eastern Orthodox faith as well as a common language and culture. Nonetheless, the small republic has a storied history of political independence, having been effectively sovereign or autonomous for over five hundred years. At the close of World War I, the Kingdom of Serbs, Croats, and Slovenes absorbed Montenegro, leaving it with no autonomy whatsoever. In 1943, Montenegro became one of six constituent republics under the Yugoslav socialist federation; although the republics were initially subjugated by a strong federal government, they gradually gained meaningful autonomy under 1960s reforms and the 1974 constitution. Still, the Montenegrin republic did not receive a full complement of republican institutions until much later.

Following the secession of Slovenia and Croatia in 1991, and Bosnia and Macedonia in 1992, Montenegro and Serbia were all that remained of rump Yugoslavia. At least partly because of its small size and relatively few resources, Montenegro remained loyal to Belgrade: Montenegrins not only voted to remain in Yugoslavia in a 1992 referendum, but their leaders staunchly defended the Milošević government. Throughout the 1990s, Montenegrin president Momir Bulatović (party loyalist and Milošević client) stood by the embattled Serbian president, offering him diplomatic cover and contributing troops to his multiple wars.[52]

Nonetheless, all was not well between Serbia and Montenegro. Partly owing to Montenegro's diminutive size (with a population of 615,000 against Serbia's 10 million), the federation was hardly a marriage of equals. Wartime sanctions against Serbia hurt the Montenegrin economy disproportionately,

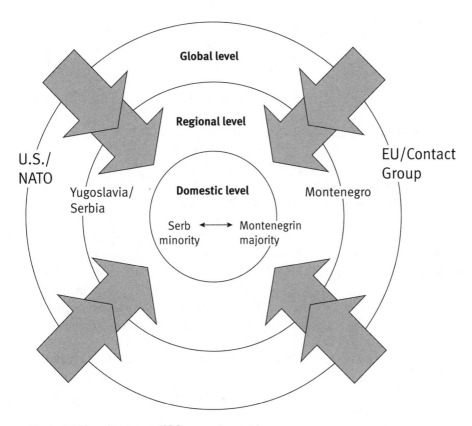

Figure 6.3 Nested security and Montenegrin secession

as the republic depended on Serbia as its most important trading partner. The Serbian-Montenegrin alliance weakened still further in the 1990s, as Milošević became increasingly isolated internationally and as domestic opposition to his rule mounted. In 1997, the republican leadership split over whether Montenegro should part ways with the federation. This case demonstrates that Montenegrin-Serb relations were nested in a wider hegemonic setting, as the destabilizing intervention of the United States in the 1990s provided Montenegro with de facto independence—such that by the 2000s not even active EU or NATO intervention could save the federation.

Regional Destabilization: U.S. Support for Montenegrins

Western governments intervened in the late 1990s to leverage the Montenegrin republic against the federal center. By aiding the Montenegrins, Western involvement insecurely nested Serbian-Montenegrin relations in an unstable regional environment—encouraging the tiny republic to escalate its demands for independence. As the United States grew increasingly hostile toward the Serbian regime, and Montenegro became effectively independent, arguments for leaving the federation gained traction in Montenegrin public debates. In early 1997, Milo Đukanović—a former protégé of Montenegrin president Bulatović and canny political operator—advocated opposition to Belgrade, declaring that "it would be completely wrong for Slobodan Milošević to remain in any place in the political life of Yugoslavia."[53] In July 1997, Đukanović launched a successful internal party revolt to replace Bulatović as president of the ruling Party of Democratic Socialists (DPS) and narrowly beat him in Montenegrin presidential elections that fall. Đukanović had run on promises of economic and political reform, an end to international isolation, and a strong place for Montenegro in the federation under the slogan, "Never alone, always [on] its own."[54] Bruised but not defeated, Bulatović and his supporters formed the breakaway Socialist People's Party (SNP), which maintained a pro-Milošević stance and became the most powerful opposition party in Montenegro.[55] Đukanović, now president of the tiny country, announced an open split with Belgrade and his former mentor, Milošević.

What accounts for the intransigent position of the new Montenegrin leadership? In the late 1990s, the international community, and particularly the United States, had seen Đukanović as a useful ally in their efforts to isolate and ultimately oust Milošević. The U.S. envoy to the Balkans Richard Gelbard had traveled to Podgorica, the Montenegrin capital, to meet Đukanović even before he became president. In the run-up to the war, Đukanović spoke with Gelbard regularly over the phone and went to Washington, where he was introduced to Secretary of State Madeleine Albright and National Security Adviser Sandy Berger.[56] Montenegro soon became the recipient of considerable foreign aid, mostly from the United States.[57] In 1999, Montenegro began receiving tens of millions of dollars in aid per year from Washington and was hailed by the State Department as a "model and stimulus for change" in the Western Balkans.[58] In 2001, the republic was allocated $89 million, making it the biggest per capita U.S. aid recipient after Israel.[59] For its part, the EU pledged 12 million British pounds in assistance.[60] Montenegro was also encouraged to establish a separate currency regime (adopting the deutschmark, and later the euro, as its main currency), which further empowered the republic against Belgrade. Its leaders enjoyed diplomatic ties with foreign governments, which treated Montenegro as a virtually independent state.[61]

In these and other ways, the international community encouraged the republic to behave as a de facto independent country. Western leaders reasoned that peeling Montenegro off from the Yugoslav federation would weaken the

Milošević regime by depriving Serbia of access to the Adriatic Sea and encircling the country with current or prospective NATO members. According to SNP spokesperson Dragan Koprivica, many local businesses and developers also had a stake in Montenegrin independence, and these interests "lined up with the interests of the international community."[62] The International Crisis Group openly advocated Montenegrin independence, calling for Western military intervention if Belgrade attempted to quell Montenegrin separatism.[63]

To further undermine the Milošević regime, the West funded the democratic opposition within Serbia.[64] The movement, led by Zoran Đinđić, began to gather steam after the 1996 local elections in which Đinđić and other opposition parties secured victories that were overturned by fiat days later. This culminated in large protests in the streets of Belgrade, unifying local NGOs, grassroots organizers, and democratic political parties in a campaign to end the Milošević regime.[65] Major-power intervention thus not only empowered the Montenegrin leadership, but also weakened the Serbian regime—creating a condition of nested *in*security on the ground.

As predicted by the model, regional destabilization exacerbated inter-republican tensions by empowering the Montenegrin minority, fueling Montenegrin separatism (Variant A). According to political analyst Dušan Janjić, "for Đukanović, it was clear that Milošević was over, that it was time to break out on his own [and] improve his image in the West."[66] Montenegro's leaders seized their moment to declare independence at the end of the Kosovo War. That summer, Đukanović presented his "Platform for a New Relationship with Serbia" to Milošević in which he explicitly called for a loose confederal state. He did not conceal his plans to make a formal declaration of independence later that year.

Exogenous Stabilization: Western Governments Push for Continued Union

The playing field changed dramatically in 2000, when Milošević was ousted and a newly accommodating leader, Vojislav Koštunica, assumed power with the promise of cooperating with the West. Western incentives to support Đukanović and his goal of Montenegrin independence evaporated almost overnight, as the new U.S. president, George W. Bush, apparently took a dim view of it. Arguments were now made that Montenegrin independence might provoke yet another conflict in the Balkans, especially since Montenegrins were internally divided on the matter (Serbs in northern Montenegro opposed independence). Others pointed out that if Montenegro were allowed to secede, this might precipitate copycat secessionist movements in Kosovo, Macedonia, and Bosnia. A third argument for preserving the federation was that the Montenegrin economy was too small and isolated to support a self-sufficient state. It is worth noting that all these arguments also applied during the Milošević regime, when the risk of violence was much greater. However, this did not stop the West from supporting de facto Montenegrin independence in the late 1990s.

The real reason for the change is that Montenegrin independence no longer fit into Western geopolitical aims in the Balkans. With Milošević gone, Washington now sought to work with the new Serbian leadership and dropped its backing for Ðukanović.[67] Whereas the United States had funded Montenegro and the Serbian democratic opposition in the 1990s, U.S. aid now went to the government in Belgrade in hopes that it would be a useful ally in the region. Western governments also believed that the pro-Western, neoliberal Montenegrin government could help promote liberalizing reforms in Serbia if it stayed *inside* the Yugoslav federation. Therefore, Western governments sought to shore up the tattered federation pursuant to EU and NATO integration.[68] In this spirit, European representatives actually scuttled an early deal between Serbian and Montenegrin representatives to hold a referendum on Montenegrin independence.[69] In November 2001, the EU General Affairs Council stated its desire for "a democratic Montenegro in a democratic FRY [Federal Republic of Yugoslavia]" and appointed Javier Solana to resuscitate the union.

The West now began to pressure both Serbia and Montenegro to compromise in order to save the union, thus exogenously stabilizing the federation. By nesting inter-republican relations in a stable regional environment, this had the effect of empowering pro-federation moderates within Montenegro. As expected, the new deal enhanced the status of the pro-Belgrade SNP, whose position now found favor with the international community.[70] Meanwhile, Solana induced Belgrade to devolve still more powers to Montenegro in an effort to undermine the Montenegrin impulse for secession. He did so by issuing a stark warning to both Serbian and Montenegrin leaders that EU accession was contingent on maintaining the federation. He cautioned Montenegrin leaders in particular against a unilateral declaration of independence, stating that Ðukanović "has to know that separation is not a rapid train to the European Union," implying that such behavior would jeopardize economic assistance and development to Montenegro.[71] In December 2001, Solana and French president Jacques Chirac traveled to Montenegro to deliver this message personally. During the visit, Chirac announced starkly, "It is my personal opinion that the European Union would not recognise an independent Montenegro."[72] Following talks with representatives of both sides, Solana's office issued a statement on February 4, 2002, that read in part, "Further fragmentation in the region would not only be contrary to the process of European integration, but would carry significant economic costs. The benefits of the bigger market will be lost, foreign investments will be discouraged and the lack of a common trade policy would be an obstacle to EU and WTO integration." The EU was determined to keep the federation together, fearing that Montenegrin secession would encourage secessionist movements elsewhere (namely Kosovo and the Republika Srpska in Bosnia and Herzegovina), provoke reactionary sentiments in post-Milošević Serbia, and trigger internal conflict between pro- and anti-independence factions within Montenegro.[73]

With the EU determined to preserve the bi-federation in the run-up to accession, the pro-federation SNP underwent a radical reversal in fortune. The new head of the SNP, Predrag Bulatović, backpedaled from his earlier acceptance of an independence referendum in Montenegro. He now informed Solana that the party was absolutely *opposed* to a referendum of independence, which he argued would destabilize Montenegro internally and could destabilize the region as a whole. Bulatović gloated to the press, "Đukanović is no longer a favorite of the international community."[74]

However, the separatist genie could not easily be put back in the bottle. The international community had clearly hoped that Montenegro would abandon its separatist agenda now that Milošević was out of office. In this, however, they were sorely disappointed. The emergence of an apparently more cooperative, more liberal Serbian government under Koštunica had zero effect on Đukanović's determination to secure an independence referendum. The young leader was little moved by the conciliatory statements of the new federal president toward Montenegro and openly questioned the sincerity of Belgrade's overtures. The West had begun to reap the consequences of having recruited Montenegro in its fight against Milošević in the 1990s. Having supported a de facto independent Montenegro, it was not easy to coax the Montenegrins back into a federal state. For instance, Đukanović's DPS refused to participate in the federal elections in the fall of 2000, leaving the pro-federal SNP with all the seats reserved for Montenegro in the federal parliament.[75] Nonetheless, public opinion in Montenegro was split on whether to remain in Yugoslavia, and Đukanović was doubtless aware that holding a referendum on independence in the early 2000s might result in defeat.

Solana now saw a chance to save the federation through devolution. Stating categorically that separation would threaten Serbia's ability to secure an association agreement with the EU, Solana induced Belgrade and Podgorica to agree to the broad outlines of a new union in 2003, which was eventually dubbed "Serbia and Montenegro." A local journalist recalled, "Solana came up with a proposal, and Belgrade accepted [it] because they did not have a clear plan for Montenegro. Serbia was too busy with itself, with internal political conflicts. Đukanović had a clear plan [for independence] from the beginning in 1997."[76] Part of why Belgrade agreed to such a loose confederation was that the new leadership understood that Montenegro was unlikely to stay in the federation in the wake of regime change. They also understood that the federal government was weakening, and that the confederation was perhaps "the best that Serbia's leaders could get."[77] The union therefore represented a compromise in which Belgrade agreed to respect an independence referendum in three years' time. In return, Podgorica agreed not to declare independence unilaterally.[78]

Confederation Postmortem

Several factors contributed to the demise of the three-year union. To begin with, its institutions were hollow, consisting only of a council of ministers and a parliament. Confederal powers were mostly limited to security and defense. The federal parliament enjoyed little credibility within Montenegro, as the domestically discredited SNP occupied all the seats that had been allocated to Montenegro; its officials were mere figureheads. Although the union had established a federal minister of foreign affairs, Montenegro maintained its own foreign minister, who met with foreign leaders abroad even though Montenegro had no formal international standing. Although it may be that devolution forestalled an untimely Montenegrin secession and was thus a qualified success,[79] it could also be argued that Montenegro might not have achieved independence in the absence of devolution. In fact, Nina Caspersen wrote that the "gradual policy of dissociation resulted in Montenegro acquiring significant attributes of statehood, but contrary to expectations, this process was not reversed with the fall of Milošević: on the contrary polarization was increased."[80] A second factor contributing to dissolution was that the EU still had no coherent single voice, as its foreign policy instrument, Common Security and Foreign Policy (CSFP), was hamstrung by collective decision-making rules at the EU level. Solana and the EU Commission for Expansion believed they should speed up the process of EU integration in the region as a way of ensuring compliance; others, however, felt that compliance had to come *prior* to EU membership.[81] As a result, the EU failed to speak with a single voice on the consequences of dissolving the federation.

More critical to the demise of the union, however, was Western support for de facto Montenegrin independence in the late 1990s. This had the effect of strengthening pro-independence forces within Montenegro, which continued to fuel separatism even *after* regime change in Belgrade in 2000.[82] In the spring of 2006, the EU broke off talks with Serbia on establishing an SAA on charges that the government was unwilling to extradite indicted war criminals to The Hague. Đukanović seized the moment to push forward his plan for independence, claiming that Montenegro was being held hostage by a recalcitrant Serbia. At this point, EU officials accepted the near inevitability of Montenegrin secession and henceforth resolved to ensure an "orderly" referendum for independence, promising that they would respect the results. Although the EU set a high bar for independence at 55 percent in favor, the referendum passed, and Montenegro achieved statehood.[83]

In the final analysis, EU efforts to save the federation were probably doomed to fail, given prior destabilization of the region by major powers in the run-up to the Kosovo War. By creating a de facto Montenegrin state in the war against Milošević, Western governments greatly empowered the republican leadership, with deleterious effects on the survival of the federation. As Nathalie Tocci wrote, "the [EU] High Representative's insistence on reconstituting federal unity between Serbia and Montenegro was resented by the latter, particularly in view of the West's (including the EU's) unreserved support for Montenegrin de facto independence before October 2000. . . . The prospect of [EU] membership was evidently not a sufficient prize to induce the Montenegrin government to make the State Union work and renounce its independence ambitions."[84]

Indeed, one could argue that the die had been cast years ago. As ICG analyst James Lyon pointed out, "The Union of 2002 was a codification on paper of what was already a de facto state. . . . The time to have saved the union was 1998 when there was a coup against the Montenegrin government."[85] Indeed, the confederation was highly unstable—by the time of the referendum, Montenegro shared only an air traffic control system and an army with Serbia. For Đukanović and his supporters, devolution was just a transitional stage on the way to secession, buying them time to secure sufficient support for a yes vote on independence. Montenegrin separatists were able to pursue, and ultimately secure, secession through the very institutional channels that had been established to *avert* this outcome.

Nonetheless, the impetus for secession clearly came from prior regional destabilization, which had empowered the Montenegrin minority in the late 1990s. EU efforts to save the federation through devolution barely slowed Montenegro's progress toward independence. This suggests that above a certain threshold of minority empowerment, conflict managers may not be able to reverse secessionist impulses, no matter how extensive the concessions are to the minority.

This chapter has examined the relationship between induced devolution and ethnic peace in three cases of mediated conflicts in the Western Balkans. While many of the starting conditions were the same—a common Titoist legacy, similar economic and political conditions, and the experience of rapid transition and collapse of the Yugoslav federation—induced devolution yielded very different outcomes in these cases. In the case of Montenegro, the republic already enjoyed de facto independence through Western (mainly U.S.) support by the time devolution was attempted. In a vain attempt to preserve what remained of the crumbling federation after Milošević was deposed in 2000, the international community induced Belgrade to devolve additional powers to the republic to satisfy Montenegrin desires for self-government and persuade the republic to stay in the federation. The relative success (or failure) of these institutions in quelling the conflict had little to do with managing ethnic fears, as Montenegrins had little to fear from Serbian intervention. In any case, the union ensured that Montenegrins enjoyed maximal autonomy (and thus protection) from the center. Neither does intervenor credibility or resources explain the outcome in this case, as perceptions of the EU remained more or less constant throughout this period.

Induced devolution may have achieved its greatest success in Macedonia, as the OFA was instrumental in ensuring peace in the newly independent state. Nevertheless, this case also suggests that devolution was far less influential than the regional power configuration in reducing conflict on the ground. In Macedonia, the international community prevailed upon the government to devolve extensive state powers to ethnic Albanian regions as a means of containing the 2001 insurgency. However, the government's progress in implementing devolution under the OFA appears far less important than the machinations of the militant leadership and their patrons in driving conflict in Macedonia at any given point. The nascent rebellion was contained only after NATO forces intervened to halt hostilities and the NLA leadership was folded into the Macedonian government. Although the government implemented devolution in Macedonia along the lines of the Ohrid agreement, giving ethnic Albanian regions greater local self-administration, this did not prevent a splinter militant group from engaging in violence periodically over the coming years, whenever events in the wider neighborhood offered an opportunity to mobilize for concessions from a relatively weak government. When the ongoing name dispute between Macedonia and Greece stalled the country's movement toward Euro-Atlantic accession in 2008, this led directly to an uptick in Macedonian nationalism and communal conflict, despite the fact that the OFA had been mostly implemented. Altogether, the pattern of internal conflict confirms that regional stability was a far stronger predictor of violence than changes or conflicts over the devolution agreement itself, consistent with the predictions of nested security. Minority fears and grievances due to Gruevski's nationalist policies have certainly played a role in the recent acceleration of ethnic tensions, but the wider regional conflict between Greece and Macedonia laid the critical groundwork for both Macedonian nationalism and the Albanian minority response.

Finally, the conflict in Kosovo cannot be understood without taking events in the wider region into account, particularly bilateral relations between Pristina and Belgrade. Belgrade's support for northern Kosovo is largely responsible for the greater intransigence of Kosovo Serbs in the north as opposed

Table 6.2 Summary evaluation of theories

Case	Minority protections / liberal government	Credibility of mediator / value of carrots and sticks	Nested security
Montenegro	*Disconfirmed* Montenegrin leaders did not moderate their demands after receiving quasi-state status under the union, with a liberal Serbian government.	*Partially confirmed* The EU used conditionality to induce Montenegrin leaders to enter into a loose confederation; this ultimately failed to prevent Montenegrin secession.	*Partially confirmed* Montenegrin leaders pressed for secession in response to Western leverage in the late 1990s; although the region was stabilized in the 2000s, Montenegro still seceded.
Albanian minority in Macedonia	*Partially confirmed* Although the minority enjoyed substantial rights in the 1990s, its leaders radicalized in 2001; however, post-2008 radicalization could be a partial response to growing signs of Macedonian nationalism.	*Confirmed* Minority leaders quickly moderated their demands after the U.S./NATO brokerage of the Ohrid agreement in 2001.	*Confirmed* The Albanian minority radicalized when the cross-border insurgency insecurely nested ethnic relations in an unstable regional environment; NATO intervention stabilized the region and induced an ethnic settlement.
Serb minority in Kosovo	*Disconfirmed* Kosovo Serbs were far more radical in the north than in the south, despite the fact that Serbs in the south had more to fear from minority discrimination.	*Partially Confirmed* Albanians viewed the U.S. and KFOR as legitimate actors, while the Serbs viewed the UN as the most legitimate actor. Predictably, this placed constraints on mediator effectiveness, but it does not explain fluctuations in conflict over this period.	*Confirmed* Serbs refused to integrate into state institutions in the north because of Belgrade's disproportionate interference in northern Kosovo; Serbs were more willing to integrate into state institutions in the south, where Belgrade enjoyed less influence.

to the south. Fears of discrimination might explain some features of conflict in Kosovo but does not explain why Serbs in the south—who faced greater threats of repression than those living in the north—began to participate at far greater levels in the Kosovo state. The credibility of the third-party mediator certainly matters, as each ethnic group had its favored third-party mediator (KFOR and NATO for the Albanians; the UN for the Serbs), but the credibility of the mediator(s) does not account for *geographical* differences in minority intransigence across Kosovo.

This analysis suggests a few things about the role of third parties in managing and containing sectarian tensions. First and foremost, hegemonic powers can clearly influence interethnic relations in the Western Balkans, and presumably more generally. In the 1990s, NATO and the United States were by far the most important conflict managers in the Western Balkans, but beginning in the 2000s, the EU assumed a greater role in cooperative conflict management. In Macedonia and Kosovo, in particular, the carrot of EU accession has proven a potent tool for encouraging governments in the region to negotiate a regional peace. The prospect of EU accession is the main reason Macedonia has sought to accommodate its minority, and has played a key role in inducing Belgrade to close its parallel institutions in Kosovo. These actions helped to securely nest minority conflicts in Kosovo and Macedonia, paving the way for greater ethnic harmony. Despite the growing role of the EU, however, the United States remains very influential in tempering government expressions of nationalism throughout the region, including Kosovo, Albania, and Macedonia. The United States and NATO have also proven capable of containing insurgencies, such as cross-border Albanian militants moving from Kosovo into south Serbia and Macedonia.

Over the longer term, prospects of integration into larger Euro-Atlantic structures might help to endogenously stabilize communal conflicts, as the states of the region identify internal incentives to keep and consolidate ethnic peace. This should decrease the political salience of ethnicity in the target states, helping to demobilize populations from ethnic cleavages and remobilize them around nonethnic political cleavages. At that point, minority and majority communities alike might foresee a future where contests over state resources are conducted through democratic institutions rather than through extra-institutional means.

7

NESTED SECURITY BEYOND EUROPE

Nested security holds that conflict mediation is much more likely to achieve success when the wider conflict environment is stabilized. I tested this proposition using intensive, over-time analysis of domestic conflict mediation under the auspices of two regional security regimes in Europe—the League of Nations and the EU/OSCE. In the four case chapters, I showed that third-party mediators tend to achieve success only once conflicts at the *regional or inter-state level* are checked or contained. This pattern holds up in both the interwar and post–Cold War periods, across different strategies of conflict management, third-party mediators, and countries—regardless of whether the minority had a history of autonomy or systematic discrimination. The upshot is that cooperative conflict management in Central and Eastern Europe was far more likely to succeed once the domestic disputes in question were securely "nested" in a stable international environment.

While qualitative case analysis demonstrated the pathways by which the wider environment can influence mediation success in Central Europe, it might also be asked whether the wider conflict environment has a similar influence on mediated conflicts *outside* the region as well.[1] Hence, the present chapter assesses the transportability of the model beyond Europe by exploring whether the stability of the neighborhood explains the variable level of violence in mediated conflicts around the world, not just within European security regimes. In this chapter, I conduct a first-cut test of the generalizability of the theory of nested security using the Managed Intrastate Low-Intensity Conflict (MILC) dataset of externally mediated low-intensity armed conflicts worldwide, dating from 1993 to 2004.[2] This dataset was chosen for analysis as one of the few available datasets of mediated civil conflicts that meets the scope conditions of the theory (see below). The aim was to restrict the analysis to low-intensity conflicts undergoing third-party mediation, since such conflicts are most responsive to soft-power conflict management. Indeed, the dataset perfectly meets the scope conditions of nested security by including only those civil conflicts around the world that are (1) minor or low-intensity (yielding fewer than one thousand battle deaths per year), and (2) mediated by external third parties using cooperative techniques such as negotiations, arbitration, or offers of conditionality. I analyze these data to determine whether regional instability (refugee flows, civil war in a neighboring country, or rivalry between the target state and a neighboring country) best accounts for the variable intensity of mediated conflicts around the world.

Although the dataset admittedly provides an incomplete test of robustness of the theory (mainly because of its short time span, which also limited the modeling choices), the results of this analysis complement the qualitative analysis in previous chapters. This analysis demonstrates that the conflict environment at the international level *is* correlated with domestic conflict intensity both (1) outside Europe, and (2) outside regional security regimes. This suggests that the theory applies to mediated conflicts worldwide, demonstrating the validity of nested security beyond the region of Central and Eastern Europe. The findings reported here, although not conclusive, support the most important prediction of nested security—that regional stability is strongly associated with the severity of conflict in the target state. Second, the cases in the quantitative analysis parallel the cases examined in the qualitative analysis: they are all low-level conflicts where third-party mediators (such as states, IGOs, and individuals) intervened cooperatively to prevent the emerging conflict from escalating to civil war. Indeed, all the qualitative cases examined in the book are low-level conflicts where mediators such as the League of Nations and the EU and OSCE sought to de-escalate communal tensions. Therefore, there is structural homogeneity between the cases chosen for qualitative analysis and those selected for quantitative analysis. Finally, by restricting the data analysis to conflicts undergoing mediation, I test for whether the features of the mediator matter more than the wider conflict environment in explaining the level of violence across these cases. Before outlining the nested security predictions to be tested in the analysis, I describe the structure of the dataset to be analyzed, including changes that were made to it.

The Data

A modified version of the Uppsala MILC dataset, v. 1.0, 1993–2004, was used for the analysis.[3] Despite the short time span of the data, MILC is one of the few available datasets of externally mediated low-intensity civil conflicts, as noted above. The Civil War Mediation (CWM) was another option, but unlike MILC, it includes information on *both* mediated and unmediated conflicts.[4] Given that the aim of this chapter is to test nested security predictions beyond Central and Eastern Europe, and since MILC is a dataset of low-intensity, mediated conflicts that therefore meets the scope conditions of the theory, I believe MILC to be among the best available datasets for the analysis. Below, I describe the original dataset and explain how and why it was transformed.

MILC is an event dataset of low-intensity conflicts waged between 1993 and 2004. It includes all armed clashes short of civil war between a government and non-state actor within a single state. Each observation is a single armed clash between the government and non-state actor, with 999 or fewer battle-related deaths. The MILC data include information on 3,471 clashes associated with seventy-six (mostly low-intensity) civil conflicts around the world. It should be noted that since the units of analysis in the MILC dataset are actually individual armed clashes, aggregating these events to conflict-years (as is done here) will cause a number of cases to surpass the 999 battle-related deaths threshold, making them civil wars. An example is the Afghanistan-Taliban conflict in 1995, which generated more than three thousand fatalities in that year, but which MILC treats as a number of distinct conflict events, each yielding fewer than one thousand deaths. Helpfully, the cases in the MILC dataset are also coded for the strategy and type of third party involved in mediating the conflict. The third-party mediator "type" can be states, groups of states, IGOs, groups of IGOs, and "other." If there is more than one mediator for a given conflict event, then that event is disaggregated into separate cases—one for each mediator.

In sum, each observation in the original MILC dataset is an armed clash between the government and a non-state actor in a conflict undergoing external mediation. The original unit of analysis in MILC is thus *conflict event–mediator*. Because I aim to identify factors associated with the degree of bloodshed in a mediated conflict, the event observations were aggregated into conflict-year observations. In doing so, all the event observations for a given set of conflict parties in a given year were aggregated into a single conflict-year observation. For each conflict-year observation, all third parties that were actively mediating that particular conflict were coded. For example, all 1995 Taliban-Afghan conflict events were aggregated to a single 1995 Taliban-Afghan conflict with two mediators—a single state and a single IGO.

Where the B side (the non-state actor) was labeled "unclear" in the original dataset, the case was aggregated with similar cases in the dataset where the B side *was* known. For example, if Croatia is coded as the A side, and the B side is coded as "unclear," and the year is 1995, then this observation is aggregated with others where the B side is identified as the Serb Republic of Krajina, as the only known armed opposition group in Croatia in 1995. However, when there were one or more unclear events in a year where at least two non-state armed actors are known to have confronted the government, these events were coded for all identified actors. For example, because both the National Liberation Army (ELN) and the Revolutionary Armed Forces of Colombia (FARC) were active against the government in Bogotá in 2004, any unclear incident, along with the information on third-party activity, is attributed to both actors. Fortunately, there were only a handful of cases in which the identity of the non-state actor was truly unclear.

The transformed conflict-year dataset consists of 229 conflict dyad-years that are associated with eighty-eight conflicts dyads. The reason the trans-formed dataset has fewer dyads than the original MILC dataset was that non-state actors with the same goals and factions of a parent group were ag-gregated into the same conflict dyad. This simplification was made because I wanted to test for the impact of the international conflict environment on the overall level of conflict between ethnic communities, rather than on the specific relationships between the state government and multiple rebel organizations.

Having outlined the structure of the transformed dataset and explained how it provides an additional test of robustness and generalizability, I turn to the predictions of nested security theory for large-N data analysis.

Theory and Hypotheses

I first outline hypotheses that can be derived from the nested security theory for large-N analysis. Broadly speaking, the model holds that the stability of the wider environment is an important facilitator of successful cooperative conflict management. If this is true, then indicators of regional instability should be correlated with indicators of communal conflict on the ground. Specifically, I hypothesize that mediated conflicts are likely to have higher ca-sualties if there is civil war in a neighboring state, rebel bases in a neighboring state, and/or significant inter-state rivalry between the host government and a neighboring state (which may be providing assistance to the rebel group). The following hypotheses (H1 through H5) outline the main predictions of the nested security model as well as important alternative accounts:

> **H1:** *If the host state is locked in a conflict with a neighboring state, then the me-diated conflict is likely to be **more** intense, other things being equal.*

Hypothesis 1 summarizes the nested security expectation that mediated con-flicts are likely to remain violent so long as there are bilateral tensions be-tween the host state and a neighboring state. This may be because the host state expects a hostile neighboring state to try to destabilize it by intervening on the side of the host state's internal challengers. The reasons for assisting an armed challenger in a neighboring state are multiple, but one important motive is that the neighboring state in question desires control over the minority region because it is valued territory. The neighboring state might also believe that supporting the internal challenger is an effective means of weakening its rival state. Whatever the reasons, I expect rivalry between the host state and neighboring country to undermine third-party efforts to de-escalate communal tensions in the host state. The second hypothesis summarizes the effects of cross-border contagion on mediated conflicts:

H2: *If there is a civil war in a neighboring state, or significant cross-border refugee flows, then the mediated conflict is likely to be **more** intense, other things being equal.*

The logic here is that organized violence on the borders of the target state will have a negative impact on the effectiveness of conflict mediation in that state. This is because armed struggles in the neighborhood typically generate cross-border flows of refugees, weapons, and fighters that can escalate civil tensions on the ground (and vice versa), despite the best efforts of conflict mediators to quell or de-escalate such conflicts. Third parties engaged in co-operative mediation are usually unable to contain the impact that civil wars in neighboring states have on the host state. Stanching the contagion effects of nearby civil wars at the state's borders often requires hard power, which mediators often cannot bring to the table. For this reason, civil war in a neighboring state is likely to escalate low-intensity conflicts, even those undergoing determined third-party mediation.

Besides the nested security hypotheses, I also test alternative hypotheses concerning the determinants of mediation success. These relate to the strategy and resources of the third-party mediator—namely, whether the third party enjoys legitimacy in the eyes of the conflict participants, and whether it has the resources to credibly signal its intent to intervene. Other alternative hypotheses are more difficult to test quantitatively, as they relate to the attitudes and perceived position of the conflict participants—namely, whether they are spoilers, or whether there is a "hurting stalemate" that creates incentives on both sides to reach a negotiated solution. The ones tested here include the following:

H3: *If the mediator is a great power, a group of states, or major international organization (a rough indicator of third-party resources and credibility), then the mediated conflict is likely to be **less** intense, other things being equal.*

The reason these conflicts are expected to be *less* intense is that when the third party is significantly more powerful than the target state, the latter is in a radically asymmetrical relationship with the mediator. This means that even if the intervention is not coercive, the third party has the means of engaging in hard-power intervention should the need arise. In this case, both conflict parties are more likely to take a powerful mediator seriously, because of the credibility of threats that it can make through coercive diplomacy.

> **H4:** *If the minority in the host state is subjected to significant discrimination prior to the conflict, then the mediated conflict is likely to be **more** intense, other things being equal.*

Hypothesis 4 summarizes the expectation that mediated conflicts are likely to be more violent—even given the presence of skilled third-party mediators—if the challenger group/minority has previously suffered discrimination at the hands of the government. In these cases, third-party mediation will be less successful in calming domestic tensions because the minority is significantly aggrieved and the state is locked into a non-accommodating position vis-à-vis the minority.

> **H5:** *If the minority in question has a history of autonomy in the target state, then the mediated conflict is likely to be **more** intense, other things being equal.*

This final hypothesis is intended to test for the possibility that intra-state tensions will be difficult to calm if the minority has a history of institutional autonomy in the host state. Under such circumstances, the minority should be more likely to push for secession or extensive autonomy because it has the institutional and symbolic resources to make a credible bid for independence. The government, for its part, is unlikely to yield to such demands, as doing so is generally seen as a significant defeat for the host state. As a consequence, civil conflicts involving historically autonomous minorities should be more difficult to de-escalate than conflicts involving minorities with no significant legacy of autonomy.

Research Design and Methods

Dependent Variable

For the purpose of this analysis, I created a new dependent variable, conflict intensity, which measures the level of violence in a given conflict-year. It is based on battle death statistics drawn from the Uppsala Armed Conflict 1946–2009 dataset.[5] It has three values: inactive conflict (0), if there were fewer than 25 battle-related deaths in a year; minor conflict (1), where battle-related deaths were between 25 and 999 in a given year; and civil war (2), where the number of battle-related deaths exceeded 1,000 per year. The dataset includes 30 inactive observations, 149 minor wars, and 31 wars (see figure 7.1). Because I am interested in the conditions under which mediated low-intensity conflicts escalate (to war) or de-escalate (to inactivity), a second dependent variable was created—a multinomial variable that captures either peace or civil war, with low-intensity conflict as the reference category. This variable will help assess whether there are associations between the independent variables and the different levels of conflict intensity.[6]

Independent Variables

To test the nested security hypotheses, I developed several proxies for regional stability. Some were obtained from the original MILC dataset; others were drawn from other conflict datasets as indicated below. I begin with the nested security variables and move on to the variables used to test alternative hypotheses.

Neighboring Rival
Rivalry is a binary variable designating whether the country containing the conflict borders a rival state; it serves as an indicator of conflict at the regional level. The theory of nested security expects inter-state confrontation (sometimes over disputed border territory) between the two countries to undermine mediation efforts.[7] This is because regional rivals very often intervene in civil conflicts within each other's borders—such as South African involvement in the internal conflicts in Angola or Zimbabwe or Russian intervention in the Georgian conflicts. Rival states in the neighborhood may provide critical assistance to one side of the conflict, intensifying the conflict even as it undergoes third-party mediation (H1).

Refugees from Neighbors
This is the logged number of refugees from neighboring countries located in the target state each year.[8] I expect the number of cross-border refugees to be positively associated with the level of conflict, and vice versa (H2).

Civil War in Neighboring State
This dummy variable captures whether there is an ongoing armed conflict between the government and a non-state armed actor in a contiguous country.[9] If the theory of nested security holds, we should see a positive relationship between the presence of civil war in a neighboring state and the level of conflict in the target state (H2). For example, civil warfare in Rwanda fed the

conflict in Congo in the 1990s, while the contemporary Syrian civil war provided a launching pad for the ISIS challenge to the Iraqi government. In sum, civil war in a neighboring state should be (imperfectly) correlated with logged refugees and significantly correlated with nested security variables—insofar as they serve as proxies for regional stability.

Variables for Alternative Hypotheses

I now outline the variables used to test alternative hypotheses for conflict mediation success.

Power Parity
This binary variable indicates whether the host state is militarily stronger (1) or weaker (0) than the third-party mediator, capturing the resources (and thus credibility) of the third-party mediator. This variable is coded by comparing the relative military capabilities of the target state and each mediator. The logic here is that third parties with superior military capacities can impose punishments if the conflict participants do not agree to a compromise settlement, improving the odds of peace.

Type of Mediator (Group of States, IGO, Group of IGOs, and Other)
To test for the possibility that third-party identity is associated with mediation success, four dummy variables were created, indicating the type of mediator in each conflict. A single conflict-year might have multiple mediators, in which case two or more of the dummies were coded 1. These variables come from the MILC dataset and are included in this analysis to ascertain whether the *type* of mediator matters in predicting the level of conflict intensity.

Neighboring State as Mediator
The information on this variable is derived from the MILC dataset. When any of the mediators is territorially contiguous to the target state, the variable is coded 1; otherwise it is coded 0. This variable is included to test for the possibility that mediator proximity is associated with lower levels of violence in the target state.

Relative Military and Economic Capacity
This variable captures whether the mediator has more power or wealth than the target state. The idea is to test for the expectation that "power mediators"—those that are able to back up threats with force or incentivize the conflict parties to negotiate—are more likely to succeed in de-escalating conflict.[10] I use the Correlates of War (COW) to obtain a measure of capabilities;[11] the

measure for GDP is taken from Gleditsch's dataset.[12] Higher military capabilities and GDP not only indicate greater state capacity, but also the ability of the third party to commit considerable resources to resolve the conflict.

Control Variables

Autonomy, Discrimination, and Power Sharing
These variables are taken from the Ethnic Power Relations (EPR) dataset and capture relative access to political power for relevant minorities during the years 1946–2005. They are dummy variables that measure, respectively, whether the group enjoyed political autonomy, suffered discrimination at the hands of the majority, or had a power-sharing agreement with the government prior to the conflict. It is expected that these variables will negatively correlate with conflict de-escalation.

Type of Conflict
This variable is taken from the MILC dataset and denotes whether the government and opposition are fighting over territory (1) or political power/control of the state center (0). It is used to control for the possibility that secessionist conflicts are more difficult for third parties to mediate because the rebels have a separate territorial base of power, making the conflicts prone to higher levels of violence.

Descriptive analysis shows that, although the dataset included a number of inactive conflicts and even full-blown civil wars, the great majority of cases

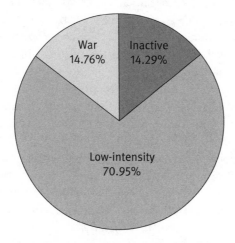

Figure 7.1 Conflicts by intensity. Number of observations: war = 31, inactive = 30, low-intensity = 149.

constitute low-intensity disputes as defined by COW's 999 battle-death threshold, even after the MILC data are aggregated to the country-year level. Since most of the civil wars in the dataset started out as minor conflicts, the data are useful for identifying conditions under which mediated low-intensity conflicts are likely to suffer higher levels of violence.[13]

Two different modeling approaches were used in the inferential analysis. In the first, the dependent variable was treated as an ordered outcome in an ordered logit model. In the second, the dependent variable was treated as a multinomial outcome in a logit link function to identify factors associated with peace as well as those associated with civil war (with low-intensity conflict as the reference category). Initially, the plan was to use a competing risk model to identify factors that increase the risk that low-level conflicts will escalate to civil war rather than de-escalate to peace, but the time series in this dataset are too short (on average 2.73 conflict-year observations per conflict), and contiguity in time series was not ensured in all cases. For this reason, a multilevel model was used in which the conflict-year observations are nested within the conflicts themselves, to try to predict the level of conflict intensity in each case. The multilevel ordered logit and multilevel multinomial logit analysis were conducted in Mplus version 7 using an uncorrected maximum likelihood estimator, a logit link function, and Monte Carlo integration.[14]

Discussion of Results

The findings of this analysis offer tentative confirmation for the nested security theory of conflict management, although they do not fully confirm the nested security hypotheses (see table 7.1). The results show that the ordinal variable of conflict intensity (DV1) is, consistent with Hypothesis 1, strongly and positively correlated with the existence of rivalry between the host state and a neighboring state—a relationship that is highly statistically significant. This suggests that mediated conflicts are likely to boast a higher level of casualties if there is regional rivalry between a (presumably interested) external neighboring state and the host government. However, if we look at the multinomial models (DV2), it becomes clear that the relationship between regional rivalry and civil war—rather than the *lack* of regional rivalry and domestic peace—is driving the first result. This offers tentative confirmation for the asymmetrical effects of nested security, namely that regional instability (here in the form of regional rivalry) may be a sufficient condition for conflict, but the *lack* of rivalry is not a sufficient condition for peace. We suspect that this is because regional instability is strongly associated with conflict escalation to war (even in the presence of conflict mediation).

However, the absence of rivalry does not appear to be associated with peace (with low-intensity conflict as the baseline), possibly because many other factors are critical to *resolving* conflict at the domestic level. In sum, we cannot conclude that resolving regional rivalry is both necessary and sufficient for peace. Regional stability may be necessary for de-escalation, but sufficient only in combination with other factors.

Hypothesis 2, on the relationship between conflict intensity and cross-border conflict contagion, finds somewhat weaker support. Although war in a neighboring state does appear to be associated with civil war (with low-intensity conflict as the reference category), the *lack* of war in a neighboring state is not a significant predictor of peace, similar to the asymmetrical effect of regional rivalry. Furthermore, the number of refugees from neighboring states fails to account for intensity of mediated conflicts. However, this negative result may be because the number of refugees from warring countries tends to accumulate over time, making the raw number of refugees a poor predictor of the intensity of conflict for any given year.

As for alternative hypotheses, mediator capability is strongly and positively associated with civil war, suggesting that if the target state is more powerful than the mediator (militarily), then the conflict is more likely to escalate to civil war. This supports the "power mediator" thesis that powerful third parties are more likely to achieve conflict de-escalation, as they are better able to get the conflict parties to submit to third-party diplomacy through a potent mix of carrots and/or sticks.

It also appears that if the mediator is an IGO or group of IGOs, then the mediated conflict is likely to suffer from more violence, even civil war. However, this may be due to the selection bias of mediators, as IGOs (such as the UN) are more likely to get involved in full-blown civil wars than in relatively mild armed conflicts. On the other hand, having a group of states as the mediator is *negatively* correlated with civil war, suggesting either that groups of states do *not* tend to get involved in civil wars, or that they—presumably because of their vested interest in solving the conflict—are better than other mediators at getting combatants to accept their mediation,[15] thereby preventing higher levels of violence.[16]

Turning to the control variables, our analysis reveals that minority discrimination is positively associated with conflict intensity, although a past history of group autonomy or power sharing is not. This squares with recent quantitative research showing that minority discrimination makes a country more prone to civil war,[17] although intensive case analysis is needed to demonstrate the ways in which minority discrimination is producing violence. Interestingly, institutions of territorial autonomy do *not* appear to be associated with conflict (de-)escalation, suggesting that minority discrimination may be a more important driver of civil violence than whether the minority has a history of autonomy.

Overall, these data suggest that *both regional rivalry and war in a neighboring country is associated with civil war in the target state, even in the presence of third-party mediation*, as stated in Hypotheses 1 and 2, respectively. This is broadly consistent with the expectations of nested security, which holds that regional instability (captured by regional rivalry and civil war in a neighboring state) is likely to undermine cooperative mediation efforts. The *lack* of regional rivalry and war in a neighboring country is not, however, associated with peace, suggesting that other factors may be more important for transforming a low-intensity conflict to a state of peace.

This chapter offers a first-cut test of whether the model of nested security helps to explain the variable success of third-party conflict mediation—not just in Central and Eastern Europe, but around the world. To assess whether the external conflict environment makes it more difficult for third-party mediators to manage low-intensity conflicts beyond Europe, I conducted quantitative analysis on a dataset of mediated low-intensity conflicts worldwide. The MILC dataset was selected for this analysis because it contains information on intra-state conflicts that are (1) mediated by third parties through cooperative techniques, and (2) low intensity (and hence good bets for cooperative interventions). These data were chosen precisely because they meet the scope conditions of the theory. Because the MILC data exclude cases of unmediated conflicts, I was also able to use these data to test alternative hypotheses outlined in the book that the mediator's identity and resources help predict whether a conflict will escalate to war or de-escalate to peace.

Using inferential analysis, I demonstrated that the nested security model can travel beyond the few Central and East European cases examined here through qualitative analysis. This analysis generally supports the nested security expectation that regional instability (captured by inter-state rivalry, civil war in a neighboring state, and cross-border refugee flows) is correlated with higher levels of violence in the target state. Moreover, it also indicates that the *absence* of these factors does not correlate with peace. These results provide tentative confirmation for the asymmetrical nature of nested security, suggesting that mediated conflicts are unlikely to end (and may even escalate) if the region is unstable. On the other hand, a stable region does not necessarily produce peace, as other factors must line up at the domestic level before peace can emerge. Another way of putting it is that the stabilization of the wider conflict environment is a necessary, but insufficient, condition for conflict reduction at the domestic level, consistent with the central expectation of nested security.

What does all this mean for policy? The most obvious takeaway is that getting the domestic institutions right is not enough to reduce intra-state conflict so long as the conflict itself is fueled by a turbulent international environment. A well-designed power-sharing or minority autonomy agreement alone is unlikely to lead to conflict reduction (although improved minority protections may help). All else being equal, it probably helps to have a relatively powerful mediator that can intervene to induce peace settlements with a judicious mix of carrots and sticks. Finally, consistent with the model's predictions, giving cooperative conflict management the best chance begins with the wider strategic environment; it is probably best achieved by neutralizing the regional setting (settling inter-state rivalries and helping to prevent conflict from spreading across borders) from the outside in—before or at the same time that intergroup conflict is mediated at the domestic level.

Table 7.1 Regression results for conflict intensity, 1993–2004

Variables	Multinomial logit		Ordered logit
	Peace (vs. low intensity)	War (vs. low intensity)	
Refugees	0.028	−0.017	0.008
Civil war	−0.045	1.11*	−0.459
Rivalry	−0.525	1.939***	1.339***
Discrimination	−0.301	0.901	1.017*
Power sharing	0.890	0.793	−0.207
Autonomy	0.416	−0.572	−0.637
Group of states	−0.280	−0.685***	−0.249
IGO	0.602	1.624*	0.420**
Group of IGOs	−0.165***	1.537	0.939*
Other mediator	1.343	−0.991	−1.083
Neighbor as mediator	0.036	0.856	0.562
Territorial conflict	0.046	−0.429	−0.004
Mediator capability	−2.385	−0.349	2.785*
Log likelihood	−176.675	−176.675	−175.868
Chi square	43.848**	43.848**	45.462***
Conflict years (level 1)	210	210	210
Conflicts (level 2)	77	77	77
Level 2 variance (mean)	−1.837	−9.962**	1.355*

Note: Reported coefficients are estimated using an uncorrected maximum likelihood estimator, a logit link function, and Monte Carlo integration.
* = $p<0.1$, ** = $p<0.05$, *** = $p<0.01$.

GREAT POWERS AND COOPERATIVE
CONFLICT MANAGEMENT

The main premise of this book is that intractable intra-state conflicts are rarely domestic affairs but instead have powerful external drivers in the wider neighborhood and beyond.[1] Indeed, many of the most entrenched conflicts around the world are nested in regional conflicts that are often themselves nested in wider hegemonic struggles. This is what makes nested civil conflicts so challenging to mediate. In view of this, it is not surprising that conflicts involving neighboring states as well as transnational and global actors often center on economically or strategically valuable territory.[2] Some of the bloodiest wars have been fought over strategically valuable transportation routes or military basing sites, territory containing precious minerals or hydrocarbon reserves, or difficult terrain that can be used to sustain guerrilla movements.[3] Conflicts intensify when the minority enjoys critical bargaining leverage from outside actors, military advantages conferred by the territory itself, or de facto or de jure autonomous status.[4] That these conflicts are so often located along contested international borders and feature cross-border groups, transnational rebels, and great-power participation often reflects the geopolitical value of the territory in question.[5]

It is this pervasive external dynamic to civil conflict that demands an "outside-in" approach to conflict management. Traditional approaches to conflict resolution emphasize the importance of domestic institutions such as power sharing or autonomy arrangements or electoral reforms to encourage issue-based voting in order to bridge communal cleavages.[6] However, institutional solutions are unlikely to promote domestic peace so long as the external environment continues to promote conflict.[7] A nested security approach to conflict management calls for addressing such disputes from the outside in—that is, neutralizing conflict dynamics in the wider neighborhood by, among other things, promoting regional cooperation among rival neighbors.[8] Because communal conflicts are so often asymmetrical, with a small rebelling group pitted against a majority-controlled state, an internal conflict is unlikely to last for decades or recur repeatedly (as so many of them do) in the absence of external lobby actors, kin groups, cross-border sanctuaries, or insurgency networks. Sever these ties and prevent external leveraging of the minority against the center, and the minority is far more likely to accommodate or compromise with the majority-controlled state. Ensure that the central government, too, is constrained or incentivized against minority discrimination, and the stage is set for a liberal peace.

Conflicts involving external actors typically occur at contact points between rival powers and recur as a function of wider regional conflict or hegemonic proxy wars.[9] Such disputes are more often easier to *manage* than they are to resolve. This means regulating the conflicts through their entire life cycle—from violent conflict prevention to postwar reconstruction. This, in turn, requires continual monitoring of tensions on the ground and adaptation to evolving conflict configurations. Regional security regimes are best suited for this purpose for several reasons. First, such regimes have institutionalized mechanisms for monitoring conflicts on an ongoing basis, and the monitors themselves are likely to have preexisting relationships with states in the region. Second, members of regional regimes have a vested interest in stabilizing their own neighborhoods, which means that both their threats and promises will be more credible to the conflict participants. Having intervened, regional actors are less likely to withdraw when the costs of engagement exceed a certain threshold; they are also likely to be familiar with the conflict dynamics in the region, a key advantage in dealing with the all-important tasks of crisis management. Finally, such regimes are likely to have the backing of regional hegemons, conferring critical leverage upon the conflict monitors.

This book examines the record of European cooperative conflict management because the regional focus offers a number of comparative controls to assess whether nested security is, as hypothesized, a critical background condition for de-escalating tensions through third-party mediation. The argument follows that unless internal conflicts are nested in stable bilateral relations, which in turn are nested in a stable regional and hegemonic environment, there can be little hope for de-escalating communal tensions on the ground. Mediators are more likely to succeed in de-escalating conflict under conditions of nested security no matter what stage the conflict is in, or how protracted the violence. In the absence of nested security, on the other hand, communal tensions will very often escalate despite the best efforts of external mediators.

The remainder of this chapter draws on the evidence marshaled in the book to draw broader inferences about the predictors of regime success. Specifically, I discuss what each European regime did well and what each did poorly; I then outline how these lessons can be used to fashion a blueprint for future security regimes both within and outside of Europe.

Lessons for Successful Cooperative Conflict Management

Before turning to regional security regimes, I identify implications of this analysis for the practice of cooperative conflict management in general. Two principles stand out in particular.

Integrating Domestic, Regional, and International Dimensions

Conflict mediators are more likely to succeed when they treat communal conflicts as an integral part of wider conflicts that extend beyond the target state's borders. Other things being equal, mediators who co-opt regional actors or contain cross-border contagion through effective border control have proven more effective in containing violence. By 1918, the Åland Island separatist movement was on the verge of violent rebellion when the League of Nations was invited to mediate the dispute. By securing a commitment from Sweden to renounce its territorial claims on the islands, even though 90 percent of the Swedish-speaking population favored annexation, the League was able to de-escalate the irredentist conflict as early as 1920. Although the Ålanders were deeply aggrieved by the League's decision, Sweden's concession was central to achieving what is considered to be one of the League's brightest successes. The agreement between Sweden and Finland has remained intact to this day, with the effect of permanently de-escalating ethnic tensions on the islands. Likewise, reining in Germany's external reach under the Versailles Treaty was critical to the early successes of autonomous institutions in Danzig, Upper Silesia, and the Saarland, whose large German populations looked to Berlin for political guidance. Subsequent revisions to the Versailles Treaty permitted the return of irredentist German foreign policy in the 1930s, triggering parallel separatist movements by German minorities in Poland and Czechoslovakia. The outsize role of Germany in escalating these conflicts in the 1930s, and the failure of the League to address Germany's predations, underscore the importance of managing "losers" of postwar settlements (more on this below).

Similar patterns can be discerned in the post–Cold War period. U.S. containment of Russian interference in the Baltics was essential for de-escalating ethnic conflicts in Latvia and Estonia in the 1990s. The Clinton administration successfully pressured Russian president Boris Yeltsin to withdraw support for the Russian-speaking minorities in the two countries, leading minority elites to moderate their calls for autonomy and separatism. With EU and NATO membership riding upon implementation of citizenship reforms recommended by the OSCE and the HCNM, Latvia and Estonia were induced to improve their treatment of the Russian minorities and ease the path to citizenship for Russian speakers who had been rendered stateless under the laws of the early 1990s. Although ethnic tensions reemerged in both countries in the mid-2000s partly as a consequence of Vladimir Putin's nationalist posturing, Moscow has so far shown little interest in reigniting hostilities with the Baltic governments, taking the wind out of the sails of extremists on both sides. In more recent years, bilateral relations have grown closer owing to common commercial interests, helping to endogenously stabilize the region. With the shadow of Moscow receding and domestic concerns looming larger, cross-ethnic voting in both states has given rise to centrist parties that appeal to both ethnic groups. Nonetheless, recent Russian interference in Georgia and Ukraine has set the Baltic majorities and Russian-speaking populations on edge; conflict managers will need to closely monitor bilateral relations in the region to prevent the resurgence of ethnic tensions in Baltics.

Co-opting Spoilers and Provocateurs

Achieving nested security may also require *co-opting* external provocateurs. Positive engagement with Austria after World War I was critical to de-escalating tensions in the German-speaking Sudetenland. Having suffered a devastating military defeat, Austria was desperately short of food and fuel. This led to a deal between Austria and Czechoslovakia whereby Vienna agreed to renounce territorial claims on German-speaking portions of lower Bohemia and Moravia in return for much-needed supplies of coal and grain from Prague. With Austria backpedaling on promises to annex the region, Sudeten irredentism gradually lost momentum, and the Czechoslovak legionnaires were able to occupy the region and bloodlessly dissolve the provisional governments.

In the conflict between Hungary and Romania over Transylvania, Italy and Austria prevailed on Hungary to open a new chapter of cooperation with Romania by implicitly promising Budapest a closer regional alliance that could extend to Germany. Desperate for the trade and security ties implied by such a pact, the recession-plagued government obligingly made overtures to Bucharest in 1933, agreeing to shelve its territorial claims in the interest of normalizing relations. In the context of warming bilateral relations between Hungary and Romania, the League of Nations succeeded in resolving long-standing compensation claims of ethnic Hungarian optants against the Romanian government.

The post–Cold War security regime has also achieved notable successes through co-optation. Although it was not a cooperative engagement, and therefore falls outside the scope of this study, Bosnia-Herzegovina serves as a vivid illustration of the value of co-opting provocateurs. The U.S. government promised Zagreb military assistance in reclaiming Serbian rebel enclaves in Croatia in return for Zagreb's agreement to sign onto and observe the Dayton Accords. Belgrade, meanwhile, was promised an end to economic sanctions so long as it severed its ties with the Bosnian Serb rebels. Despite the fact that communal tensions continue to persist nearly two decades after the end of the war, Bosnia has been virtually violence-free since 1995, with fewer than a thousand remaining peacekeeping troops under the command of European Union Force Althea (EUFOR). Under present conditions, there is an extremely low probability of a return to violence. The co-optation of Zagreb and Belgrade was one of the biggest milestones in ending the three-year war. In the Baltics, too, the United States successfully co-opted external provocateurs. The Clinton administration used aid to induce Russia to withdraw its troops from their military bases in the Baltics, effectively removing Russia's most important lever of influence from the region. Later, the United States prevailed on Moscow to assume a noninterventionist stance toward co-ethnics in Latvia and Estonia in return for additional financial assistance and a consultative status with NATO. This all points to the importance of what Timothy Sisk has called "powerful peacemaking"—the use of awesome sanctions and incentives to leverage the conflict participants into a peace deal.[10]

Long-term co-optation of spoilers and provocateurs might be achieved by integrating them into common security institutions—ideally, the very same regional security regimes engaged in conflict management. The post–Cold War conflicts between Hungary and its neighbors over the status of ethnic Hungarians in Slovakia and Romania were effectively neutralized once the three states were inducted into NATO and the EU. As members of a common security regime, Hungary and its neighbors have managed their border disputes fairly well. Indeed, it is revealing that the most contentious communal conflicts in post–Cold War Europe have been along international borders that separate one sphere of hegemonic influence from another. The conflicts between Serbia and its neighbors and between Russia and the Baltic states have straddled the borders of, or were poorly covered by, Europe's security organizations. Currently, the most dangerous European conflicts are situated along the virtual border between the EU/NATO and Russia—the Ukrainian, Georgian, and Moldovan conflicts. In these peripheral zones, the regional regimes' conflict-regulation mechanisms have far lower chances of success than they would otherwise have.

Building Regional Security Regimes

Can we build effective cooperative conflict management regimes outside Europe? The historical record suggests that systemic war or region-wide transition may be a necessary condition for the creation of robust security regimes. This was true not only of the League of Nations and post–Cold War regimes, but also of their nineteenth-century predecessor, the Concert of Europe. Indeed, all three European security regimes emerged as a response to systemic war. The Concert of Europe was established in 1815 to stabilize the Continent and redistribute lands that Napoleon Bonaparte had acquired through war. Although its meetings were convoked on a strictly "as needed" basis, it was the first permanent international organization designed to manage conflict in continental Europe more or less indefinitely—and did so for decades. The Concert enjoyed the critical backing of members of the Quadruple Alliance that had defeated Napoleon, including Austria, Prussia, the United Kingdom, and the Russian Empire (France later became the fifth member of the Concert). As the nineteenth century progressed, the Concert powers used the regime to manage the gradual collapse of the Ottoman Empire—new southeastern European states were recognized in return for commitments to provide protections to certain minorities. In 1830, Britain, France, and Russia recognized an independent Greece in return for its commitment to protect its Muslim minority; these provisions were reaffirmed when Greece expanded in 1863. The Concert powers successfully arbitrated a number of crises related to the emergence of new states in the Balkans as well as the division of Africa between competing colonial powers.

One hundred years after the creation of the Concert, the League of Nations was established to manage imperial collapse after the First World War.[11] Following the Armistice of November 1918, the four Allied powers were faced with the task of constructing viable nation-states from the wreckage of four imperial powers—Russia, Turkey, Austria-Hungary, and Germany. The new and expanded states in Central Europe—Yugoslavia, Czechoslovakia, Romania, and Poland—had all been wartime allies of the Entente powers. Fortunately for Czech, Romanian, Polish, and Serb nationals, their statehood was seen as a key means by which the Allied powers could fulfill an overriding war aim: checking German, Russian, and (to a lesser degree) Bulgarian and Hungarian territorial ambitions. Then, because the new and enlarged state borders left millions of people outside their putative national homes, the Allied powers established a permanent organization to manage the repercussions of these border changes. The Covenant of the League of Nations laid out a system of minority protections to manage national conflicts that threatened the postwar order.

The post–Cold War security regime had very similar origins. The regime was designed to manage the political and security externalities from the imploding Soviet empire and neighboring communist states. By 1992, fifteen fledgling states stood where the Soviet Union once was. Meanwhile, Yugoslavia had separated into five pieces, and Czechoslovakia had split into its constituent Czech and Slovak Republics. Already by the early 1990s, violent communal conflicts raged in Bosnia, Croatia, Moldova, Abkhazia, South Ossetia, Nagorno-Karabakh, Tajikistan, and Uzbekistan. Still other places threatened violence, including Kosovo, Vojvodina, Macedonia, Montenegro, Transylvania, Chechnya and Dagestan, the Baltic states, and Tatarstan. As in earlier periods, Western powers attempted to shore up the collapsing states for as long as possible. In 1991, the European Community (EC) announced that it supported self-determination insofar as it was exercised within "existing frontiers which can only be changed by peaceful means and by common agreement."[12] As Yugoslavia too began to disintegrate, giving rise to the Croatian and Bosnian Wars, Western governments scrambled to fashion an ad hoc security regime to identify and monitor emerging conflict zones in Europe. Acting as conflict monitors, the OSCE provided long-term missions on the ground, while the HCNM provided crisis management through shuttle diplomacy. The Council of Europe served a supporting role in monitoring brewing conflicts. Enforcers of the system included NATO, the EU, and major Western governments.

What this history suggests is that regional security regimes are most likely to emerge in the wake of massive geopolitical disruption, leading (regional) hegemons to create security institutions to restore stability to a region plagued by dangerous power vacuums. This fits the description of numerous regions today, including Ukraine and its neighbors, the South Caucasus, and Central Asia—where conflicts over still-transitioning countries continue to threaten the peace of Eurasia. Backers of a Caspian region security regime might include the EU and/or Russia. Over the longer term, more consolidated regional security regimes may emerge in South or Southeast Asia to manage separatism in states such as China, India, Pakistan, the Philippines, and Indonesia, or in the Middle East and North Africa to contain cross-border insurgencies and secessionist struggles.

It is possible to create regional security regimes even in the absence of imperial collapse. Since the end of the Cold War, regional organizations around the world have begun to build capacities for early warning and conflict prevention over a given territorial remit; available tools include early conflict warning mechanisms, preventive deployment of peace forces, and preventive diplomacy. Since 1998, the United Nations Development Programme has assisted the African Union in developing the Peace and Security Directorate and the Peace and Security Council for conflict prevention. ASEAN established the Regional Forum in 1989 to facilitate peaceful dialogue and resolve disputes in the region before they turn violent. The Union of South American Nations recently committed to preventive diplomacy, and other regional organizations have begun to establish mechanisms for preventive action, as evidenced by the 2000 Biketawa Declaration of the Pacific Island Forum, the 2001 Inter-American Democratic Charter, the 2005 Charter of the Francophonie, and the 2008 Charter of the OIC. The question is whether these organizations have the necessary teeth for preventing the escalation of violence—particularly in war-torn regions such as sub-Saharan Africa and the Middle East and North Africa (MENA). Despite the proliferation of regimes on paper, in practice contemporary conflict management has a strongly ad hoc character, with multiple conflict managers sometimes working at cross-purposes or along multiple tracks.[13] Greater coordination among third parties seeking to manage hot spots around the world might be achieved through greater institutionalization—which might necessitate global or regional hegemons taking a lead role. Like the EU/OSCE and the League of Nations before it, in order to succeed, security regimes depend to a large extent on the backing of regional or global hegemons.

Determinants of Regime Success

Having explored the lessons from interwar and post–Cold War Europe for successful cooperative conflict management, what can we now say about the conditions for conflict management regime success?

Cooperation between Mediators and Enforcers

Close cooperation between regime monitors and enforcers is a hallmark of successful cooperative conflict management. The task of the monitors is twofold. First, they serve an "early warning" function, using indicators such as conflict contagion across borders or external interference into conflict zones to alert the enforcers to impending violence on the ground. Their second function is as "first responders"—deploying "good offices" for third-party mediation or technical solutions (such as legal fixes) to contain conflicts in the early stages. In this, they are equipped with a network of legal advisers, diplomats, and other support staff who serve as a first line of defense against conflict escalation.

The enforcers act as the second line of defense, assuming control of the situation once it has passed a certain threshold of violence; this is where major powers play a critical role. Enforcement of regional security regimes is vital for two reasons. First, the implicit threat of intervention by major powers lends authority to the monitors and provides incentives for target governments to cooperate with the dispute-resolution process. Monitors are better able to induce compliance in the presence of a credible threat of enforcement such as direct military force, economic or military sanctions, or the withholding of aid or membership in valued international organizations.

The record of the League of Nations demonstrates the vital importance of cooperation between monitors and enforcers. Violent uprisings in Upper Silesia (a border region disputed by Germany and Poland) in 1919 and 1920 were addressed by a League-appointed commission, which used a popular plebiscite to partition the territory. The crisis was ultimately resolved through close cooperation between the Conference of Ambassadors and the League of Nations. Following the division of the region between Germany and Poland, an Allied peacekeeping force was deployed there, keeping the peace until the Second World War. Teschen, another energy-rich region, contested by Poland and Czechoslovakia, was also successfully partitioned through intensive League mediation backed by Great Power enforcement. Finally, Britain (a Great Power enforcer) was instrumental in persuading Finland and Sweden to accept League of Nations mediation of the Åland Islands dispute.

Cooperation between monitors and enforcers has also been central to mediation success in the post–Cold War period. For example, the OSCE high commissioner effectively de-escalated communal tensions in Estonia in 1993 by engaging in shuttle diplomacy between the Russophone cities (Narva and Sillamäe), Tallinn, and Moscow. Moscow and the Russian autonomists cooperated with the high commissioner largely because of the intervention of a U.S. ambassador, which gave considerable weight to the high commissioner's diplomacy. In Macedonia, too, the high commissioner experienced far greater success once NATO and the EU linked his language and education reforms to the country's eventual membership in Euro-Atlantic organizations. By contrast, the *lack* of cooperation between the high commissioner and peace enforcers in Kosovo severely undercut the high commissioner's ability to persuade both sides to arrive at a compromise solution in the 1990s.

Robust Enforcement by Great Powers

Lacking hard-power capacity, cooperative security regimes are unlikely to succeed in containing escalating violence. To date, no such regime has deployed enforcement beyond what its member states have provided voluntarily, on a case-by-case basis.

The League security regime was particularly beset by problems of enforcement. Its ability to function was compromised at birth by the failure of U.S. president Woodrow Wilson to secure the Senate's ratification of League membership. To compound the problem, the League covenant provided for no enforcement powers whatsoever. The French favored a system with maximum guarantees of peace on the Continent. Having fought three land wars with

Germany over the past one hundred years, the French were convinced that an effective military was necessary to check the ambitions of revisionist powers. However, the United States and Britain opposed giving the League such powers, arguing that their publics would never accept military entanglements in continental Europe.[14] This meant that the use of "sticks" by the League depended entirely on the ad hoc decisions of the Great Powers to provide such sticks.

Despite the world's focus on Geneva as the face of the League of Nations, the real power in the interwar period rested with the Allies. This is manifested by the League Council's inability to resolve disputes that required a costly military intervention. League mediation between Russia and Poland over the Vilnius region dragged on for years before a final resolution was reached in 1927. Tensions between Greece and Turkey triggered a bloody war, leading to brutal ethnic cleansing of Greeks from the Anatolian peninsula. In the Caucasus, the fledgling Armenian Republic appealed for assistance against Turkish forces that were amassing on that country's border. The Allies attempted to delegate Armenia's petition to the League, but Geneva protested that it had no means of forcibly ejecting hostile powers. The League Council therefore turned to the United States, which had the greatest capacity to solve the crisis. By the time the United States formally declined to intervene, the unfortunate republic had already been overpowered and absorbed by Russia's Bolshevik government. With the League bereft of political and military support from the United States—and Britain and France reluctant to extend security guarantees to the newest members of the League—the League of Nations was helpless to resolve the thorniest conflicts of the interwar period.

The League of Nations was in fact compelled to rely on the consent of its most powerful members to enforce its decisions. The League covenant mandated that its members enforce the borders of the postwar order as well as the sovereignty of all its members (Article 10). However, the League itself still had no direct mandate for enforcement under the covenant. On occasion, the League was able to implement an institution through the implicit or explicit threat of force, but only when a national state offered to provide military assistance to the League in that instance. Decisions to backstop League interventions, where they occurred, were made on a voluntary basis by the states themselves. Throughout the interwar period, the Conference of Ambassadors (the Allied powers) met to discuss various military threats that arose. These meetings were convened at the discretion of the Allies, and their decisions superseded those of the League. The League was tasked with resolving either the smallest problems or the biggest problems that the Allies wished to ignore.

In the end, the regime posed little impediment to German expansion in the late 1930s. With France and Britain distancing themselves from security complexes in the region, the Reich was afforded the requisite space to plan attacks against its neighbors and engage in systematic slaughter of vulnerable groups. By the time the Allies perceived the full extent of Hitler's ambitions, the minorities regime (along with the League itself) had lost all relevance in European security affairs. In the end, the inconsistent support of France and Britain, the nonparticipation of the United States, the limited commitment of the major powers to protect threatened states, and the increasingly divergent interests of the major powers struck a fatal blow to the League security regime.[15]

By contrast, the post–Cold War regime has enjoyed far more robust enforcement by the major powers. After initially taking a hands-off approach to the collapse of communism across Eastern Europe, the West became far more interventionist when the Bosnian War began to send hundreds of thousands of asylum seekers into Western Europe. European governments first sought to establish an independent conflict-management mechanism through the West European Union, but in the face of U.S. opposition eventually accepted a subordinate position as an independent security pillar under NATO. In the 1990s, the United States assumed the lead role in the European security regime, beginning with U.S.-led NATO strikes on Bosnian Serb positions in 1994–95. The United States also spearheaded economic sanctions against Yugoslavia to induce Belgrade to cut off supplies to the Serb rebels. In 1995, American diplomats successfully pressured the combatants and their regional patrons to sign the Dayton Peace Agreement in Paris, deploying sixty thousand NATO peacekeepers to enforce the accords. Most dramatically, the United States was the primary intervenor in the showdown with Milošević over Kosovo—culminating in an extended NATO bombing campaign upon Yugoslav territory. Upon Serbian withdrawal from Kosovo, the United States took a leading role in providing security to the Kosovo protectorate, with the UN managing the political transition. The United States and NATO also contained the cross-border insurgency from Kosovo to Macedonia in 2001—mediating the Ohrid Framework Agreement and overseeing its implementation.

Under the George W. Bush administration in the early 2000s, the United States began to withdraw from the European security regime. At the same time, the EU accelerated its efforts to establish an independent military capacity with the Common Security and Defense Policy (CSDP).[16] In 2004, a seven-thousand-troop EU force (EUFOR) replaced the NATO force in Bosnia; according to agreement, it would make use of existing NATO bases and infrastructure. The EU has since assumed nearly full control over the international administration of Bosnia, with the Bosnian EU special representative double-hatted as the Bosnian high commissioner. The United States continues to maintain a presence there, with U.S. and NATO bases throughout the region, including a large U.S. base in Kosovo and an indefinite mandate for the U.S.-led NATO peacekeeping force, KFOR. However, it has handed off most of its hard security tasks to the EU. The UN transitional authority in Kosovo has closed up shop, and the government of Kosovo has taken over the core functions of the state. The EU Rule of Law Mission in Kosovo provides legal, advisory, and technical assistance to the government. The 2000s thus witnessed the general retrenchment of the United States (and NATO) from Central and Eastern Europe in favor of the Caspian Sea and Central Asia. At the same time, the EU has developed a more centralized regional security regime, including both monitoring and robust enforcement capacities. The OSCE and the HCNM have seen many of their functions taken over by the EU and are currently casting about for a new role in the European security architecture of the twenty-first century.

In general, the comparison of the interwar and post–Cold War regimes suggests that the more consistent major-power enforcement of the latter played a significant role in its overall stronger record of conflict mediation (particularly when considering the cases of the Baltics and Macedonia). Benjamin Miller writes that "by placing limitations on local military capabilities and by constructing an effective arms control regime, the great powers can constrain regional actors' ability to resort to force."[17] Indeed, great-power constraints are often essential to maintaining peace in turbulent neighborhoods. The more recent conflicts in Georgia and Ukraine demonstrate that even where regime monitors are deployed to the fullest extent of their mandates, gaps in major-power enforcement can fatally weaken the capacity of regional security regimes.

Managing the Losers in the New System

The effective functioning of any security regime requires building consensus among the principals over whether and how to intervene in every case. This means that veto players represent a constant threat to derail the regime's activities. The interwar regime had formidable veto players—Germany and Russia in particular. With its war-making capacity still largely intact, it seemed clear that the occupation of Germany was needed to prevent revisionism and to consolidate the new post–World War I order. Since Germany's Rhine region was considered a strategic location, it was believed that the Allied powers should occupy this region. Weary of war, however, neither the U.S. public nor its leaders had much appetite for the occupation and withdrew their troops as soon as possible.

Having gained a permanent seat on the League Council in 1926, Germany was able to gum up the system by continually seizing the Council to deliberate the transgressions of its archrival, Poland. Russia, too, worked to obstruct League operations within its own sphere of interest. At the Genoa Conference of 1922, the Great Powers tried in vain to co-opt Germany and Russia in a collective European security system, only to look on helplessly as the two countries secretly negotiated their own agreement on bilateral trade and diplomatic relations prior to the convening of the conference.[18]

Similarly, the veto players of the post–Cold War regime have been its biggest losers—Russia and Serbia. For the past two decades, these two governments have been among the greatest obstacles to the smooth operation of cooperative conflict management in the region. Serbia was largely responsible for triggering the violence in the Bosnian and Croatian wars and, later on, the conflict in Kosovo. It was clearly necessary to co-opt Belgrade into the conflict-management process. Serbian cooperation in ending the Bosnian War was mainly secured through promises of ending sanctions against Yugoslavia. Although Serbia continued to foment tensions in Kosovo and Montenegro into the 2000s, these conflicts were also greatly ameliorated once the EU began accession negotiations with Serbia in 2005.

Turning to Russia, it is clear that integrating the Baltics into Western security structures was a serious blow to Russia's great-power aspirations. Not only did the newly independent states contain large Russian-speaking populations, but they were former Soviet Republics. Russia objected strenuously to NATO expansion to Central Europe and the Balkans; the Yeltsin government warned ominously that NATO enlargement to former Warsaw Pact countries would be met with hostility. Moscow also vehemently opposed the NATO war over Kosovo and insisted on a coequal role in the postwar administration through the United Nations. Western governments managed Russian obstructionism partly through promises of assistance (in the case of the Baltics) and partly through UN institutions (in the case of Kosovo). Russia accepted NATO expansion to Central Europe and the Baltics in return for a consultative status in NATO as well as commitments of state aid during the financially turbulent 1990s.

Russia has acted as a far greater impediment to conflict management in the Caucasus and Central Asia, as a direct or indirect participant in the territorial conflicts of Transnistria, Nagorno-Karabakh, and South Ossetia and Abkhazia, Crimea and Eastern Ukraine. In none of these interventions were the rights of Russian minorities the central impetus for Russian intervention. This speaks to the formidable geopolitical stakes of nested conflicts. The OSCE and the HCNM, which operate with the consent of the conflict participants, have enjoyed limited success in addressing disputes in the Commonwealth of Independent States, where government consent has been less than forthcoming. Integrating all involved regional players into robust security organizations may be the answer—not only for constraining intervening kin states, but also for inducing host states to improve their treatment of beleaguered minorities.[19] It is no accident that the internal conflicts in the Balkans became much easier to manage once the regional players began accession negotiations with NATO and the EU. Altogether, this strongly suggests that the co-optation of provocateurs and veto players is critical to the success of domestic conflict reduction.

Proactive Rather Than Reactive

Regional security regimes cannot be the leaders in global conflict management so long as they fail to take on powerful troublemakers. If they fail to address the regional imbalances that create a condition of nested *in*security at the domestic level, such regimes cannot hope to de-escalate emerging communal tensions on the ground.

The first several years of the League's history were disappointing for those who had hoped that the new organization would secure permanent peace on the Continent. In the early 1920s, the Soviets and the Poles waged sporadic battles over the location of their international boundary. At the same time, a Kemalist revolution raged in Turkey, leading to a bloody war with Greece. Germany and Austria, meanwhile, struggled to cope with near-revolutionary social upheaval, and France and Britain bickered over Allied occupation of the Rhineland.[20] There were serious tensions between Romania and Hungary over Transylvania; between Yugoslavia and Italy over Dalmatia and the city-port Fiume (Rijeka); between Poland and Germany over Upper Silesia; and between Poland and Czechoslovakia over Teschen. To complicate matters, Soviet Russia and a nationalist Turkey threatened to destabilize enemy countries and crush fledgling states on their borders.[21] In each of these conflicts, the League either failed to intervene or simply institutionalized power realities on the ground because it relied on consensus decision-making and had no independent means of enforcing its decisions. In 1922, the League even failed to protest French and Belgian occupation of the industrial Ruhr region of Germany—because France was a permanent member of the Council, and Britain did not want to alienate the Continental power by sanctioning it.

The late 1920s and early 1930s represented the high point of League efficacy, bringing a new mood of internationalism to the capitals of Europe. The new governments of Britain and France proclaimed that the League covenant would serve as the "keystone of its foreign policy."[22] They decided that the League Council would meet at regular intervals, four times a year; state foreign ministers attended the Council and Assembly meetings regularly. A forum began to form between the Great Powers and smaller states, lending it the appearance of something akin to a world government. People began to speak excitedly of "the atmosphere of Geneva."[23] By the early 1930s, the Minorities Department staff had more than doubled, and the budget for the Minorities Section increased from 175,000 to more than 333,000 Swiss francs.[24] Between 1921 and 1929, no fewer than 150 Committees of Three were formed to consider petitions; by 1931, 525 petitions for redress had been sent to the League.[25] In a number of cases, including those of the Hungarians in Transylvania and the conflicts in Upper Silesia, the League's interventions were deemed successful.

As the regime's veto players grew more powerful in the 1930s, the League increasingly catered to their interests. Petitions from Germany and Hungary concerning co-ethnics in neighboring countries began to increase in frequency, leading the German and Hungarian minorities to radicalize their demands accordingly. From 1929 onward, the League Council was primarily occupied with meeting the demands of revisionist states and veto players, who continued to radicalize despite the best efforts of League authorities.[26]

In many ways, today's European security regime is also largely reactive, basing its mediations on the prevailing balance of power in each national struggle. For example, the EC affirmed its support for the territorial integrity of Yugoslavia so long as Belgrade enjoyed the upper hand in the conflicts. When Croatia and Slovenia effectively broke free, the EC recognized their independence. In 1991, the Badinter Commission hedged its earlier position by declaring that the secessionist movements could take place only along *internal republican* borders. However, the EU tentatively recognized Kosovo independence (*not* an internal republican border) in 2008 because of strong U.S. backing. In Bosnia, the Dayton Accords institutionalized the final battle lines at the end of the war, and the EU green-lighted a popular referendum on Montenegrin independence when it could no longer keep the rump Yugoslavia together. While some territorial conflicts were successfully managed *within* the borders of existing states, other secessionist movements succeeded in gaining statehood and recognition by Europe's security organizations. The most striking cases of success (the Åland Islands for the League and the Baltics and Macedonia for the EU/OSCE) were cases in which the regime's enforcers identified the problem early and moved quickly to neutralize it (for example, by containing cross-border conflict dynamics or co-opting external provocateurs). In most cases, success requires that the regime act early and *proactively* rather than *reactively*.

Scholars of interwar Europe have written extensively on the "failure" of the League security regime. The conventional view was that the system was still-born because of the lack of enforcement powers. A more generous assessment is that the League *did* succeed insofar as it managed a series of territorial disputes in the 1920s, while responding to hundreds of minority complaints, thereby lending the regime legitimacy in the eyes of the participants, including the losers of the system. Evidence for this is that numerous minorities and national homeland governments—many of whom had initially rejected the League's authority—ultimately accepted League arbitration.

Today, many scholars have arrived at a more balanced view of the League's record, which is that the minorities regime was only one piece of the machinery needed for effective conflict management. As one scholar put it, "The twenty-year life-span granted to the League of Nations was not sufficient to establish a completely new legal system and procedure," noting that the region was "marked by political and social conflicts of almost unprecedented magnitude."[27] Moreover, collective-security regimes require both monitors and enforcers to work; and by the 1930s, the League increasingly operated in the absence of major-power backstopping. The analysis in this book demonstrates that the League succeeded where it enjoyed Great Power leverage to "nest" ethnic relations at the domestic level in stable regional environments. As noted by a well-known scholar of the League, "The 'Geneva system' was not a substitute for great-power politics . . . but rather an adjunct to it. It was only a mechanism for conducting multinational diplomacy whose success or failure depended on the willingness of the states, and particularly the most powerful states, to use it."[28]

What hope does this offer for the future of European conflict management? There is some evidence that the post–Cold War regime has already avoided the mistakes of the past. Whereas in the interwar period France and Britain enforced League decisions in an ad hoc manner, the current regime enjoys the backing of NATO and the EU. In Europe today, there is a regularized permanent force structure in place, as well as a procedure for evaluating and prescribing responses to each conflict. There was no such force structure available to the League, the authorities of which depended on ad hoc decisions by national governments to provide troops, logistical support, and other resources to back up their decisions where needed. This meant that the League could not respond in a timely manner to the Lithuanian capture of Memel nor to the Polish capture of Vilnius, nor did it intercede in a timely fashion to halt the violent Silesian uprisings in the early 1920s. In the current period, by contrast, NATO was able to respond quickly to conflict contagion from Kosovo to Macedonia, effectively containing it.

Despite improvements over earlier models, the current European security regime remains dependent on the proactive engagement of the major powers. It took NATO more than two years to intervene forcefully to end the Bosnian War, by which time tens of thousands had died and hundreds of thousands had taken flight. The international community also failed to prevent the ethnic cleansing of Serbs from Kosovo in the early days of the transitional administration and during the 2004 pogrom against Serb civilians by Albanian extremists. International programs of minority return and property restitution in Croatia, Bosnia, and Kosovo were similarly handicapped by the reluctance of administrators and peacekeepers to ensure that refugees could return safely to their prewar homes and rebuild their lives. Farther east, Europe's security regime failed to forestall a Russian incursion into South Ossetia in 2008 and did little to prevent Russian forces from effectively annexing Crimea or ginning up violence in the eastern regions of Ukraine in 2014. What this shows is that even the most technically proficient international mediation is unlikely to achieve success in the absence of proactive hegemonic engagement.

What does this say for regional security regimes beyond Europe? Such regimes are clearly permitted, if not encouraged, under international law. Chapter 8, Article 53, of the UN Charter states: "The Security Council shall, where appropriate, utilize such regional arrangements or agencies for enforcement action under its authority." Beyond Europe, the most elaborated regime is in Africa. The conflict-management mechanism under the Organization for African Unity has been replaced by the African Union's Permanent Security Council, an organization composed of fifteen African states, to provide collective security and early warning of crisis situations. In Asia, the ASEAN Regional Forum is the closest to a regional security regime, with nineteen member countries, including Russia, the EU, Canada, the United States, and Australia. Although dedicated to preventive diplomacy, it is at present merely a deliberative forum in which member states meet to exchange security concerns. To be effective, it would have to have the active backing of China and Japan, at minimum. A third region badly in need of a security regime is the Middle East and North Africa—where all or most domestic conflicts are embedded in intractable regional conflicts.

To establish effective regional security regimes, three features must be present. First, a decision-making body must be established that can cope with internal veto players as well as member-state aggression. Second, a regularized, independent enforcement mechanism must be created with the full backing of regional hegemons and/or great powers. Finally, the regime must engender cooperation between monitors and enforcers to provide effective conflict management at all stages of the conflict—from preventive diplomacy to postwar reconstruction. Whether such regimes can be developed depends on the willingness of regional hegemons to invest in missions of long-term conflict management, which are costly and do not always serve the hegemon's immediate interests. Securing significant investment from regional powers, while protecting against exploitation, remains the most difficult task for the designers of regional security regimes. Yet it is also critical for preventing communal tensions from escalating to internecine civil and inter-state war.

NOTES

Introduction

1. OSCE 2014.
2. Loiko 2014.
3. Oliver 2014.
4. Mihai Gribincea, interview with the author, The Hague, Netherlands, November 14, 2002. In Georgia, the OSCE mission was not renewed after 2008.
5. This book uses Stephen Krasner's definition of international regime as a "set of implicit or explicit principles, norms, rules, and decision-making procedures around which actors' expectations converge in a given area of international relations" (Krasner 1982, 3). *International security regimes* consist of a set of principles, norms, rules and decision-making procedures for ensuring stability and peace within a given supra-state territorial remit.
6. *Mediators* or *conflict managers* are third parties that intervene in a conflict to restore stability to a conflict state and/or region. I use the terms *mediations* and *cooperative interventions* interchangeably when referring to third parties that intervene with the explicit intent to reduce the conflict. Mediations themselves may involve one or more third parties working separately or in concert. External conflict managers can be individual diplomats, state governments, international organizations, or regional associations; they may be unilateral or multilateral, ad hoc or undertaken under the rubric of security regimes. It goes without saying that they are nonparticipants in the conflict. For more on the value of third-party involvement in managing conflicts see Asal et al. 2005.
7. For an authoritative overview of minority rights and self-determination in international law see Hannum 1996. See also Wippman 1998. For historical reviews of the principle of self-determination see especially Cassese 1995 and Buchheit 1978. See Preece 1997, and Krasner 1999, chapter 3, for concise overviews of minority rights in Europe from the 1555 Peace of Augsburg to the 1995 Dayton Accords. See also Muldoon 1983 for detailed surveys of minority protections in Westphalia and other international treaties.
8. These territories were to retain the religion they had practiced in 1624, even if this went against the wishes of the then ruler.
9. Strauss 1949.
10. Under the 1878 Treaty of Berlin, European powers guaranteed the sovereignty of new Balkan states—including Serbia, Romania, and Montenegro—in return for pledges by each state that it would respect the rights of its ethnic and religious minorities (Toynbee and Israel 1967, 978, Article IV). The 1881 International Convention of Constantinople included provisions for Muslims living in areas of Greek control (Lerner 1991, 7–8). As before, minority protections were included as a security consideration rather than out of a real concern for the people on the ground. Primarily, the Great Powers wanted to ensure

stability of the Balkan region and prevent the out-migration of disgruntled or persecuted minorities to Western Europe (see Krasner 1982, 84–90, for a detailed discussion of these treaties).

11. The Organization for Security and Co-operation in Europe (formerly the Conference on Security and Co-operation in Europe) was originally established as a Cold War–era institution to help member states from both the East and West blocs find solutions to common problems. At the end of the Cold War, it was renamed the OSCE and simultaneously given a more institutionalized status with a well-elaborated mechanism for conflict prevention and crisis management; today it has fifty-seven members and is the largest such organization in the world. The High Commissioner on National Minorities is an organization operating under the OSCE that uses "quiet diplomacy" and other technical methods to resolve emerging sectarian conflicts that threaten to spill over state borders. For a comprehensive overview of the OSCE conflict and dispute resolution mechanisms see Bothe, Ronzitti, and Rosas 1997.

12. Robinson et al. 1943, 35. It should be noted that, despite these defects, the postwar settlement placed far fewer nationals outside their "homeland" states than did the prewar borders (Galántai 1992, 13).

13. Galántai 1992, 19–22.

14. Sharp 1979, 175.

15. Although the resulting document is known as the Treaty of Versailles, almost all the negotiations took place within Paris itself. The draft treaty was signed on June 28, 1919, by German leaders in Versailles; subsequent treaties modeled after this one were signed by Austria in September 1919 in Saint-Germaine-en-Laye; Bulgaria in November 1919 in Neuilly; Hungary in June 1920 in the Grand Trianon; and Turkey in August 1921 in Sèvres.

16. Headlam-Morley 1972, 109–10, as cited in Raitz von Frentz 1999, 64.

17. Naimark 2002; Eberhardt 2003; Hayden 1996.

18. Both the UN Charter and the 1948 Universal Declaration of Human Rights give precedence to individual and state rights over those of groups. Moreover, minority rights were generally limited to *integrationist* rights (e.g., the prohibition against nondiscrimination) at the end of World War II. For an enumeration of UN covenants dealing with minorities see Hannum 1996.

19. M. E. Brown 1996, 12.

20. See, for example, Kaplan 1994; Van Evera 1994; M. E. Brown 1993; Mearsheimer 1990; Snyder 1993.

21. European Community 1991; emphasis mine.

22. See Trbovich 2008 for an excellent account of this episode. See also Caplan 2005; Gow 1997; Conversi 1998; Wolff 2008.

23. In 1995, the CSCE was formally renamed the Organization for Security and Co-operation in Europe.

24. Pamphlet No. 9 of the UN Guide for Minorities, 2.

25. Hannum 2001; Oberleitner 1999.

26. These criteria drew heavily on the standards set by the OSCE and the Council of Europe (Hughes and Sasse 2003, 9).

27. See, in particular, Carr 1946. For more contemporary arguments see Krasner and Froats 1998; Joffe 1992; Kupchan and Kupchan 1995.

28. Stone 1932, vii.

29. Ackerman 2000; Kemp 2001; Lund 1996; Bothe, Ronzitti, and Rosas 1997; Zaagman 1999; Horváth 2002; Lahelma 1999.

30. Hopmann 2003.

31. Warren Christopher, Intervention at the North Atlantic Council of Ministerial Meeting at Noordwijk, Netherlands, May 30, 1995, U.S. Department of State *Dispatch 6*, No. 23 (June 5, 1995), 471–74.

32. Steiner 2005, 299.

33. Krasner 1999, 96.

1. The Promises and Pitfalls of Cooperative Conflict Management

1. I use "intra-state," "communal," "civil," and "substate" conflicts interchangeably to refer to disputes between the groups within a state, be they based on ethnic or ideological grounds. The empirical portion of the book applies the model to the specific conflicts between ethnic minorities and the dominant group or state center in interwar and postcommunist Central and Eastern Europe.

2. The terms "mediation," "cooperative intervention," and "cooperative conflict management" are used interchangeably to denote noncoercive third-party interventions aimed at de-escalating disputes before they generate more violence—cooperative techniques are usually (although not always) employed in the early stages of the conflict. By contrast, *conflict resolution* is intended to halt armed hostilities once significant violence has already emerged, and *post-conflict reconstruction* aims to rebuild war-torn societies and prevent the reemergence of armed hostilities. All these techniques fall under the broad rubric of conflict management. While cooperative techniques can and have been used to manage both violent and nonviolent conflict, they are mostly reserved for the early (largely nonviolent) stage of conflict.

3. Lederach 1997, 73–74.

4. United Nations, "Secretary-General Says Proposals in His Report on Africa Require New Ways of Thinking, of Acting" (1998), un.org, Press Release SG/SM/6524, April 16, 1998 para. 5, http://www.un.org/press/en/1998/19980416.SGSM6524.html.

5. United Nations, General Assembly / Security Council, "Identical letters dated 21 August 2000. . . ." http://unrol.org/files/brahimi%20report%20peacekeeping.pdf.

6. Some of these NGOs directly mediate internal conflicts, whereas others are advocacy organizations. For more on this see Wolff and Yakinthou 2012.

7. For a summary of these efforts see Ackermann 2003; Björkdahl 2002; Brown and Rosecrance 1999; Carment and Schnabel 2003; Carment and James 1998; Lund, Rasamoelina, and Network 2000.

8. Regan, Frank, and Aydin 2009, 142–43.

9. Zartman and Touval 2007; Touval and Zartman 1985; Young 1972.

10. Stedman 1995; Lund 1995, 14. Of course, where multiple parties intervene in a single conflict, there is a countervailing risk of competing intervention agendas and poor coordination.

11. Boulding 1989. Cooperative interventions aim at de-escalating substate conflicts without the use of force and include technical assistance or "good offices" for mediation or arbitration (Crocker, Hampson, and Aall 2004); electoral engineering (Horowitz 1985; Reilly and Reynolds 1999); and political conditionality (Vachudova 2005; Kelley 2004a, 2004b). Coercive techniques of conflict management involve force or threat of force, including economic compellence (Stedman 1996), peace enforcement (Haass 1994; Cooper and Berdal 1993; Snow 1993; Jakobsen 1996; Kaufmann 2007, 1998, 1996; Downes 2004), and peacekeeping missions (Durch 1996; Fortna 2004).

12. The U.S. Army defines "low-intensity" conflicts as "the level of hostilities or use of military power that falls short of a full-scale conventional or general war." I adopt the

Uppsala Conflict Data Program (UCDP) measure of low-intensity conflict as any militarized dispute that generates fewer than twenty-five deaths per year.

13. On the moral hazard of intervention see especially Kuperman 2001 and Jenne 2007.

14. Ayres 2000; Toft 2009; Regan, Frank, and Aydin 2009. It should be noted that Toft and others, including Chapman, Thomas, and Roeder (2007), have been highly critical of negotiated solutions to conflicts, arguing that decisive military victories have proven more durable.

15. The following chapter outlines the precise indicators that will be used to measure shifts in communal tensions.

16. Buhaug and Gleditsch 2008; Gleditsch 2007.

17. Modelski 1964, 18.

18. Goertz 1995.

19. Uppsala Conflict Data Program (UCDP) armed conflict dataset, as cited in Harbom and Wallensteen 2005, 629.

20. Adamson 2006, 2005; Salehyan 2009; Davis and Moore 1997; Gleditsch 2007; Checkel 2013; Zartman and Touval 2007; Touval and Zartman 1985.

21. Lischer 2003, 2005; Salehyan and Gleditsch 2006; Salehyan 2007; Lake and Rothchild 1998.

22. See especially Weiner 1996.

23. Salehyan 2009, 15–17.

24. Saideman 1997, 2001.

25. Salehyan 2009.

26. Hill and Rothchild 1992, 1986; Hill, Rothchild, and Cameron 1998.

27. Beissinger 2002; Weyland 2012; Lotan et al. 2011.

28. Goertz and Diehl 1993.

29. See, for example, Toft 2003.

30. Cunningham 2006, 2011.

31. M.E. Brown 1993; Lake and Rothchild 1998.

32. Mylonas 2012; Davis and Moore 1997; Saideman and Ayres 2000; Cetinyan 2003.

33. Saideman and Ayres 2008; Heraclides 1991.

34. See the following chapter for a more extensive discussion of this argument.

35. A "minority" is defined as a group that is numerically inferior to the politically dominant group in the state. "State," "majority," "dominant group," and "central or host government" are used interchangeably throughout the book to refer to the state center with which the minority bargains.

36. Bercovitch 1992, 8.

37. Ban Ki-Moon delivered a report to the UNSC recommending that a mediation capacity be established under the auspices of the UN; this led to a General Assembly resolution to that effect in July 2011. UNSG, "Enhancing Mediation and Its Support Activities," UN Doc. S/2009/189, April 8, 2009; UNGA Res., UN Doc. A/RES/65/283, July 28, 2011.

38. Wallensteen 2014, 16–17.

39. "Regional security regimes" are akin to Buzan and Wæver's "regional security complex" (Buzan and Wæver 2003; see also Lake and Morgan 1997a, 1997b) but are defined more narrowly. State governments establish regional security regimes to provide hard security in a geographically delimited space. The regime's strength and scope are determined by its architects and enforcers—usually regional, and sometimes extra-regional, state powers. By contrast, regional security complexes are defined more broadly to encompass human security, identity, and societal security, as well as hard security.

40. Engberg 2014, 81.

41. Bercovitch and Gartner 2006, 348.

42. Hansen, Mitchell, and Nemeth 2008.

43. See also Diehl et al. 2003.

44. Chigas, McClintock, and Kamp 1996; Peck 2001.

45. Engberg 2014, 81.

46. Lake and Morgan 1997a, 5.

47. Wallensteen and Bjurner 2014, appendix 2.

48. The ASEAN member states established the ASEAN Regional Forum in 1994 to promote peace in the region through "dialogue and cooperation." The twenty-seven ARF member countries include the ten ASEAN member countries as well as ten "dialogue partners" (Australia, Canada, China, the EU, India, Japan, New Zealand, ROK, Russia, and the United States) and seven other Southeast Asian countries. In 2011, the ministers agreed to establish a work plan for developing a preventive diplomacy capacity (http://aseanregionalforum.asean.org/).

49. Kioko 2003.

50. MINA (Miraj Islamic News Agency), http://mirajnews.com/asia/3141-oic-launches-peace-security-and-mediation-unit-at-its-headquarters.html. See also Wolff and Dursun-Ozkanca 2012.

51. While it is true that European powers have engaged in conflict management outside the region—for example, UK intervention in Sierra Leone, France in Mali, and EU interventions in the Democratic Republic of the Congo—these efforts do not compare to their decades-long investment of resources and military engagement in the Balkans.

52. Raghavan 2014.

53. Diehl 2008.

54. ECOMOG was established in 1990 by the Economic Community of West African States (ECOWAS) to coordinate multilateral military interventions; to date, it has intervened in civil wars in Liberia, Sierra Leone, and Guinea-Bissau.

55. Nevertheless, lessons from past conflicts in the region may indeed influence mediation success. I discuss these issues in the final chapter, where I address "lessons learned" in the establishment of the regimes as well as the conduct of mediators within each regime.

56. See Walter 1999; Fearon 1998; Lake and Rothchild 1996; Walter 1997, 2002.

57. Stedman 1996; Zahar 2005; Reno 1998.

2. The Theory of Nested Security

1. Lund 1996.

2. Krasner 1999, 104.

3. Kydd 2003, 2006; Touval and Zartman 1985; Carnevale and Arad 1996; and Svensson 2009.

4. See Touval and Zartman 1985. See Diehl and Greig 2012, chap. 4, for good overviews of mediator traits and behavior hypothesized to improve the chances of mediator success. Although explicitly focused on the resolution of violent conflict, much of this literature also has applications for the prevention of deadly conflict.

5. Ratner 2000, 694; see also Kemp 2001.

6. Huber 1994, 3.

7. It should be noted that Ratner identifies a number of endogenous and exogenous preconditions for the success of "normative mediation," including the cooperation of the host government and external kin state, as well as a friendly normative environment.

8. Kelley 2004a, 2004b.

9. Vachudova 2005.

10. There are skeptics who question the impact of EU conditionality. See, for example, Vermeersch 2003. Others note that conditionality can work only under a narrow set of conditions. Namely, the promise of rewards must be credible, the rewards significant and imminent, and the conditions clearly articulated and binding (Schimmelfennig and Sedelmeier 2005a, chap. 1).

11. Jenne 2007.

12. Csergő 2007.

13. Early conditionality scholarship focused on the lending practices of international financial institutions. The concept of conditionality took on a new meaning in the post–Cold War period as NATO, the European Community, and the Council of Europe prepared for eastward expansion. At a 1993 meeting in Copenhagen, it was decided that prospective members to the EC must meet a set of conditions known as the "Copenhagen criteria" before they could be admitted to the EC. There are a number of mechanisms by which European standards and norms have been propagated outside EU borders, including norms transfer (Checkel 2001; Börzel and Risse 2003), lesson-drawing (Dolowitz and Marsh 2000), and external incentives (Schimmelfennig 2000; Kelley 2003; Kelley 2004a, 2004b; Vachudova 2005). For a useful overview of this literature see Schimmelfennig and Sedelmeier 2005a, chap. 1.

14. Kaufman 2006; R. Taylor 2001.

15. The mediation literature on civil war takes a more symmetrical approach to conflict management, arguing that mediation is more likely to yield peace when the conflict is protracted, the combatants are at an impasse and are willing to accept a compromise (Bercovitch 1984; Bercovitch and Houston 1996). Breakthroughs can be expected where the conflict is "ripe" for resolution or where there is a "hurting stalemate," such that neither party can prevail in conflict and therefore both have an incentive to search for a peaceful solution (Zartman 2001; Pruitt 1997). These factors are less relevant for conflict settings short of mass violence.

16. Salehyan 2009; Salehyan and Gleditsch 2006.

17. Suhrke and Noble 1977; M. E. Brown 1993; Lake and Rothchild 1998; Carment and James 1995, 1997; Brecher and Wilkenfeld 1997.

18. Sarkees, Wayman, and Singer 2003, 62.

19. Midlarsky 1992; Rosenau 1964.

20. Huth 2009; Hensel 1996; Holsti 1991.

21. Fair 2005; Wayland 2004; Jenne 2003.

22. Gleditsch and Beardsley 2004, 899.

23. Gleditsch, Salehyan, and Schultz 2008, 480.

24. On the regional nature of civil conflict see Bercovitch and Fretter 2004.

25. Lemke 1996, 82.

26. Saideman 1998, 2001.

27. Davis and Moore 1997.

28. Lemke 2002.

29. Weiner 1996.

30. Jenne 2007, 2004; Thyne 2006; Elbadawi and Sambanis 2002.

31. I am grateful to Stuart Kaufman for raising this point.

32. For more on these competing theories of mobilization see Cederman, Min, and Wimmer 2010; Kaufman 2001; Jenne 2007; Saideman and Ayres 2000; Collier and Hoeffler 2004; Birnir 2007.

33. Demmers 2007.

34. Jenne 2004, 2007; Cetinyan 2003.

35. Beardsley 2011.

36. Although endogenous stabilization usually follows exogenous stabilization, the two processes might occur consecutively or simultaneously. However, endogenous stabilization does not occur in every case. In so-called "frozen conflicts" (such as South Ossetia, Abkhazia, and Transnistria), for example, stabilization is entirely exogenous; as predicted, the participants of the conflict remain mobilized in such settings with the lines of conflict frozen.

37. O'Donoghue and Punch 2003, 78.

3. Preventive Diplomacy in Interwar Europe

1. The treaties could not be contravened without majority consent of the League Council. In some treaties, membership in the League was made contingent upon the state's compliance with the mandated minority protections. Although this may resemble EU/NATO membership conditionality, League membership was not valuable enough to the target states to adequately leverage League diplomacy.

2. Sir James Headlam-Morley, *A Memoir of the Paris Peace Conference, 1919* (London: Methuen, 1972), 109, as cited in Lund 1996 and Ratner 2000, 64.

3. It should be noted, however, that Jewish minorities in CEE enjoyed the support of Jewish organizations in the West, which lobbied for their protection.

4. Of the 314 petitions submitted on behalf of ethnic Germans in Poland, approximately 50 complaints were taken up by the League, only a few of these were brought before the Council, and none were satisfactorily resolved, according to minority leaders (Blanke 1993, 130, 132).

5. Jenne 2007, 2004; Cetinyan 2003.

6. Macartney 1968, 372–73.

7. Mazower 2004.

8. Raitz von Frentz 1999.

9. Fink 2006.

10. Scheuermann 2000.

11. Pedersen 2007, 1093.

12. Krasner and Froats 1998; Krasner 1999.

13. Northedge 1986; Walters 1986.

14. Krasner 1999, 94–95.

15. Blanke 1993.

16. The Germans in Poland were not a monolithic group. The overwhelming majority of Germans resided in western Poland and strongly identified with Germany. However, the minority of Germans in former Habsburg-controlled Galicia and former Russian-controlled regions identified less strongly with Germany (Komjathy and Stockwell 1980, 71–72; Jaworski 1991, 170–74). The Germans of Upper Silesia and Danzig had special arrangements under the League and so are not dealt with here.

17. The Sudeten German case narrative draws substantially from Jenne 2007, chap. 3.

18. Bugajski 1994, 294.

19. Wingfield 1989, 5.

20. Dietrich Vogt, *Der grosspolnische Aufstand 1918–1919* (Marburg: Herder-Institut, 1980), 21, quoted in Blanke 1993, 11.

21. Wiskemann 1956, 95.

22. "Poslední zprávy, Němci v Čechách budou 'osvobozeni'" [Latest news: Germans in the Czech lands will be "liberated"], *Lidové Noviny*, November 22, 1919; emphasis mine.

23. Komjathy and Stockwell 1980, 3. Only cultural, educational, or religious organizations were permitted to have contact with *Volksdeutsche*, and the activities of these organizations were strictly monitored by the host governments.

24. Raitz von Frentz 1999, 143.

25. There are two important reasons why Germany extended greater support to ethnic Germans in Poland than in Czechoslovakia. Besides the fact that the Sudeten Germans suffered less discrimination, Germany had a territorial claim on western Poland that it did not have on the Sudeten region (which had been part of Austria). Second and relatedly, Germany had a more antagonistic relationship with Poland than it did with Czechoslovakia; Berlin therefore had a vested interest in supporting Poland's internal enemies.

26. Lippelt 1971, 328.

27. Stachura 1998, 61.

28. Raitz von Frentz 1999, 145–46.

29. Komjathy and Stockwell 1980, 67.

30. Blanke 1993, 41–43.

31. Chief Bureau of Statistics of the Republic of Poland, *Concise Statistical Year-Book of Poland*, 1937 (Warsaw: Chief Bureau of Statistics, 1937), cited by Komjathy and Stockwell 1980, 74.

32. Blanke 1993, 13.

33. Komjathy and Stockwell 1980, 18.

34. "Minority states" were the new or newly enlarged states that signed treaties at the end of World War I committing them to protect their national minorities as a condition of international recognition.

35. Campbell 1975, 82–83.

36. It was largely because of this law that almost half of all German state employees (excluding teachers) lost their jobs between 1921 and 1930 (Campbell 1975, 82).

37. Campbell 1975, 82.

38. Masaryk 1933, 19–22.

39. "Naši němci o rozhodnutí konference" [Our Germans on the conference decision], *Lidové Noviny*, May 11, 1919.

40. Bugajski 1994, 295.

41. Stachura 1998, 70–71.

42. Adam Próchnik, *Pierwsze piętnostolecie Polski niepodległy* (Warsaw: Książka i Wiedza, 1957), 279, quoted in Blanke 1993, 10.

43. Blanke 1993, 13.

44. Ibid., 15–17. Stachura notes that, despite Poland's draconian policies in western Poland, Germans in Poland were "allowed extensive freedom to use their own language and organize their own press, cultural associations, libraries, sports clubs, schools, cooperatives, even banks. From time to time the cash strapped Polish government even provided limited funding for some of these activities." They were also permitted to establish their own parties and contest elections, with German representatives in the Sejm and the Senate (Stachura 1998, 72).

45. Fink 1972.

46. Healam-Morley memorandum, February 7, 1922, PRO, London, FO 371, W1030/48/98, as cited in Fink 1972, 335.

47. Raitz von Frentz 1999, 130–31.

48. Eser 2007.

49. Polonsky 1972, 90.

50. Mair 1928, 119–25.

51. Raitz von Frentz 1999; emphasis mine.

52. Kurt Doß, *Zwischen Weimar und Warschau. Ulrich Rauscher. Deutscher Gesandter in Polen 1922–1930. Eine politische Biographie* (Düsseldorf: Droste, 1984), 125, quoted in Raitz von Frentz 1999, 174.

53. Raitz von Frentz 1999, 167.
54. Kopecek 1996, 69.
55. Campbell 1975, 164.
56. Spuler 1953, 512–13.
57. *Národní Shromáždění*, 374.
58. Ibid., 1192.
59. Chmelař 1926, 70–71.
60. Wingfield 1989, 82–83.
61. Campbell 1975, 202.
62. Roberts 1953, 587–88.
63. Weinberg 1995, 42.
64. Von Riekhoff 1971, 310.
65. Ibid., 295.
66. Blanke 1993, 66–67; Raitz von Frentz 1999, 147–48.
67. Raitz von Frentz 1999, 149–50; Blanke 1993, 67.
68. Lippelt 1971.
69. Von Riekhoff 1971, 164.
70. Ibid., 171.
71. Lippelt 1971.
72. Torzecki 1989, 148.
73. Kacprzak 2007.
74. Von Riekhoff 1971, 214.
75. Robinson et al. 1943, 251.
76. Stresemann to all German Missions, Berlin, March 18, 1927, 3147/1550/D658541–46, as cited in Fink 1972, 341–42.
77. Ratliff 1988, 180.
78. Raitz von Frentz 1999, 186.
79. Wiskemann 1956, 34.
80. Komjathy and Stockwell 1980.
81. The SdP declared that although the memorandum was an inadequate solution to Sudeten German problems, they would not obstruct its implementation (Hodža 1942, 145). In this way, the SdP could take credit for the successes of the German activists while remaining in opposition.
82. Bierschenk 1954, 34.
83. Eser 2007, 40.
84. Polonsky 1972, 377.
85. Cited in Leslie 1983, 183.
86. Officially, the document was not called a pact, but a declaration. In Germany, it is also known as Piłsudski-Hitler-Pakt.
87. Raitz von Frentz 1999.
88. Horak 1961, 111.
89. Fink 2006.
90. Cornwall 2007, 138–39.
91. Komjathy and Stockwell 1980, 39.
92. Polonsky 1972, 377.
93. Raitz von Frentz 1999, 253–54.
94. Kees 1994, 114–17.
95. Although the country was given the name Yugoslavia only in 1929, I use this name throughout the interwar period for the sake of convenience.
96. Zeidler 2003, 80.
97. I do not examine the Hungarian minority in Yugoslavia because the League did not actively mediate this conflict.

98. Rouček 1971, 140.
99. Magda 1995, 148.
100. Meeting of the Hungarian delegation, May 10, 1920, in Francis Deák and Dezső Ujváry, eds., *Papers and Documents Relating to the Foreign Relations of Hungary*, vol. 1, *1919–1920* (Budapest: Royal Hungarian Ministry for Foreign Affairs, 1939), 920, as cited in Cameron J. Watson, "Ethnic Conflict and the League of Nations: The Case of Transylvania, 1918–1940," *Hungarian Studies* 9 (1–2): 173–80.
101. Mair 1928, 153.
102. According to one scholar, "Czechoslovakia alone made efforts to enforce the principles laid down in the international minority treaty in its own legislation. Romania and Yugoslavia did their best to negate the treaty's effects" (Szarka 2004, 24).
103. Johnson 1985, 104.
104. These losses were somewhat counterbalanced by the establishment of a Hungarian faculty at Charles University in Prague and an increase in the absolute number of Hungarian language primary schools in the early 1920s.
105. Fischer-Galati 1995, 189.
106. Treaty of Trianon, Article 63, para. 4, http://www.gwpda.org/versa/tri1.htm.
107. [The Basic Principles of the Union of Transylvania's Three Nations] in Elemér Gyárfás, *Erdélyi problémák* [Transylvanian problems] (Cluj-Kolozsvár, 1921), as cited in Balogh 1998, 225, fn6.
108. Szarka 2004, 27–28; emphasis mine.
109. Balogh 1998, 247.
110. Note for the British Representatives at the Council of the League of Nations on the Question of the Expropriation by the Romanian Government of the Property of the Hungarian Optants, Foreign Office, June 27, 1923, C 11257/164/37, in C. Seton-Watson, ed., Confidential Print, series F, vol. 2 (1923–June 1930), 45, in Watson 1994, 174.
111. Watson 1994, 176.
112. Sir Austen Chamberlain to Sir C. Barclay (Budapest), Foreign Office, December 3, 1925, C 15583/261/21, in C. Seton-Watson, ed., Confidential Print, series F, vol. 2, 184, as cited in Watson 1994, 175.
113. *Times* (London), June 23, 1927, as cited in Watson 1994, 176.
114. Rouček 1971, 144–45.
115. Lord Rothermere, formerly Harold Harmsworth, ran an editorial in the *Daily Mail* in June 21, 1927, in which he advocated the return to Hungary of territories it had lost under the Treaty of Trianon.
116. Sakmyster 1980, 50.
117. *Budapesti Hírlap*, January 5, 1933, as cited in Lorman 2005, 295, fn17.
118. Sakmyster 1980, 38–40, 43.
119. Az Est, January 27, 1933; FO 371/16820, 203–9, as cited in Lorman 2005, 298, fn31.
120. Johnson 1985, 229, 253.
121. Hungarian State Archives, Department K, 63, 27/1, November 15, 1932, as cited in Lorman 2005, 293, fn12.
122. Scheuermann 2000, 341.
123. Imre Mikó, *Huszonkét év: Az Erdélyi Magyarság politikai története 1918. December 1-től 1940. Augusztus 30-ig* (Budapest, 1941), as cited in Lorman 2005, 303–7.
124. Macartney 1937, 339.
125. Balogh 1998, 251.
126. Blomqvist 2008, 267.
127. Lorman 2005, 305–6.

128. Ibid., 314.
129. Macartney 1937, 152.
130. Ibid., 183.
131. Ibid.
132. Jelenik 1995, 210.
133. Romsics 1995, 140.

4. Induced Devolution in Interwar Europe

1. *Official Journal, League of Nations*, Special Supplement, no. 3, August 1920, 27, as cited in Barros 1968, 62.
2. Ibid., 27–29, as cited in Barros 1968, 69.
3. Williams 2007, 92–93.
4. P. M. Brown 1921, 268–69.
5. Barros 1968, 92.
6. *Official Journal, League of Nations*, Special Supplement, no. 1, August 1920, 5, in P. M. Brown 1921, 269.
7. The British Foreign Office believed that Finland should relinquish the islands to Sweden in exchange for the territory of Eastern Karelia (Barros 1968). Other proposals included pressuring the Finns to give up the islands or instituting a kind of "Finno-Swedish condominium" over the islands (ibid., 149).
8. Walters 1986, 104.
9. Ibid., 103–4.
10. *Official Journal, League of Nations*, Special Supplement, no. 3, October 1920, 14, point 2.
11. Emphasis mine. *Official Journal, League of Nations*, Special Supplement, no. 3, October 1920, 6.
12. Proposition for the first Autonomy Act, Ålands lagsamling (Mariehamn: Ålands landskapsstyrelse, 2001), 741, trans. Rhodri Williams, in Williams 2007, 94.
13. Padelford and Andersson 1939, 477.
14. Walters 1986, 105.
15. Pekka Kalevi Hämäläinen, *Nationalitetskampen och språkstriden i Finland, 1917–1939* (Helsingfors: Hofer Schildts Förlang, 1968), 34, as cited in Williams 2007, 93.
16. Barros 1968, 341, 337.
17. It was called Klaipėda region in Lithuanian; Memelland in German. Roughly seventy thousand Germans lived in German-speaking Memel; residents of the hinterland mainly spoke Lithuanian.
18. For instance, after Lithuania protested against the commanding general's anti-Lithuanian stance, he was replaced by a civilian high commissioner (Gade 1924).
19. Lord 1923, 56.
20. Safronovas 2009.
21. Vareikis 2001.
22. Eberhardt 2003, 40.
23. Gade 1924, 413.
24. Safronovas 2009.
25. Gade 1924, 413.
26. Safronovas 2009.
27. Cf. Gade 1924, 413; Lord 1923, 56.

28. Gustainis 1939, 615; Akzin 1937, 500.

29. The Conference of Ambassadors of the Principal Allied and Associated Powers was an organization of the victorious Entente Powers formed in January 1920 to manage the peace after World War I. It was the successor to the Supreme War Council, which was founded in 1917 to facilitate preliminary discussions among the Allied powers about the terms of the armistice and peace treaties. The Conference of Ambassadors met on an ad hoc basis during the interwar period, working alongside the League. It often made important decisions concerning the interwar security architecture, as the League Assembly was hamstrung by a unanimity voting requirement, and the League itself had no enforcement powers.

30. Walters 1986, 304.

31. Dean 1935, 696.

32. Vareikis 2001, 64.

33. Walters 1986, 449–50.

34. Kalijarvi 1936, 209.

35. Dean 1935, 696; Nikžentaitis 1996, 765.

36. Dean 1935, 696.

37. Nikžentaitis 1996, 770.

38. Ibid., 770–79.

39. Gustainis 1939, 615.

40. Nikžentaitis 1996, 777; Dean 1935, 696.

41. Nikžentaitis 1996, 778, 780; Kalijarvi 1936, 210.

42. Kalijarvi 1936; Latimer 1935, 11.

43. Gustainis 1939, 615.

44. Dean 1935, 697.

45. Walters 1986, 305.

46. Latimer 1935, 11.

47. Gustainis 1939, 616.

48. Latimer 1935, 10.

49. Quoted from Smogorzewski 1934, 299.

50. Karl Halfar, Danzig und Gdingen, *Erde und Wirtschaft* 5 (1931), as cited by Van Cleef 1933, 103.

51. Von Riekhoff 1971, 367.

52. Walters 1986, 453–54.

53. Latimer 1936, 7.

54. Ibid., 5.

55. Ibid., 7; BSK 1939.

56. Von Riekhoff 1971, 366–67.

57. Walters 1986, 618.

58. Latimer 1936, 6.

59. Lipski 1968, 214, cited by Prazmowska 1992, 80–81.

60. Stahn 2008.

61. Levine 1973.

62. Lipski 1968, 442.

63. Levine 1973.

64. Ibid., 451.

65. "Danzig, Germany and Poland," *Bulletin of International News* (1939) 16 (17): 12–18, 14.

66. Prazmowska 1983, 178.

67. Browning 2004, 31.

5. Preventive Diplomacy in Post–Cold War Europe

1. The HCNM was placed under the auspices of the Conference on Security and Co-operation in Europe (CSCE), which was founded in 1975 with the signing of the Helsinki Final Act to help the East and West to solve inter-state disputes through dialogue. In 1994, the CSCE formally changed its name to the Organization for Security and Co-operation in Europe (OSCE), at which point it assumed the character of a collective security organization. This chapter uses both abbreviations where appropriate.

2. In the course of this work, the high commissioner is mandated to report confidentially to the CSCE chairman-in-office (CSO)—the head of the OSCE who is responsible for the coordination of all the organization's missions and activities. A *formal* early warning is believed to compromise the effectiveness of preventive diplomacy and is therefore used only as a last resort.

3. Conflict Management Group 1993, 6. Roma minorities were not deemed a security risk and therefore did not fall under the HCNM mandate.

4. Vollebaek 2012, 7.

5. Whereas a permanent OSCE mission might be established in a target state to deal more intensively with an internal conflict, the high commissioner serves more as a troubleshooter, traveling to crisis areas on short notice to mediate disputes that have already reached a boiling point.

6. In the course of these mediations, the high commissioner facilitates constructive and continuous dialogue between the disputant parties. The advisers of the HCNM are to assist the target states in designing legislation aimed at integrating the minorities into their respective states and thereby quelling the conflict. So far as possible, the high commissioner conducts mediations confidentially—to encourage target states to utilize HCNM services and promote open exchanges between the feuding sides without fear of popular backlash or reputational costs. Insofar as the minority's external kin state has been involved, the high commissioner consults both target and kin governments in the course of the mediation. As a general rule, the high commissioner encourages target governments to improve their treatment of beleaguered minorities, while admonishing minority leaders and their external patrons to accept compromise solutions to a conflict.

7. It is worth noting two additional features of the HCNM. First, the high commissioner can intervene only with the consent of the target state, as the OSCE has no enforcement mechanism. Second and relatedly, the high commissioner is to maintain strict neutrality in all interventions. In observing these rules, the HCNM closely follows the principles of preventive diplomacy.

8. As of now, only Albania has been admitted to NATO (2009); none have yet been admitted to the EU.

9. The Copenhagen criteria were set forth by the European Council (an institution of the European Union that is made up of the heads of the EU member states) in 1993; the first criterion was that candidate countries demonstrate "stability of institutions guaranteeing democracy, the rule of law, human rights, and respect for and protection of minorities" (European Council 1993). As noted below, this criterion has been widely faulted for its vagueness. The *acquis communautaire* is a French term that refers to the entire body of European Community laws, including rules, policies, objectives, and case law. During accession negotiations, candidate countries must demonstrate that they are in compliance with the *acquis*.

10. Dimitrina Petrova, interview by the author, European Roma Rights Center headquarters, Budapest, October 3, 2002.

11. Marcin Czapliński, interview by the author, The Hague, November 15, 2002.

12. There are two reasons why popular support on the ground is believed vital to the success of such endeavors. First, a public that perceives a realistic opportunity for accession to valued international organizations is more likely to elect a reform-minded government that will respond positively to the international community (Vachudova 2005, chap. 6). It is no accident that the HCNM's greatest success was achieved in the Baltic countries, which "had the best claim to be in Europe." One member of an OSCE mission to the Baltics observed, "Europe had the most to lose by ceding them back to Russia. . . . People cared about getting them in. [This] was seen as a touchstone for the success of the West" (Falk Lange, interview by the author, The Hague, November 15, 2002). Second, if accession is viewed as a realistic possibility, then the government can justify the costs of enacting liberal reforms and avoid the political fallout from a potentially humiliating capitulation. For example, the Latvian president was able to fend off accusations from extremists that he was pandering to Russia or the Russian speakers by pointing out that amending the citizenship law was a strict precondition of EU membership.

13. Pippan 2004; Kelley 2003, 38–41.

14. Schimmelfennig and Sedelmeier 2005b, 13–14.

15. Sasse 2008; Schulze 2010; Rechel 2008; Vermeersch 2003; Hughes, Sasse, and Gordon 2004, chap. 1.

16. Csergő 2007.

17. Sasse 2008.

18. Lepingwell 1994; Simonsen 2001.

19. This figure is from 1991 (Dreifelds 1994, 9).

20. Muižnieks 2006, 120, 129.

21. Meri 1992.

22. Simonsen 2001, 775.

23. Bungs 1992.

24. *Christian Science Monitor*, June 29, 1993, quoted in Ott, Kirch, and Kirch 1996, 21.

25. Kemp 2001, 141–42, 153.

26. Letter to Georgs Andrejevs, minister for foreign affairs of the Republic of Latvia, CSCE Communication 8/94, December 10, 1993.

27. "Russia Sharpens Rhetoric against Estonia," *Summary of Daily News Briefs, Central and Eastern Europe, RFE/RL*, vol. 2, no. 27 (1993): 17, in Huber 1994, 2.

28. It is worth noting that Russia's security threats and delayed troop withdrawals were extended to Lithuania as well, despite the fact that Vilnius had enacted a relatively inclusivist citizenship law and had no salient conflicts with its Russian minority (Kauppila 1999, 30). That Moscow had lumped Lithuania in with the other two republics suggests that its posture was driven more by international and domestic political considerations than by a determination to protect its compatriots where they needed it (as Russian speakers were relatively well treated in that country).

29. Huber 1994, 2–3, 7.

30. Bungs 1992.

31. Chigas, McClintock, and Kamp 1996, 55.

32. Author interview, Aleksei Semjonov, Director, Legal Information Centre for Human Rights, Tallinn, Estonia, December 3, 2008.

33. It should be noted that the U.S. position on NATO expansion evolved over the 1990s, from a commitment to nonexpansion to a determination to enlarge, despite Moscow's strenuous objections. This change was at least partly due to behind-the-scenes lobbying by concerned Nordic countries as well as the Baltic countries themselves.

34. Chigas, McClintock, and Kamp 1996, 18.

35. Ibid., 20.

36. Kemp 2001, 154.

37. *New York Times*, July 7, 1994, as cited in Dreifelds 1996.
38. Kelley 2004a, 167.
39. Pabriks and Purs 2001, 123–24.
40. Aleksei Semjenov, director, Legal Information Centre for Human Rights, Tallinn, Estonia, interview with the author, December 3, 2008.
41. Ash 2000.
42. Nadein 1997.
43. Letter to Valdis Birkavs, minister for foreign affairs of Latvia, April 13, 1999, as cited in Kemp 2001, 163.
44. Lange interview.
45. Pettai and Kallas 2009.
46. Lange interview. According to Lange, the missions were closed because the Clinton administration believed that NATO expansion to the Baltic countries (which would be announced the following year) would be easier to sell to Congress if they were no longer under formal HCNM supervision.
47. Larrabee 2003, 55.
48. Neil Melvin, interview by the author, The Hague, November 12, 2002.
49. Morozov 2004, 322.
50. Galbreath and Lašas 2011, 264.
51. Lamoreaux and Galbreath 2008, 7, 9.
52. Romanova 2009, 150–51.
53. Coffey 2013.
54. Kārkliņa and Lieģis 2006, 148.
55. Viktor Kaluzhny, Regnum, August 30, 2006, as quoted in Latvia's MFA "Press Review," August 31, 2006, cited by Kārkliņa and Lieģis 2006, 151.
56. Spruds 2009, 226–27.
57. Dombrovsky, Vanags, and Muižnieks 2006, 99, 103–9.
58. Estonian Ministry of Foreign Affairs, "Number of Foreign Tourists Doubled in Ten Years," *Estonian Review*, September 26, 2012, http://www.vm.ee/?q=en%2Fnode%2F15465.
59. Tabuns 2010, 258–59.
60. Estonian Ministry of Foreign Affairs, http://www.vm.ee/estonia/kat_399/pea_172/4518.html, as cited in "State Integration Programme 2008–2013 Final Report on Needs and Feasibility Research," http://www.meis.ee/bw_client_files/integratsiooni_sihtasutus/public/img/File/raamatukogu_uuringud/Lopparuanne_LISA_5_2_uuringute_lopparuanne_ENG.pdf, p. 7.
61. *Baltic Course*, "Estonia's Russian-Speaking Population Becomes Increasingly Alienated from the State," Tallinn, September 15, 2010, http://www.baltic-course.com/eng/education/?doc=31621, as cited in Włodarska 2011, 46, fn29.
62. Tabuns 2010, 257. It is noteworthy that there has been more ethnic segregation in the political sphere, where (in contrast to Estonia) ethnic Russians vote for Russian parties; however, this is likely due to the larger size of the Russian minority in Latvia.
63. Tolvaišis 2011, 114–15.
64. Edgar Savisaar, "Kakim mne viditsya budushchee Russkogo voprosa" [How I see the future of the Russian question], April 20, 2011, http://www.keskerakond.ee/savisaar/rus/2011/04/20/, as cited in Tolvaišis 2011, 125.
65. "Keskerakond on mitte-eestlaste seas jätkuvalt populaarseim partei" [The Centre Party is still the most popular party for non-Estonians], *Postimees*, September 23, 2012, http://www.postimees.ee/982022/keskerakond-on-mitte-eestlaste-seas-jatkuvalt-populaarseim-partei.
66. Straumanis 2011.
67. Schwirtz 2011.

68. Schulze 2010.
69. Włodarska 2011, 45–46.
70. The Sandžak Muslims are a territorially concentrated group in southern Serbia bordering on Montenegro and Kosovo. The region was considered a security threat because of the group's ethnic ties to Kosovo and Montenegrin Muslims, their location in the border region, and their compact settlement pattern. However, since the region has shown no signs of ethnic tensions that could lead to violence, I do not deal with this group separately.
71. Since the Yugoslav Republic of Macedonia achieved independence, Athens has opposed its use of the name Macedonia, claiming that doing so implies territorial claims on the northern territories of Greece, also known as Macedonia. The dispute has been temporarily resolved with Skopje's agreement to use the name Former Yugoslav Republic of Macedonia (FYROM) in international settings. However, this interim solution has failed to satisfy either side, with Skopje insisting on going by the Republic of Macedonia, and Athens vowing to block the country's accession to international organizations if Skopje fails to change the country's official name. For good summaries of the two-decade conflict see Vangeli 2011 and Mavromatidis 2010. I use the term Macedonia for the sake of simplicity.
72. It would be years, however, before the country obtained diplomatic recognition, because of a drawn-out dispute over the country's name.
73. Kemp 2001, 199–200.
74. Croatia, Slovakia, and Romania passed similar clauses, to the considerable consternation of their minorities.
75. The main Albanian party has been included in every government since independence.
76. Kemp 2001, 201.
77. Sokalski 2003, 95.
78. Kiro Gligorov, president of the Republic of Macedonia, interview, June 6, 1996, Skopje, as cited in Ackermann 2003.
79. See UNPREDEP mission profile, http://www.un.org/Depts/DPKO/Missions/unpred_p.htm.
80. Sokalski 2003, 108.
81. Stevo Pendarovski, national security adviser to the president, 2001–9, interview by the author, Skopje, July 23, 2013.
82. Sokalski 2003, 184–85.
83. Kemp 2001, 183–84.
84. Ibid., 187.
85. Ibid., 189.
86. Sokalski 2003, 191.
87. Pendarovski interview.
88. Dennis Blease, commander of NATO's Mission in the Republic of Macedonia (2004–5) and military adviser to President Martti Ahtisaari during Kosovo status negotiations (2006–7), interview by Dane Taleski, Skopje, September 16, 2011.
89. Biljana Vankovska, professor of security and peace studies, Cyril and Methodius University, Skopje, interview by the author, Skopje, April 6, 2004.
90. Grant 1999, 1–28.
91. The OSCE reestablished its missions in Serbia after the regime change in 2000.
92. Karsten Friis, OSCE field officer, interview by the author, Belgrade, April 8, 2005.
93. *RFE/RL*, May 30, 2001.
94. Hislope 2003, 129.
95. Pendarovski interview.

96. Xhemil Shahu, UNHCR Albanian field officer and Emergency Management Group protection officer, interview by the author, Tirana, April 5, 2003.

97. Mihai Gribincea, HCNM political adviser, interview by the author, The Hague, November 14, 2002.

6. Induced Devolution in Post–Cold War Europe

1. Mallet 2009.

2. Europe is not the only region where territorial autonomy has been used as a means of settling internal violent conflict. Wolff and Weller (2005) review a large and growing number of internal conflicts to which territorial self-governance has been applied, including Colombia, Mexico, and Nicaragua in Latin America; Iraq, India, Indonesia, Papua New Guinea in the Middle East and Asia; and Sudan and Tanzania in sub-Saharan Africa.

3. For arguments in favor of autonomy as a conflict management device see Hannum 1996; Nordquist 1998; Lapidoth 1996; Ghai 2000; Lijphart 1977; and McGarry and O'Leary 1993.

4. See, for example, Cornell 2002; Suny 1993; Slezkine 1994; Bunce 1999; Roeder 1991, 2011; Hale 2000; King 2001; and Brancati 2006.

5. Jenne, Saideman, and Lowe 2007; Saideman and Ayres 2000; Fearon and Laitin 2003; Treisman 1997; Toft 2003; and Siroky and Cuffe 2014.

6. See Wolff (2010, 10) for an excellent discussion of the distinction between devolution and decentralization—two of the many forms of territorial solutions to conflict he labels territorial self-government (TSG).

7. Global IPD Project 2004, 7.

8. Gurr 1970, 1993.

9. Manchevski 2001.

10. Phillips 2004, 80–81.

11. Muhamed Zekiri, editor in chief, Alsat-M TV, interview by the author, Skopje, July 21, 2013.

12. British Helsinki Human Rights Group (BHHRG) 2001, 3.

13. Scott Taylor, "Thanks to Uncle Sam, the Macedonians Are No Match for Us," August 29, 2001, http://www.globalresearch.ca/articles/TAY108A.html.

14. *Hamburger Abendblatt*, June 28, 2001.

15. Stojan Andov, Speaker of Macedonian Parliament, 2000–2002, interview by the author, Skopje, July 21, 2013.

16. Ali Ahmeti, interview by the author, Tetovo, Macedonia, July 22, 2013.

17. Ljupcho Ristovski, head of unit, Sector for European Integration, Government of Macedonia, interview by the author, Skopje, April 2, 2004.

18. Ristovski interview.

19. Islam Yusufi, assistant to the national security adviser, cabinet of the president of Macedonia, interview by the author, Skopje, April 7, 2004.

20. International Crisis Group 2011, 14. The report also notes, however, that decentralization has not gone as far as envisioned by the OFA, largely owing to the lack of municipal capacity as well as inadequate funding for many municipalities.

21. ISA Consulting 2007.

22. Pickering 2006, 21.

23. Vachudova 2005.

24. Taleski 2010, 198.

25. Boris Georgievski, "Ghosts of the Past Endanger Macedonia's Future," *Balkan Insight*, October 27, 2009, http://www.balkaninsight.com/en/article/ghosts-of-the-past-endanger-macedonia-s-future.

26. Miki Trajkovski, "Ohrid Agreement Faces Criticism, 11 Years Later," *SETimes.com*, August 22, 2012, http://www.setimes.com/cocoon/setimes/xhtml/en_GB/features/setimes/features/2012/08/22/feature-03.

27. *Economist* 2012.

28. Taleski 2010, 201.

29. Gallup Balkan Monitor 2010, 17.

30. Ahmeti interview.

31. U.S. Embassy Tirana 2013.

32. Nikolaos Chountis, rapporteur for Albanian accession to the EU, December 13, 2012, http://www.europarl.europa.eu/news/en/pressroom/content/20121207IPR04413/html/Albania-yes-to-EU-candidate-status-but-under-certain-conditions.

33. International Crisis Group 2011.

34. Although estimates vary, analysts generally put the ethnic Serb population in postwar Kosovo at 100,000 to 120,000, with one-third in the north and two-thirds in the south; however, the divide is approaching parity, since the Serb population in the south is mostly older and rural.

35. International Crisis Group 2002b.

36. Purvis 2000.

37. International Crisis Group 2002b.

38. On July 19, 1999, the federal government of Yugoslavia instituted a Serbian National Assembly, which would "protect national interests and property of Serbs in Kosovo and Metohija." Essentially, the idea was to gather people loyal to Milošević under a single institution that would play a game with KFOR and UNMIK according to Belgrade's instructions. See *Glas Javnosti* 1999.

39. International Crisis Group 2002b.

40. Filip Ejdus, assistant professor at the Faculty of Political Sciences, University of Belgrade, interview by the author, Pristina, July 16, 2013.

41. To see the full text of the plan go to http://www.unosek.org/unosek/en/status proposal.html.

42. International Crisis Group 2012, 14–15.

43. Stojic 2008.

44. Subotić 2010, 607; see also Obradović-Wochnik and Wochnik 2012.

45. International Crisis Group 2012, 13.

46. International Crisis Group 2009, 12.

47. International Crisis Group 2012, 2.

48. Isak Vorgućić, interview by the author, Radio KIM studio, Gračanica, Kosovo, July 16, 2013.

49. "UN Officer Dies after Kosovo Riot," BBC News, March 18, 2008, http://news.bbc.co.uk/1/hi/world/europe/7300015.stm.

50. Bojan Vasić, interview by the author, Mitrovica, Kosovo, July 18, 2013.

51. Bo-Ewert Linne, director of the OSCE regional office in Pristina, interview by the author, Mitrovica, Kosovo, July 18, 2013.

52. Bulatović had been brought to power by Milošević in 1989 and maintained his allegiance to the Serbian government until an internal split in 1997.

53. Stojan Cerović, "Serbia and Montenegro: Reintegration, Divorce or Something Else?," Special Report, United States Institute for Peace, 2001, 3, as cited in Caspersen 2003, 107.

54. European Stability Initiative, "Autonomy, Dependency, Security: The Montenegrin Dilemma," Podgorica: ESI Report, 2000, 6, as cited in Caspersen 2003, 107.

55. For a detailed account of this episode see International Crisis Group 2000b.

56. Harden 1999.

57. Đukanović, in particular, enjoyed the support of the U.S. government. In July 1999 he was invited by the United States to a European summit in Sarajevo on reconstructing the Balkans, whereas Serbian and Yugoslav representatives had been barred from attending.

58. Dajkovic 2001.

59. Belgrade received no U.S. aid during this time; the State Department instead funded the democratic opposition. Eli J. Lake, "Montenegro Fears Support May Lessen," United Press International, April 11, 2001.

60. Foreign aid has primarily benefited a small circle of politically connected elite. Because of a dearth of employment opportunities in a stagnant economy, many Montenegrins turned to smuggling cigarettes, a business that has flourished with the complicity of the government. Tobacco smuggling has been said to account for as much as 50 percent of Montenegro's GDP and was also used to pay government pensions and salaries; this revenue was critical for carving out republican autonomy in the mid-1990s.

61. U.S. secretary of state Madeleine Albright met with Đukanović on multiple occasions.

62. Dragan Koprivica, SNP spokesperson, interview by the author, Podgorica, Montenegro, September 14, 2007.

63. International Crisis Group 2000a.

64. For more on Western support for the Serbian opposition movement see Bunce and Wolchik 2011, chap. 4.

65. Many of these organizations enjoyed financial backing, training, and diplomatic support from the international community.

66. Dušan Janjić, president of the Forum for Ethnic Relations, interview by the author, Belgrade, September 11, 2003.

67. Dan Briody wrote that Đukanović traveled to Washington in early 2001 to secure support from the new Bush administration for Montenegrin independence. Although he failed to secure an audience with Secretary of State Colin Powell, he did manage to meet with the former defense secretary under Ronald Reagan, Frank Carlucci, who tried (unsuccessfully) to arrange a personal meeting with Powell to plead the case for Montenegrin independence (Briody 2003, 132–35).

68. The EU had its own reasons to rein in Montenegrin autonomy. According to the *Financial Times Deutschland*, cigarette smuggling alone cost the EU an estimated 15 billion euros between 1999 and 2001. Italy had a particular interest in cracking down on the renegade republic, which was suspected of having ties to crime families in Italy whose activities were draining tax revenue out of Italian coffers.

69. International Crisis Group 2002a.

70. Although Bulatović had lost his position as party leader because of his previous association with Milošević, a new leader had come to the helm of the party, Pedrag Bulatović (no relation to Momir).

71. International Crisis Group 2002a, 6.

72. Tadic 2001.

73. Tocci 2007, 80.

74. Bond and Robson 2003. At this point, the international community began to make overtures toward the SNP, which earlier seemed doomed to disappear with the crumbling Yugoslav state. The SNP had come to be seen as a bridge to build up the moribund federation.

75. The issue of the union created splits in the new Serbian leadership as well. FRY president Koštunica, whose position depended on the existence of Yugoslavia, called for a

"functioning if minimal federal state," whereas Serbian prime minister Zoran Đinđić was willing to accept a loose confederation. There is some evidence that Đinđić only really cared about Montenegro insofar as the issue influenced the speed of Serbian accession to the EU (Goran Svilanović, foreign minister of Serbia and Montenegro, 2000–2004, interview by the author, Belgrade, September 12, 2007).

76. Dejan Anastasijević, independent journalist, interview by the author, Belgrade, September 10, 2007.

77. Svilanović interview.

78. Nenad Koprivica, executive director, Center for Democracy and Human Rights, interview by the author, Podgorica, Montenegro, September 14, 2007.

79. Keane 2004, 504.

80. Caspersen 2003, 106.

81. At an Institute for Security Studies–sponsored conference in Paris before the signing of the agreement, a further dispute emerged between Solana, who favored maintaining the federation by getting Belgrade to offer Montenegro a confederal status, and Romano Prodi and others who saw the federation as an institutional stepping-stone to eventual Montenegrin secession.

82. Janjić interview.

83. The Đukanović government then set out to ensure a "yes" vote on the referendum by ensuring that Montenegrins residing in Serbia could not vote in the referendum, whereas Montenegrins living abroad (who were by and large pro-separatists) were encouraged to travel to Montenegro (some allegedly flown in at the expense of the government) to vote. Dragan Koprivica interview.

84. Tocci 2007, 92–93.

85. James Lyon, International Crisis Group analyst, interview by the author, Belgrade, September 11, 2007.

7. Nested Security beyond Europe

1. This means examining an individual conflict from the point at which outside parties begin their mediation efforts and recording shifts in conflict intensity on the ground over time. If such shifts are preceded by shifts in the regional or hegemonic conflict environment in the direction predicted by the model, and if the conflict participants on the ground also indicate (through words and/or actions) that their behavior was motivated by shifts in the external conflict environment, then this provides significant confirmation for the nested security model.

2. The data analysis is drawn from Erin K. Jenne, Milos Popovic, and Levente Littvay, "Nested Security as a Prerequisite for Third Party Conflict Mediation: A Data Analysis of Mediated Civil Conflicts, 1993–2004," paper prepared for presentation at Third Parties and Ethnic Conflict: The Impact of Transnational Actors on Ethnic Civil Wars Workshop, Central European University, Budapest, July 1–2, 2013.

3. Melander, Möller, and Öberg 2009.

4. DeRouen, Bercovitch, and Pospieszna 2011.

5. Gleditsch et al. 2002. It should be noted that we lack information on the status of the conflicts beyond the final year of the dataset (2004).

6. Because the effects of mediation might not be felt right away, models were also run on a third dependent variable that captures the level of violence for the following year (leading conflict intensity), as well as a fourth dependent variable that codes for changes in conflict intensity over time (conflict intensity change). The latter variable is coded by subtracting

the ordinal variable (conflict intensity) from conflict intensity coded for the following year (leading conflict intensity). To illustrate, a low-intensity conflict (0) that has escalated the following year (1) is coded 1 (escalation); the same conflict that stays the same the following year is coded 0 (no change), and a low-intensity conflict that has become inactive the following year is coded −1 (de-escalation). These tests yielded little in the way of results.

7. Hensel 1996.

8. These data are borrowed from Salehyan and Gleditsch 2006.

9. Salehyan and Gleditsch 2006.

10. Touval 1975; Touval and Zartman 1985.

11. Singer, Bremer, and Stuckey 1972.

12. K.S. Gleditsch 2002.

13. Only nine cases in the dataset started out as civil wars in the 1993–2004 period of analysis. These include Afghan-Taliban in 1995, Afghan–Northern Alliance in 1996, Chad-MDJT in 2000, Congo-AFDL in 1996, Congo-RCD in 1998, Georgia-Abkhazia, India-NDFP in 2001, Sudan-SPLN in 1995, and Yemen-DRY in 2001.

14. Mplus User's Guide, Statistical Analysis with Latent Variables, September 2012, http://www.statmodel.com/download/usersguide/Mplus%20user%20guide%20Ver_7_r3_web.pdf. Missing data were corrected with multiple imputation using R's PAN package (Schafer 2001); m = 1000 imputations were used. This m = 1000 is considered very high, as the literature recommends only m = 10 imputations for multilevel models in PAN. But for many of the estimates, the rate of missing information was too high when a lower number of imputations was used. Therefore, the number of imputations was increased to get the rate of missing information below 5 percent for all estimates. Cases with missing data on the dependent variable were discarded, as these cases offered no substantive information for the analysis. Results are unbiased under the MAR assumption—as opposed to the more restrictive MCAR assumption made when cases are excluded from the analysis because of missing data (Rubin 1976). Some of the missing data in this analysis is structural, and while it "feels" wrong to impute values that theoretically could not exist, these imputations do not contribute to the estimates or their certainty one way or another. In these instances, results remain unbiased under the MAR assumption.

15. Greig and Regan 2008.

16. Kydd 2003, 2006.

17. Cederman, Min, and Wimmer 2010; Wimmer, Cederman, and Min 2009; Wimmer 2012.

Great Powers and Cooperative Conflict Management

1. Salehyan 2009, 2008.

2. Toft 2003.

3. Collier and Hoeffler 2004; Lujala 2010; Fearon and Laitin 2003; Lujala, Gleditsch, and Gilmore 2005; Ross 2004; Klare 2002.

4. Jenne 2004, 2007; Jenne, Saideman, and Lowe 2007; Saideman and Ayres 2000; Treisman 1997; Roeder 1991, 2011.

5. Salehyan 2007; Salehyan and Gleditsch 2006; Lischer 2003; Lischer 2005.

6. Harris, Reilly, and Anstey 1998; Lijphart 1977; Horowitz 1991.

7. Zahar 2005.

8. Salehyan 2009.

9. Thompson 1995; Miller and Kagan 1997.

10. Sisk 2009.

11. The League regime consisted of (1) the Assembly, where each member state had one vote; (2) the Council, which had permanent members (the Great Powers) and nonpermanent members; (3) the Secretariat, which provided administrative support; and (4) the Permanent Court of International Justice, which served as the League's primary judicial organ (Åkermark 1997, 102).

12. European Communities Declaration on the "Guidelines on the Recognition of New States in Eastern Europe and the Soviet Union," quoted in Hannum 2001, 411.

13. Harsch (2015) observes that the degree of cooperation between the UN and NATO in managing three conflicts has been mostly ad hoc and mostly dependent on the extent to which the organizations relied on one another's resources.

14. Walters 1986, 86.

15. Krasner and Froats 1998; Steiner 1993; Dunbabin 1993.

16. The CSDP was formerly the European Security and Defense Policy (ESDP), which was subordinated to the EU. Its predecessor was the European Security and Defense Identity, created by the Western European Union as a pillar under NATO in Berlin. This illustrates the development over time of a European defense arm separate from NATO. Fearing that NATO might become obsolete, the United States concluded the "Berlin Plus" agreement, whereby the EU promised to coordinated its actions with NATO and not to duplicate the role played by NATO.

17. Miller 2005, 235.

18. Walters 1986, 162–68.

19. Mylonas 2013, 195.

20. Northedge 1986, 71.

21. Walters 1986, 83–84.

22. Ibid., 264.

23. Ibid., 296.

24. *League of Nations Official Journal* 10, no. 7 (July 1929): 1144, fn1.

25. Walters 1986; Macartney 1937, 370–423.

26. Following the 1938 Anschluss, Sudeten German leader Konrad Henlein reacted to Germany's signals of nationalist intent by ratcheting up his demands against the Czechoslovak state. The Czechs responded by offering concessions to the minority in hopes of heading off a looming crisis. Although the government had largely addressed ethnic German grievances—even offering the minority broad territorial autonomy—Sudeten German leaders remained unsatisfied. In June 1938, the government of Czech prime minister Milan Hodža presented Sudeten German leaders with a plan for decentralization that would have created de facto federalization along ethnic lines. The plan was, however, summarily rejected by the Sudeten German leadership (Hodža 1942, 147–78).

27. Robinson et al. 1943, 260.

28. Steiner 2005.

REFERENCES

Ackermann, Alice. 2000. *Making Peace Prevail: Preventing Violent Conflict in Macedonia.* Syracuse, NY: Syracuse University Press. http://search.ebscohost.com/login.aspx?direct=true&scope=site&db=nlebk&db=nlabk&AN=33858.

———. 2003. "The Idea and Practice of Conflict Prevention." *Journal of Peace Research* 40 (3): 339–47.

Adamson, Fiona B. 2005. "Globalisation, Transnational Political Mobilisation, and Networks of Violence." *Cambridge Review of International Affairs* 18 (1): 31–49.

———. 2006. "Crossing Borders: International Migration and National Security." *International Security* 31 (1): 165–99.

Åkermark, Athanasia Spiliopoulou. 1997. *Justifications of Minority Protection in International Law.* London: Martinus Nijhoff.

Akzin, Benjamin. 1937. "Choices before the Baltic States." *Foreign Affairs* 15 (3): 495–508.

Ash, Timothy Garton. 2000. "Kosovo: Was It Worth It?" *New York Review of Books,* September 21. http://www.nybooks.com/articles/archives/2000/sep/21/kosovo-was-it-worth-it/.

Ayres, R. William. 2000. "A World Flying Apart? Violent Nationalist Conflict and the End of the Cold War." *Journal of Peace Research* 37 (1): 105–17.

Balogh, Piroska. 1998. "Transylvanianism: Revision or Regionalism?" In *Geopolitics in the Danube Region: Hungarian Reconciliation Efforts, 1848–1998,* edited by Ignác Romsics and Béla K. Király, 243–62. Budapest: Central European University Press.

Barros, James. 1968. *The Aland Islands Question: Its Settlement by the League of Nations.* New Haven, CT: Yale University Press.

Beardsley, Kyle. 2011. *The Mediation Dilemma.* Ithaca, NY: Cornell University Press.

Beissinger, Mark R. 2002. *Nationalist Mobilization and the Collapse of the Soviet Union.* Cambridge: Cambridge University Press.

Bercovitch, Jacob. 1984. *Social Conflicts and Third Parties: Strategies of Conflict Resolution.* Boulder, CO: Westview Press.

———, ed. 1992. "The Structure and Diversity of Mediation in International Relations." In *Mediation in International Relations: Multiple Approaches to Conflict Management,* edited by Jacob Bercovitch and Jeffrey Z. Rubin. New York: St. Martin's Press.

Bercovitch, Jacob, and Judith Fretter. 2004. *Regional Guide to International Conflict and Management from 1945 to 2003.* Washington, DC: CQ Press.

Bercovitch, Jacob, and Scott Sigmund Gartner. 2006. "Is There Method in the Madness of Mediation? Some Lessons for Mediators from Quantitative Studies of Mediation." *International Interactions* 32 (4): 329–54.

Bercovitch, Jacob, and Allison Houston. 1996. "The Study of International Mediation: Theoretical Issues and Empirical Evidence." In *Resolving International Conflicts: The Theory and Practice of Mediation,* ed. by Jacob Bercovitch. Boulder: Lynne Rienner.

217

Bierschenk, Theodor. 1954. *Die Deutsche Volksgruppe in Polen 1934–1939.* Würzburg: Holzner.

Birnir, Jóhanna Kristín. 2007. *Ethnicity and Electoral Politics.* Cambridge: Cambridge University Press.

Björkdahl, Annika. 2002. *From Idea to Norm: Promoting Conflict Prevention.* Vol. 125. Lund: Department of Political Science, Lund University.

Blanke, Richard. 1993. *Orphans of Versailles: The Germans in Western Poland, 1918–1939.* Lexington: University Press of Kentucky.

Blomqvist, Anders. 2008. "Hungarian Elite Strategy and Discourse in Interwar Romania." *Regio—Minorities, Politics, Society* 1:265–70.

Bond, Paul, and Tony Robson. 2003. "Political Disaffection Spreads throughout the Former Yugoslavia." *World Socialist Web Site.* January 31. http://www.wsws.org/en/articles/2003/01/mont-j31.html.

Börzel, Tanja A., and Thomas Risse. 2003. "Conceptualizing the Domestic Impact of Europe." In *The Politics of Europeanization,* edited by Keith Featherstone and Claudio Radaelli, 57–80. Oxford: Oxford University Press.

Bothe, Michael, Natalino Ronzitti, and Allan Rosas. 1997. *The OSCE in the Maintenance of Peace and Security: Conflict Prevention, Crisis Management, and Peaceful Settlement of Disputes.* The Hague: Kluwer Law International.

Boulding, Kenneth E. 1989. *Three Faces of Power.* Newbury Park, CA: Sage Publications.

Brancati, Dawn. 2006. "Decentralization: Fueling the Fire or Dampening the Flames of Ethnic Conflict and Secessionism?" *International Organization* 60 (03): 651–85.

Brecher, Michael, and Jonathan Wilkenfeld. 1997. "The Ethnic Dimension of International Crises." In *Wars in the Midst of Peace: The International Politics of Ethnic Conflict,* edited by David Carment and Patrick James, 164–93. Pittsburgh: University of Pittsburgh Press.

Briody, Dan. 2003. *The Iron Triangle: Inside the Secret World of the Carlyle Group.* Hoboken, NJ: John Wiley & Sons.

British Helsinki Human Rights Group (BHHRG). 2001. *Report: Macedonia in Crisis.* Helsinki: British Helsinki Human Rights Group (BHHRG) Report.

Brown, Michael E. 1993. *Ethnic Conflict and International Security.* Princeton, NJ: Princeton University Press.

———. 1996. *The International Dimensions of Internal Conflict.* Cambridge, MA: MIT Press.

Brown, Michael E., and Richard N. Rosecrance. 1999. *The Costs of Conflict: Prevention and Cure in the Global Arena.* Vol. 118. Lanham, MD: Rowman & Littlefield.

Brown, Philip Marshall. 1921. "The Aaland Islands Question." *American Journal of International Law* 15 (2): 268–72.

Browning, Christopher R. 2004. *The Origins of the Final Solution: The Evolution of Nazi Jewish Policy, September 1939–March 1942.* Comprehensive History of the Holocaust. Lincoln: University of Nebraska Press.

BSK. 1939. "Poland's Foreign Trade: Danzig and Gdynia." *Bulletin of International News* 16 (10): 18–20.

Buchheit, Lee C. 1978. *Secession: The Legitimacy of Self-Determination.* New Haven, CT: Yale University Press.

Bugajski, Janusz. 1994. *Ethnic Politics in Eastern Europe: A Guide to Nationality Policies, Organizations, and Parties.* New York: M. E. Sharpe.

Buhaug, Halvard, and Kristian Skrede Gleditsch. 2008. "Contagion or Confusion? Why Conflicts Cluster in Space." *International Studies Quarterly* 52 (2): 215–33.

Bunce, Valerie. 1999. *Subversive Institutions: The Design and the Destruction of Socialism and the State*. Cambridge: Cambridge University Press.

Bunce, Valerie J., and Sharon L. Wolchik. 2011. *Defeating Authoritarian Leaders in Postcommunist Countries*. Cambridge: Cambridge University Press.

Bungs, Dzintra. 1992. "Zotov, Veterans Threaten Latvia." *RFE/RL Research Report* 199.

Buzan, Barry, and Ole Wæver. 2003. *Regions and Powers: The Structure of International Security*. Cambridge: Cambridge University Press.

Campbell, Gregory F. 1975. *Confrontation in Central Europe: Weimar Germany and Czechoslovakia*. Chicago: University of Chicago Press.

Caplan, Richard. 2005. *Europe and the Recognition of New States in Yugoslavia*. Cambridge: Cambridge University Press. http://search.ebscohost.com/login.aspx?direct=true& scope=site&db=nlebk&db=nlabk&AN=149833.

Carment, David, and Patrick James. 1995. "Internal Constraints and Interstate Ethnic Conflict: Toward a Crisis-Based Assessment of Irredentism." *Journal of Conflict Resolution* 39 (1): 82–109.

——. 1997. "Secession and Irredenta in World Politics: The Neglected Interstate Dimension." In *Wars in the Midst of Peace: The International Politics of Ethnic Conflict*, edited by David Carment and Patrick James, 194–231. Pittsburgh: University of Pittsburgh Press.

——, eds. 1998. *Peace in the Midst of Wars: Preventing and Managing International Ethnic Conflicts*. Columbia: University of South Carolina Press.

Carment, David, and Albrecht Schnabel. 2003. *Conflict Prevention: Path to Peace or Grand Illusion?* New York: United Nations Publications.

Carnevale, Peter J., and Shannon Arad. 1996. "Bias and Impartiality in International Mediation." In *Resolving International Conflicts: The Theory and Practice of Mediation*, edited by J. Bercovitch, 39–53. London: Lynne Rienner Publishers.

Carr, Edward Hallett. 1946. *The Twenty Years' Crisis, 1919–1939: An Introduction to the Study of International Relations*. London: Macmillan.

Caspersen, Nina. 2003. "Elite Interests and the Serbian-Montenegrin Conflict." *Southeast European Politics* 4 (2–3): 104–21.

Cassese, Antonio. 1995. *Self-Determination of Peoples: A Legal Reappraisal*. Cambridge: Cambridge University Press.

Cederman, Lars-Erik, Brian Min, and Andreas Wimmer. 2010. "Why Do Ethnic Groups Rebel? New Data and Analysis." *World Politics* 62 (1): 87–119.

Cetinyan, Rupen. 2003. "Ethnic Bargaining in the Shadow of Third-Party Intervention." *International Organization* 56 (03): 645–77.

Chapman, Thomas, and Philip G. Roeder. 2007. "Partition as a Solution to Wars of Nationalism: The Importance of Institutions." *American Political Science Review* 101 (04): 677–91.

Checkel, Jeffrey T. 2001. "Why Comply? Social Learning and European Identity Change." *International Organization* 55 (03): 553–88.

——, ed. 2013. *Transnational Dynamics of Civil War*. New York: Cambridge University Press.

Chigas, Diana, Elizabeth McClintock, and Christophe Kamp. 1996. "Preventive Diplomacy and the Organization for Security and Cooperation in Europe: Creating Incentives for Dialogue and Cooperation." In *Preventing Conflict in the Post-Communist World: Mobilizing International and Regional Organizations*, edited by Abram Chayes and Antonia Handler Chayes, 25–95. Brookings Occasional Papers. Washington, DC: Brookings Institution.

Chmelař, Josef. 1926. *Political Parties in Czechoslovakia*. Prague: Orbis.

Coffey, Luke. 2013. "U.S.-Baltic Relations: Laying the Groundwork for Deeper Cooperation." Heritage Foundation. August 21. http://www.heritage.org/research/reports/2013/08/us-baltic-relations-laying-the-groundwork-for-deeper-cooperation.

Collier, Paul, and Anke Hoeffler. 2004. "Greed and Grievance in Civil War." *Oxford Economic Papers* 56 (4): 563–95.

Conflict Management Group. 1993. *Early Warning and Preventive Action in the CSCE : Defining the Role of the High Commissioner on National Minorities*. Cambridge: Conflict Management Group.

Conversi, Daniele. 1998. *German-Bashing and the Breakup of Yugoslavia*. Seattle: Henry M. Jackson School of International Studies, University of Washington.

Cooper, Robert, and Mats Berdal. 1993. "Outside Intervention in Ethnic Conflicts." *Survival* 35 (1): 118–42.

Cornell, Svante E. 2002. "Autonomy as a Source of Conflict: Caucasian Conflicts in Theoretical Perspective." *World Politics* 54 (2): 245–76.

Cornwall, Mark. 2007. "The Henlein Movement in Czechoslovakia, 1933–1938." In *Czechoslovakia in a National and Fascist Europe, 1918–1948*, edited by Mark Cornwall and R.J.W. Evans, 123–42. Oxford: Oxford University Press.

Crocker, Chester A., Fen Osler Hampson, and Pamela R. Aall. 2004. *Taming Intractable Conflicts: Mediation in the Hardest Cases*. Washington, DC: United States Institute of Peace Press.

Csergő, Zsuzsa. 2007. *Talk of the Nation: Language and Conflict in Romania and Slovakia*. Ithaca, NY: Cornell University Press.

Cunningham, David E. 2006. "Veto Players and Civil War Duration." *American Journal of Political Science* 50 (4): 875–92.

——. 2011. *Barriers to Peace in Civil Wars*. Cambridge: Cambridge University Press.

Dajkovic, Alex N. 2001. "A 'Model' for the Balkans." *Z Magazine*, January 1. https://zcomm.org/zmagazine/a-model-for-the-balkans-by-alex-n-dajkovic/.

Davis, David R., and Will H. Moore. 1997. "Ethnicity Matters: Transnational Ethnic Alliances and Foreign Policy Behavior." *International Studies Quarterly* 41 (1): 171–84.

Dean, Edgar Packard. 1935. "Again the Memel Question." *Foreign Affairs* 14 (3): 695–97.

Demmers, Jolle. 2007. "New Wars and Diasporas: Suggestions for Research and Policy." *Journal of Peace, Conflict & Development*, no. 11. http://germanium.cen.brad.ac.uk/ssis/peace-conflict-and-development/issue-11/PCD-ISSUE-11-ARTICLE_-New-Wars-and-Diasporas_-Joell-Demmers.pdf.

DeRouen, Karl, Jacob Bercovitch, and Paulina Pospieszna. 2011. "Introducing the Civil Wars Mediation (CWM) Dataset." *Journal of Peace Research* 48 (5): 663–72.

Diehl, Paul F. 2008. "Peacekeeping and Beyond." In *The Sage Handbook of Conflict Resolution*, edited by Jacob Bercovitch, Victor Kremenyuk, and I. William Zartman, p. 537. Sage Publications.

Diehl, Paul F., and J. Michael Greig. 2012. *International Mediation*. Cambridge: Polity Press.

Diehl, Paul F., Joseph Lepgold, Kanti Bajpai, Victor D. Cha, John S. Duffield, Benjamin Miller, Carolyn M. Shaw, and I. William Zartman, eds. 2003. *Regional Conflict Management*. Boulder, CO: Rowman & Littlefield.

Dolowitz, David P., and David Marsh. 2000. "Learning from Abroad: The Role of Policy Transfer in Contemporary Policy-Making." *Governance* 13 (1): 5–23.

Dombrovsky, Vyacheslav, Alf Vanags, and Nils Muižnieks. 2006. "Latvian-Russian Economic Relations." In *Latvian-Russian Relations: Domestic and International Dimensions*, 98–109. Riga: University of Latvia.

Downes, Alexander B. 2004. "The Problem with Negotiated Settlements to Ethnic Civil Wars." *Security Studies* 13 (4): 230–79.

Dreifelds, Juris. 1994. "Environmental Resources and Constraints in the Former Soviet Republics. National Council for Soviet and East European Research." Unpublished manuscript. Washington, DC. http://www.ucis.pitt.edu/nceeer/1994-807-04-22-Dreifelds.pdf.

——. 1996. *Latvia in Transition.* Cambridge: Cambridge University Press.

Dunbabin, J.P. 1993. "The League of Nations' Place in the International System." *History* 78 (254): 421–42. doi:10.1111/j.1468-229X.1993.tb02252.x.

Durch, William J. 1996. *UN Peacekeeping, American Politics, and the Uncivil Wars of the 1990s.* New York: St. Martin's Press.

Eberhardt, Piotr. 2003. *Ethnic Groups and Population Changes in Twentieth-Century Central-Eastern Europe: History, Data, and Analysis.* Armonk, NY: M. E. Sharpe.

Economist. 2012. "Stir It Up." April 14. http://www.economist.com/node/21552606.

Elbadawi, I., and N. Sambanis. 2002. "How Much War Will We See? Explaining the Prevalence of Civil War." *Journal of Conflict Resolution* 46 (3): 307.

Engberg, Katarina. 2014. "Trends in Conflict Management." In *Regional Organizations and Peacemaking: Challengers to the UN?*, 72–85. London: Routledge.

Eser, Ingo. 2007. "'Loyalität' als Mittel der Integration oder Restriktion? Polen und seine deutsche Minderheit 1918–1939" [Loyalty as means of integration or restriction? Poland and her German minority, 1918–1939]. In *Staat, Loyalität und Minderheiten in Ostmittel- und Südosteuropa 1918–1941* [State, loyalty, and minorities in Central-Eastern and Southern Europe, 1918–1941], edited by Peter Haslinger and Joachim von Puttenkammer, 17–44. München: Oldenbourg.

European Community. 1991. *Declaration on the "Guidelines on the Recognition of New States in Eastern Europe and in the Soviet Union" (16 December 1991).* Brussels: European Community.

European Council. 1993. *Conclusions of the Presidency, Copenhagen, 21–22 June 1993.* DOC SN180/93, para. 7.

Fair, Christine C. 2005. "Diaspora Involvement in Insurgencies: Insights from the Khalistan and Tamil Eelam Movements." *Nationalism and Ethnic Politics* 11 (1): 139.

Fearon, James D. 1998. "Bargaining, Enforcement, and International Cooperation." *International Organization* 52 (02): 269–305. doi:10.1162/002081898753162820.

Fearon, James D., and David D. Laitin. 2003. "Ethnicity, Insurgency, and Civil War." *American Political Science Review* 97 (01): 75–90.

Fink, Carole. 1972. "Defender of Minorities: Germany in the League of Nations, 1926–1933." *Central European History* 5 (4): 330–57.

——. 2006. *Defending the Rights of Others: The Great Powers, the Jews, and International Minority Protection, 1878–1938.* Cambridge: Cambridge University Press.

Fischer-Galati, Stephen. 1995. "Trianon and Romania." In *Trianon and East Central Europe: Antecedents and Repercussions*, edited by Béla K. Király and László Veszprémy, 185–99. New York: Columbia University Press.

Fortna, Virginia Page. 2004. *Peace Time: Cease-Fire Agreements and the Durability of Peace.* Princeton, NJ: Princeton University Press.

———. 2008. *Does Peacekeeping Work? Shaping Belligerents' Choices after Civil War*. Princeton, NJ: Princeton University Press.

Gade, John A. 1924. "The Memel Controversy." *Foreign Affairs* 2 (3): 410–20.

Galántai, József. 1992. *Trianon and the Protection of Minorities*. Budapest: Corvina Books.

Galbreath, David J., and Ainius Lašas. 2011. "The 'Baltic' Factor in EU-Russian Relations: In Search of Coherence and Co-operation in an Era of Complexity." *Journal of Contemporary European Studies* 19 (2): 261–72. doi:http://dx.doi.org/10.1080/14782804.2011.580914.

Gallup Balkan Monitor. 2010. "Insights and Perceptions: Voices of the Balkans." http://www.balkan-monitor.eu/index.php/dashboard.

Ghai, Yash P. 2000. *Autonomy and Ethnicity: Negotiating Competing Claims in Multi-Ethnic States*. Cambridge: Cambridge University Press.

Glas Javnosti. 1999. "Serbian National Assembly to Be Established." July 20. http://arhiva.glas-javnosti.rs/arhiva/1999/07/20/srpski/vest-dana.shtm.

Gleditsch, Kristian Skrede. 2002. "Expanded Trade and GDP Data." *Journal of Conflict Resolution* 46 (5): 712–24. doi:10.1177/0022002702046005006.

———. 2007. "Transnational Dimensions of Civil War." *Journal of Peace Research* 44 (3): 293.

Gleditsch, Kristian Skrede, and Kyle Beardsley. 2004. "Nosy Neighbors Third-Party Actors in Central American Conflicts." *Journal of Conflict Resolution* 48 (3): 379–402.

Gleditsch, Kristian Skrede, Idean Salehyan, and Kenneth Schultz. 2008. "Fighting at Home, Fighting Abroad: How Civil Wars Lead to International Disputes." *Journal of Conflict Resolution*. http://jcr.sagepub.com/content/early/2008/04/01/0022002707313305.short.

Gleditsch, Nils Petter, Peter Wallensteen, Mikael Eriksson, Margareta Sollenberg, and Halvard Buhaug. 2002. "Armed Conflict, 1946–2001: A New Dataset." *Journal of Peace Research* 39 (5): 615–37.

Global IPD Project. 2004. *A Profile of Internal Displacement: Macedonia*. Geneva: Global IPD Project.

Goertz, Gary. 1995. *Contexts of International Politics*. Cambridge: Cambridge University Press.

Goertz, Gary, and Paul F. Diehl. 1993. "Enduring Rivalries: Theoretical Constructs and Empirical Patterns." *International Studies Quarterly* 37 (1): 147–71.

Gow, James. 1997. *Triumph of the Lack of Will: International Diplomacy and the Yugoslav War*. New York: Columbia University Press.

Grant, Rebecca. 1999. *The Kosovo Campaign: Aerospace Power Made It Work*. Arlington, VA: Air Force Association.

Greenhill, Kelly M., and Solomon Major. 2006/7. "The Perils of Profiling: Civil War Spoilers and the Collapse of Intrastate Peace Accords." *International Security* 31 (3): 7–40.

Greig, J. Michael, and Patrick M. Regan. 2008. "When Do They Say Yes? An Analysis of the Willingness to Offer and Accept Mediation in Civil Wars." *International Studies Quarterly* 52 (4): 759–81.

Gurr, Ted R. 1970. *Why Men Rebel*. Princeton, NJ: Princeton University Press.

———. 1993. *Minorities at Risk*. Washington, DC: United States Institute of Peace Press.

Gustainis, Valentine. 1939. "Lithuania: The First Twenty Years." *Slavonic and East European Review* 17 (51): 606–17.

Haass, Richard N. 1994. *Intervention: The Use of American Military Force in the Post–Cold War World*. Washington, DC: Carnegie Endowment for International Peace Press.

Hale, Henry E. 2000. "The Parade of Sovereignties: Testing Theories of Secession in the Soviet Setting." *British Journal of Political Science* 30 (01): 31–56.

Hannum, Hurst. 1996. *Autonomy, Sovereignty, and Self-Determination: The Accommodation of Conflicting Rights*. Philadelphia: University of Pennsylvania Press.

——. 2001. "International Law." In *Encyclopedia of Nationalism*, edited by Alexander Motyl, 1:405–19. San Diego, CA: Academic Press.

Hansen, Holley E., Sara McLaughlin Mitchell, and Stephen C. Nemeth. 2008. "IO Mediation of Interstate Conflicts Moving beyond the Global versus Regional Dichotomy." *Journal of Conflict Resolution* 52 (2): 295–325.

Harbom, L., and P. Wallensteen. 2005. "Armed Conflict and Its International Dimensions, 1946–2004." *Journal of Peace Research* 42 (5): 623–35.

Harden, Blaine. 1999. "Playing Chicken with Milosevic." *New York Times*, April 25, magazine. http://www.nytimes.com/1999/04/25/magazine/playing-chicken-with-milosevic.html.

Harris, P., B. Reilly, and M. Anstey. 1998. *Democracy and Deep-Rooted Conflict: Options for Negotiators*. Stockholm: International IDEA.

Harsch, Michael. 2015. *The Power of Dependence: NATO-UN Cooperation in Crisis Management*. Oxford: Oxford University Press.

Hayden, Robert M. 1996. "Schindler's Fate: Genocide, Ethnic Cleansing, and Population Transfers." *Slavic Review* 55 (4): 727–48.

Headlam-Morley, James. 1972. *A Memoir of the Paris Peace Conference, 1919*. Edited by Agnes Headlam-Morley. London: Methuen.

Hensel, Paul R. 1996. "Charting a Course to Conflict: Territorial Issues and Interstate Conflict, 1816–1992." *Conflict Management and Peace Science* 15 (1): 43–73. doi:10.1177/073889429601500103.

Heraclides, Alexis. 1991. *The Self-Determination of Minorities in International Politics*. London: F. Cass.

Hill, Stuart, and Donald Rothchild. 1986. "The Contagion of Political Conflict in Africa and the World." *Journal of Conflict Resolution* 30 (4): 716–35.

——. 1992. "The Impact of Regime on the Diffusion of Political Conflict." In *The Internationalization of Communal Strife*, edited by Manus I. Midlarsky, 189–203. New York: Routledge.

Hill, Stuart, Donald Rothchild, and Colin Cameron. 1998. "Tactical Information and the Diffusion of Peaceful Protests." In *The International Spread of Ethnic Conflict: Fear, Diffusion, and Escalation*, edited by David A. Lake and Donald S. Rothchild, 61–88. Princeton, NJ: Princeton University Press.

Hislope, Robert. 2003. "Between a Bad Peace and a Good War: Insights and Lessons from the Almost-War in Macedonia." *Ethnic and Racial Studies* 26 (1): 129–51. doi:10.1080/0141987002000025306.

Hodža, Milan. 1942. *Federation in Central Europe*. London: Jarrold's Publishers.

Holsti, Kalevi J. 1991. *Peace and War: Armed Conflicts and International Order, 1648–1989*. Cambridge: Cambridge University Press. http://www.google.com/books?hl=en&lr=&id=XeRWvk3TP_gC&oi=fnd&pg=PR12&dq=holsti+&ots=oAm-l6QwUD&sig=nUWrMpRgBsOnA7Mn4Gt3Ldiokwc.

Hopmann, Terrence P. 2003. "Managing Conflict in Post–Cold War Eurasia: The Role of the OSCE in Europe's Security 'Architecture.'" *International Politics* 40 (1): 75–100. doi:10.1057/palgrave.ip.8800009.

Horak, Stephan. 1961. *Poland and Her National Minorities, 1919–1939*. New York: Vantage Press.

Horowitz, Donald L. 1985. *Ethnic Groups in Conflict*. Berkeley: University of California Press.

———. 1991. *A Democratic South Africa? Constitutional Engineering in a Divided Society*. Berkeley: University of California Press.

Horváth, István. 2002. "Facilitating Conflict Transformation: Implementation of the Recommendations of the OSCE High Commissioner on National Minorities to Romania, 1993–2001." CORE Working Paper 8: 1–142.

Huber, Konrad J. 1994. "Averting Inter-Ethnic Conflict: An Analysis of the CSCE High Commissioner on National Minorities in Estonia, January–July 1993." In *Conflict Resolution Program of the Carter Center of Emory University's Working Paper Series* 1 (2).

Hughes, James, and Gwendolyn Sasse. 2003. "Monitoring the Monitors: EU Enlargement Conditionality and Minority Protection in the CEECs." *Journal on Ethnopolitics and Minority Issues in Europe* 1 (1): 1–36.

Hughes, James, Gwendolyn Sasse, and Claire Gordon. 2004. "Europeanization and Regionalization in the EU's Enlargement to Central and Eastern Europe." Houndmills, UK: Palgrave.

Huth, Paul. 2009. *Standing Your Ground: Territorial Disputes and International Conflict*. Ann Arbor: University of Michigan Press. http://www.google.com/books?hl=en& lr=&id=NIAc-R5fgQoC&oi=fnd&pg=PR1&dq=paul+huth&ots=Gkl67xOmpY& sig=Oi1xn60Hn_lbutLfkOYEUSsK9BU.

International Crisis Group. 2000a. "Montenegro: In the Shadow of the Volcano." March 21. http://www.crisisgroup.org/en/regions/europe/balkans/montenegro/ 089-montenegro-in-the-shadow-of-the-volcano.aspx.

———. 2000b. "Montenegro's Socialist People's Party: A Loyal Opposition?" April 28. http://www.crisisgroup.org/en/regions/europe/balkans/montenegro/ 092-montenegros-socialist-peoples-party-a-loyal-opposition.aspx.

———. 2002a. "Still Buying Time: Montenegro, Serbia and the European Union." May 7. http://www.crisisgroup.org/en/regions/europe/balkans/montenegro/129-still- buying-time-montenegro-serbia-and-the-european-union.aspx.

———. 2002b. "UNMIK's Kosovo Albatross: Tackling Division in Mitrovica." June 3. http://www.crisisgroup.org/en/regions/europe/balkans/kosovo/131-unmiks-kosovo- albatross-tackling-division-in-mitrovica.aspx.

———. 2009. "Serb Integration in Kosovo: Taking the Plunge." May 12. http://www. crisisgroup.org/en/regions/europe/balkans/kosovo/200-serb-integration-in- kosovo-taking-the-plunge.aspx.

———. 2011. "Macedonia: Ten Years after the Conflict." August 11. http://www. crisisgroup.org/en/regions/europe/balkans/macedonia/212-macedoni a-ten-years-after-the-conflict.aspx.

———. 2012. "Setting Kosovo Free: Remaining Challenges." September 10. http://www. crisisgroup.org/en/regions/europe/balkans/kosovo/218-setting-kosovo-free- remaining-challenges.aspx.

ISA Consulting. 2007. "Kosovo: Armed for Independence." The International
Relations and Security Network, ETH Zurich. November.
http://www.isn.ethz.ch/Digital-Library/Articles/Detail/?ots59
1=4888caa0-b3db-1461-98b9-e20e7b9c13d4&lng=en&id=51982.

Jackson Preece, Jennifer. 1997. "Minority Rights in Europe: From Westphalia to
Helsinki." *Review of International Studies* 23 (01): 75–92.

Jakobsen, P. V. 1996. "National Interest, Humanitarianism or CNN: What Triggers
UN Peace Enforcement after the Cold War?" *Journal of Peace Research* 33 (2):
205–15.

Jaworski, Rudolf. 1991. "German Minorities in Interwar Poland and Czechoslovakia." In
*Comparative Studies on Governments and Non-dominant Ethnic Groups in Europe,
1850–1940.* Vol. 5, *Ethnic Groups in International Relations,* edited by Paul Smith,
Kalliopa Koufa, and Arnold Suppan, 169–85. New York: NYU Press.

Jelenik, Yeshayahu. 1995. "Trianon and Czechoslovakia: Reflections." In *Trianon and East
Central Europe: Antecedents and Repercussions,* edited by Béla Király and László
Veszprémy, 201–16. New York: Columbia University Press.

Jenne, Erin K. 2003. "Sri Lanka: A Fragmented State." In *State Failure and State Weakness
in a Time of Terror,* edited by Robert I. Rotberg, 219–44. Washington, DC:
Brookings Institution Press.

——. 2004. "A Bargaining Theory of Minority Demands: Explaining the Dog That Did
Not Bite in 1990s Yugoslavia." *International Studies Quarterly* 48 (4): 729–54.
doi:10.1111/j.0020–8833.2004.00323.x.

——. 2007. *Ethnic Bargaining: The Paradox of Minority Empowerment.* Ithaca, NY: Cornell
University Press.

Jenne, Erin K., Stephen S. Saideman, and Will Lowe. 2007. "Separatism as a Bargaining
Posture: The Role of Leverage in Minority Radicalization." *Journal of Peace Research*
44 (5): 539–58. doi:10.1177/0022343307080853.

Joffe, Josef. 1992. "Collective Security and the Future of Europe: Failed Dreams and Dead
Ends." *Survival: Global Politics and Strategy* 34 (1): 36–50.

Johnson, Owen V. 1985. *Slovakia, 1918–1938: Education and the Making of a Nation.* New
York: Columbia University Press.

Kacprzak, Paweł. 2007. *Niemiecka mniejszość narodowa w Polsce w latach 1919–1939*
[German minority in Poland between 1919 and 1939]. Edited by Wydawnictwo
Państwowej Wyższej Szkoły Zawodowej. Wydziału: Studia Lubuskie.

Kalijarvi, Thorsten. 1936. "The Problem of Memel." *American Journal of International Law*
30 (2): 204–15.

Kaplan, Robert D. 1994. "The Coming Anarchy." *Atlantic Monthly* 273 (2): 44–76.

Kārkliṇa, Rasma, and Imants Lieģis. 2006. "Latvia and Russia within the Broader
International Context." In *Latvian-Russian Relations: Domestic and
International Dimensions,* edited by Nils Muižnieks, 148–57. Riga: University of
Latvia.

Kaufman, Stuart J. 2001. *Modern Hatreds: The Symbolic Politics of Ethnic War.* Ithaca, NY:
Cornell University Press.

——. 2006. "Escaping the Symbolic Politics Trap: Reconciliation Initiatives and Conflict
Resolution in Ethnic Wars." *Journal of Peace Research* 43 (2): 201–18.

Kaufmann, Chaim D. 1996. "Possible and Impossible Solutions to Ethnic Civil Wars."
International Security 20 (4): 136–75.

——. 1998. "When All Else Fails: Ethnic Population Transfers and Partitions in the Twentieth Century." *International Security* 23 (2): 120–56.

——. 2007. "An Assessment of the Partition of Cyprus." *International Studies Perspectives* 8 (2): 206–23.

Kauppila, Laura Eleonoora. 1999. "The Baltic Puzzle: Russia's Policy towards Estonia and Latvia." Helsinki: University of Helsinki. http://ethesis.helsinki.fi/julkaisut/val/yhtei/pg/kauppila/thebalti.pdf.

Keane, Rory. 2004. "The Solana Process in Serbia and Montenegro: Coherence in EU Foreign Policy." *International Peacekeeping* 11 (3): 491–507. doi:10.1080/13533310 42000249064.

Kees, T. 1994. "'Polnische Greuel'—der Propagandafeldzug des Dritten Reiches gegen Polen." Master's thesis, Philosophische Fakultät, Universität des Saarlandes.

Kelley, Judith G. 2003. "Does Domestic Politics Limit the Influence of External Actors on Ethnic Politics?" *Human Rights Review* 4 (3): 34–54.

——. 2004a. *Ethnic Politics in Europe: The Power of Norms and Incentives*. Princeton, NJ: Princeton University Press.

——. 2004b. "International Actors on the Domestic Scene: Membership Conditionality and Socialization by International Institutions." *International Organization* 58 (03): 425–57.

Kemp, Walter A. 2001. *Quiet Diplomacy in Action: The OSCE High Commissioner on National Minorities*. The Hague: Kluwer Law International.

King, Charles. 2001. "The Benefits of Ethnic War: Understanding Eurasia's Unrecognized States." *World Politics* 53 (04): 524–52.

Kioko, Ben. 2003. "The Right of Intervention under the African Union's Constitutive Act: From Non-interference to Non-intervention." *International Review of the Red Cross* 85 (852): 807–26. doi:10.1017/S0035336100179948.

Klare, Michael T. 2002. *Resource Wars: The New Landscape of Global Conflict*. New York: Owl Books.

Komjathy, Anthony, and Rebecca Stockwell. 1980. *German Minorities and the Third Reich: Ethnic Germans of East Central Europe*. New York: Holmes & Meier.

Kopecek, Herman. 1996. "Zusammenarbeit and Spoluprace: Sudeten German–Czech Cooperation in Interwar Czechoslovakia." *Nationalities Papers* 24 (1): 63–78.

Krasner, Stephen D. 1982. "Structural Causes and Regime Consequences: Regimes as Intervening Variables." *International Organization* 36 (2): 185–205.

——. 1999. *Sovereignty: Organized Hypocrisy*. Princeton, NJ: Princeton University Press.

Krasner, Stephen D., and Daniel T. Froats. 1998. "Minority Rights and the Westphalian Model." In *The International Spread of Ethnic Conflict: Fear, Diffusion, and Escalation*, 227–50. Princeton, NJ: Princeton University Press.

Kupchan, Charles A., and Clifford A. Kupchan. 1995. "The Promise of Collective Security." *International Security* 20 (1): 52–61.

Kuperman, Alan J. 2001. *The Limits of Humanitarian Intervention: Genocide in Rwanda*. Washington, DC: Brookings Institution Press.

Kydd, Andrew. 2003. "Which Side Are You On? Bias, Credibility, and Mediation." *American Journal of Political Science* 47 (4): 597–611.

——. 2006. "When Can Mediators Build Trust?" *American Political Science Review* 100 (3): 449–62.

Lahelma, Timo. 1999. "The OSCE's Role in Conflict Prevention: The Case of Estonia." *Helsinki Monitor* 10 (2): 19–38. doi:10.1163/157181499X00032.

Lake, David A., and Patrick M. Morgan. 1997a. "The New Regionalism in Security Affairs." In *Regional Orders: Building Security in a New World*, edited by David A. Lake and Patrick M. Morgan, 3–19. University Park: Pennsylvania State University Press.

———. 1997b. *Regional Orders: Building Security in a New World*. University Park: Pennsylvania State University Press.

Lake, David A., and Donald S. Rothchild. 1996. "Containing Fear: The Origins and Management of Ethnic Conflict." *International Security* 21 (2): 41–75.

———. 1998. *The International Spread of Ethnic Conflict: Fear, Diffusion, and Escalation*. Princeton, NJ: Princeton University Press.

Lamoreaux, Jeremy W., and David J. Galbreath. 2008. "The Baltic States as 'Small States': Negotiating the 'East' by Engaging the 'West.'" *Journal of Baltic Studies* 39 (1): 1–14. doi:http://dx.doi.org/10.1080/01629770801908697.

Lapidoth, Ruth. 1996. *Autonomy: Flexible Solutions to Ethnic Conflicts*. Washington, DC: United States Institute of Peace Press.

Larrabee, F. Stephen. 2003. *NATO's Eastern Agenda in a New Strategic Era*. Santa Monica, CA: Rand Corp.

Latimer, Hugh. 1935. "The Elections in Memel." *Bulletin of International News* 15 (25): 9–11.

———. 1936. "The Problem of Danzig." *Bulletin of International News* 13 (2): 3–14.

Lederach, John Paul. 1997. *Building Peace: Sustainable Reconciliation in Divided Societies*. Washington, DC: United States Institute of Peace Press.

Lemke, Douglas. 1996. "Small States and War: An Expansion of Power Transition Theory." In *Parity and War: Evaluations and Extensions of the War Ledger*, edited by Jacek Kugler and Douglas Lemke, 77–92. Ann Arbor: University of Michigan Press.

———. 2002. *Regions of War and Peace*. Cambridge: Cambridge University Press.

Lepingwell, John W.R. 1994. "The Russian Military and Security Policy in the 'Near Abroad.'" *Survival* 36 (3): 70–92. doi:10.1080/00396339408442751.

Lerner, Natan. 1991. *Group Rights and Discrimination in International Law*. International Studies in Human Rights, vol. 15. Dordrecht: M. Nijhoff.

Leslie, R.F., ed. 1983. *The History of Poland since 1863*. 1st paperback ed., with epilogue. Soviet and East European Studies. Cambridge: Cambridge University Press.

Levine, Herbert S. 1973. "The Mediator: Carl J. Burckhardt's Efforts to Avert a Second World War." *Journal of Modern History* 45 (3): 439–55.

Lijphart, Arend. 1977. *Democracy in Plural Societies: A Comparative Exploration*. New Haven, CT: Yale University Press.

Lippelt, Helmut. 1971. "'Politische Sanierung': Zur deutschen Politik gegenüber Polen 1925/26 [Political reconstruction: On Germany's Polish policy, 1925–26]." *Vierteljahrshefte für Zeitgeschichte* 19 (4): 323–74.

Lipski, Józef. 1968. *Diplomat in Berlin, 1933–39*. Edited by Waclaw Jedrzejewicz. New York: Columbia University Press.

Lischer, Sarah K. 2003. "Collateral Damage: Humanitarian Assistance as a Cause of Conflict." *International Security* 28 (1): 79–109. doi:10.1162/016228803322427983.

———. 2005. *Dangerous Sanctuaries: Refugee Camps, Civil War, and the Dilemmas of Humanitarian Aid*. Ithaca, NY: Cornell University Press.

Loiko, Sergei L. 2014. "Captive Observers in Ukraine Meet Journalists under Eyes of Gunmen." *Los Angeles Times*, April 27. http://articles.latimes.com/2014/apr/27/world/la-fg-wn-ukraine-captives-new-conference-20140427.

Lord, R. H. 1923. "Lithuania and Poland." *Foreign Affairs* 1 (4): 38–58.

Lorman, Tom. 2005. "Missed Opportunities? Hungarian Policy towards Romania, 1932–1936." *Slavonic and East European Review* 83 (2): 290–317.

Lotan, Gilad, Erhardt Graeff, Mike Ananny, Devin Gaffney, Ian Pearce, et al. 2011. "The Arab Spring: The Revolutions Were Tweeted; Information Flows during the 2011 Tunisian and Egyptian Revolutions." *International Journal of Communication* 5:31.

Lujala, Päivi. 2010. "The Spoils of Nature: Armed Civil Conflict and Rebel Access to Natural Resources." *Journal of Peace Research* 47 (1): 15–28. doi:10.1177/0022343309350015.

Lujala, Päivi, Nils Petter Gleditsch, and Elisabeth Gilmore. 2005. "A Diamond Curse? Civil War and a Lootable Resource." *Journal of Conflict Resolution* 49 (4): 538–62.

Lund, Michael S. 1995. "Underrating Preventive Diplomacy." *Foreign Affairs* 74:160–63.

———. 1996. *Preventing Violent Conflicts: A Strategy for Preventive Diplomacy.* Washington, DC: United States Institute of Peace Press.

Lund, Michael S., Guenola Rasamoelina, and SWP-Conflict Prevention Network. 2000. *The Impact of Conflict Prevention Policy: Cases, Measures, Assessments.* Baden-Baden: Nomos Verlagsgesellschaft.

Macartney, Carlile Aylmer. 1937. *Hungary and Her Successors: The Treaty of Trianon and Its Consequences, 1919–1937.* London: Oxford University Press.

———. 1968. *National States and National Minorities.* New York: Russell & Russell.

Magda, Ádám. 1995. "Complete Encirclement: The Establishment of the Little Entente." In *Hungarians and Neighbors in Modern Times, 1867–1950*, edited by Ferenc Glatz, 143–49. New York: Columbia University Press.

Mair, Lucy. 1928. *The Protection of Minorities: The Working and Scope of the Minorities Treaties under the League of Nations.* London: Christophers.

Mallet, Victor. 2009. "Flimsier Footings." *Financial Times*, August 18. http://www.ft.com/cms/s/0/de6c00f0–8c25–11de-b14f-00144feabdc0.html#axzz2EgBtDlBZ.

Manchevski, Milcho. 2001. "Nato Gave Us This Ethnic Cleansing." *Guardian*, August 15, sec. World News. http://www.theguardian.com/world/2001/aug/15/comment.

Masaryk, Tomáš Garrigue. 1933. *Cesta demokracie I* [The path of democracy, vol. 1]. Prague: Spisy TGM.

Mavromatidis, Fotis. 2010. "The Role of the European Union in the Name Dispute between Greece and FYR Macedonia." *Journal of Contemporary European Studies* 18 (1): 47–62.

Mazower, Mark. 2004. "The Strange Triumph of Human Rights, 1933–1950." *Historical Journal* 47 (2): 379–98.

McGarry, John, and Brendan O'Leary, eds. 1993. *The Politics of Ethnic Conflict Regulation: Case Studies of Protracted Ethnic Conflicts.* London: Routledge.

Mearsheimer, John J. 1990. "Back to the Future: Instability in Europe after the Cold War." *International Security* 15 (1): 5–56.

Melander, Erik, Frida Möller, and Magnus Öberg. 2009. "Managing Intrastate Low-Intensity Armed Conflict, 1993–2004: A New Dataset." *International Interactions* 35 (1): 58–85. doi:10.1080/03050620902743887.

Meri, H. E. Lennart. 1992. *Speech by H. E. Lennart Meri, President of the Republic of Estonia to the Royal Institute of International Relations Palais d'Egmont.* Brussels: Office of the President of the Republic. http://vp1992–2001.president.ee/eng/k6ned/K6ne.asp?ID=9516.

Midlarsky, Manus I. 1992. *The Internationalization of Communal Strife*. London: Routledge.

Miller, Benjamin. 2005. "When and How Regions Become Peaceful: Potential Theoretical Pathways to Peace." *International Studies Review* 7:229–67.

Miller, Benjamin, and Korina Kagan. 1997. "The Great Powers and Regional Conflicts: Eastern Europe and the Balkans from the Post-Napoleonic Era to the Post–Cold War Era." *International Studies Quarterly* 41 (1): 51–85. doi:10.1111/0020–8833.00033.

Modelski, George. 1964. "International Relations of Internal War." In *International Aspects of Civil Strife*, edited by James N. Rosenau, 14–44. Princeton, NJ: Princeton University Press.

Morozov, Viatcheslav. 2004. "Russia in the Baltic Sea Region: Desecuritization or Deregionalization?" *Cooperation and Conflict* 39 (3): 317–31. doi:10.1177/0010836704045207.

Muižnieks, Nils. 2006. "Russian Foreign Policy towards 'Compatriots' in Latvia." In *Latvian-Russian Relations: Domestic and International Dimensions*, edited by Nils Muižnieks, 119–30. Riga: University of Latvia.

Muldoon, James B. 1983. "The Development of Group Rights." In *Minority Rights: A Comparative Analysis*, edited by Jay A. Sigler, 31–66. Westport, CT: Greenwood Press.

Mylonas, Harris. 2013. *The Politics of Nation-Building: Making Co-nationals, Refugees, and Minorities*. New York: Cambridge University Press.

Nadein, Vladimir. 1997. "Moscow Gives in to Washington." *Izvestia*, May 6.

Naimark, Norman M. 2002. *Fires of Hatred: Ethnic Cleansing in Twentieth-Century Europe*. Cambridge, MA: Harvard University Press.

Národní Shromáždě ní: Republiky Československé v Prvém Desítiletí. 1928. Prague: Presidency of the Chamber of Deputies and Presidency of the Senate.

Newman, Edward, and Oliver Richmond. 2006. "Peace Building and Spoilers." *Conflict, Security & Development* 6 (1): 101–10.

Nikžentaitis, Alvydas. 1996. "Germany and the Memel Germans in the 1930s (on the Basis of Trials of Lithuanian Agents before the Volksgerichtshof, 1934–45)." *Historical Journal* 39 (03): 770–83. doi:10.1017/S0018246X00024560.

Nordquist, Kjell-Åke. 1998. "Autonomy as a Conflict-Solving Mechanism: An Overview." In *Autonomy: Applications and Implications*, edited by Markku Suksk, 59–77. The Hague: Kluwer Law International.

Northedge, F.S. 1986. *The League of Nations: Its Life and Times, 1920–1946*. New York: Holmes and Meier.

Oberleitner, Gerd. 1999. "Monitoring Minority Rights under the Council of Europe's Framework Convention." In *Minority Rights in the New Europe*, edited by Peter Crumper and Steven Charles Wheatley, 71–88. The Hague: Kluwer Law International.

Obradović-Wochnik, Jelena, and Alexander Wochnik. 2012. "Europeanising the 'Kosovo Question': Serbia's Policies in the Context of EU Integration." *West European Politics* 35 (5): 1158–81.

O'Donoghue, Thomas A., and Keith F. Punch. 2003. *Qualitative Educational Research in Action: Doing and Reflecting*. London: Routledge.

Oliver, Spencer. 2014. "Can Europe's Security Watchdog Survive the Crisis in Ukraine?" Organization for Security and Co-operation in Europe, Parliamentary Assembly,

News and Media, Op-Eds, May 15. http://www.oscepa.org/news-a-media/op-eds/1744-can-europe-s-security-watchdog-survive-the-crisis-in-ukraine.

OSCE (Organization for Security and Co-operation in Europe). 2014. "OSCE to Send Military and Civilian Personnel to Ukraine." OECD. http://www.osce.org/sg/116093.

Ott, Attiat F., Aksel Kirch, and Marika Kirch. 1996. "Ethnic Anxiety: A Case Study of Resident Aliens in Estonia (1990–1992)." *Journal of Baltic Studies* 27 (1): 21–46.

Pabriks, Artis, and Aldis Purs. 2001. *Latvia: The Challenges of Change.* London: Routledge.

Padelford, Norman J., and K. Gosta A. Andersson. 1939. "The Aaland Islands Question." *American Journal of International Law* 33 (3): 465–87.

Peck, Connie. 2001. "The Role of Regional Organizations in Preventing and Resolving Conflict." In *Turbulent Peace: The Challenges of Managing International Conflict,* edited by Chester A. Crocker, Fen Osler Hampson, and Pamela Aall, 561–83. Washington, DC: U.S. Institute of Peace Press.

Pedersen, Susan. 2007. "Back to the League of Nations." *American Historical Review* 112 (4): 1091–1117.

Pettai, Vello, and Kristina Kallas. 2009. "Estonia: Conditionality amidst a Legal Straightjacket." In *Minority Rights in Central and Eastern Europe,* edited by Bernd Rechel, 104–18. London: Routledge.

Phillips, John. 2004. *Macedonia: Warlords and Rebels in the Balkans.* New Haven, CT: Yale University Press.

Pickering, Paula M. 2006. "Explaining Support for Non-nationalist Parties in Post-conflict Societies in the Balkans." Unpublished ms., forthcoming in *Europe-Asia Studies,* http://people.wm.edu/~pmpick/research/ExplainingSupportEASPickering.pdf.

Pippan, Christian. 2004. "The Rocky Road to Europe: The EU's Stabilisation and Association Process for the Western Balkans and the Principle of Conditionality." *European Foreign Affairs Review* 9 (2): 219–45.

Polonsky, Antony. 1972. *Politics in Independent Poland, 1921–1939: The Crisis of Constitutional Government.* Oxford: Clarendon Press.

Prazmowska, Anita J. 1983. "War over Danzig? The Dilemma of Anglo-Polish Relations in the Months Preceding the Outbreak of the Second World War." *Historical Journal* 26 (01): 177–83. doi:10.1017/S0018246X00019658.

———. 1992. "The Role of Danzig in Polish-German Relations on the Eve of the Second World War." In *The Baltic and the Outbreak of the Second World War,* edited by John Hiden and Thomas Lane, 74–94. Cambridge: Cambridge University Press.

Preece, Jennifer Jackson. 1997. "National Minority Rights vs. State Sovereignty in Europe: Changing Norms in International Relations?" *Nations and Nationalism* 3 (3): 345–64.

Pruitt, Dean G. 1997. "Ripeness Theory and the Oslo Talks." *International Negotiation* 2 (2): 237–50.

Purvis, Andrew. 2000. "A Bridge Too Far in Kosovo." *Time,* March 6. http://content.time.com/time/world/article/0,8599,2051106,00.html.

Raghavan, Sudarsan. 2014. "Record Number of U.N. Peacekeepers Fails to Stop African Wars." *Washington Post,* January 3.

Raitz von Frentz, Christian. 1999. *A Lesson Forgotten: Minority Protection under the League of Nations; The Case of the German Minority Poland, 1920–1934.* Berlin-Hamburg-Münster: LIT Verlag.

Ratliff, William Grant. 1988. "Faithful to the Fatherland: Julius Curtius and Weimar Foreign Policy, 1920–1932." PhD dissertation, graduate faculty, Texas Tech University.

Ratner, Steve R. 2000. "Does International Law Matter in Preventing Ethnic Conflict?" *New York University Journal of International Law and Politics* 32 (3): 591–698.

Rechel, Bernd. 2008. "What Has Limited the EU's Impact on Minority Rights in Accession Countries?" *East European Politics & Societies* 22 (1): 171–91.

Regan, Patrick, Richard Frank, and Aysegul Aydin. 2009. "Diplomatic Interventions and Civil War: A New Dataset." *Journal of Peace Research* 46 (1): 135–46.

Reilly, Ben, and Andrew Reynolds. 1999. *Electoral Systems and Conflict in Divided Societies.* Vol. 2. Washington, DC: National Academy Press.

Reno, William. 1998. *Warlord Politics and African States.* Boulder, CO: Lynne Rienner.

Roberts, Henry L. 1953. "The Diplomacy of Colonel Beck." In *The Diplomats, 1919–1939*, edited by Gordon Alexander Craig and Felix Gilbert, 579–614. Princeton, NJ: Princeton University Press.

Robinson, Jacob, Oscar Karbath, Max S. Laserson, Nehemiah Robinson, and Marc Vichniak. 1943. *Were the Minority Treaties a Failure?* New York: Institute of Jewish Affairs.

Roeder, Philip G. 1991. "Soviet Federalism and Ethnic Mobilization." *World Politics* 43 (2): 196–232. doi:http://dx.doi.org/10.2307/2010471.

——. 2011. *Where Nation-States Come From.* Princeton, NJ: Princeton University Press.

Romanova, Tatiana. 2009. "Energy Policy of Russia: Still in a State of Flux." In *Energy: Pulling the Baltic Sea Region Together or Apart?*, edited by Andris Spruds and Toms Rostoks, 122–56. Riga: Zinātne.

Romsics, Ignác. 1995. "Italy and the Plans for a Romanian-Hungarian Agreement." In *Trianon and East Central Europe: Antecedents and Repercussions*, edited by Béla K. Király and László Veszprémy, 107–48. New York: Columbia University Press.

Rosenau, James N. 1964. *International Aspects of Civil Strife.* Princeton, NJ: Princeton University Press.

Ross, Michael L. 2004. "How Do Natural Resources Influence Civil War? Evidence from Thirteen Cases." *International Organization* 58 (01): 35–67.

Rouček, Joseph S. 1971. *Contemporary Roumania and Her Problems: A Study in Modern Nationalism.* New York: Arno Press and the New York Times.

Rubin, Donald B. 1976. "Inference and Missing Data." *Biometrika* 63 (3): 581–92. doi:10.1093/biomet/63.3.581.

Safronovas, Vasilijus. 2009. "Die Rolle des Schützenverbandes Litauens bei der Besetzung des Memelgebietes 1923. Die Tilsiter Akte und der 'Aufstand' als Symbole des Legitimationsmythos." *Annaberger Annalen: Jahrbuch über Litauen und deutsch-litauenische Beziehungen* 17:5–40.

Saideman, Stephen M. 1997. "Explaining the International Relations of Secessionist Conflicts: Vulnerability versus Ethnic Ties." *International Organization* 51 (04): 721–53.

——. 1998. "Inconsistent Irredentism? Political Competition, Ethnic Ties, and the Foreign Policies of Somalia and Serbia." *Security Studies* 7 (3): 51–93.

——. 2001. *The Ties That Divide: Ethnic Politics, Foreign Policy, and International Conflict.* New York: Columbia University Press.

Saideman, Stephen M., and R. William Ayres. 2000. "Determining the Causes of Irredentism: Logit Analyses of Minorities at Risk Data from the 1980s and 1990s." *Journal of Politics* 62 (04): 1126–44.

——. 2008. *For Kin or Country: Xenophobia, Nationalism, and War.* New York: Columbia University Press.

Sakmyster, Thomas L. 1980. *Hungary, the Great Powers, and the Danubian Crisis, 1936–1939.* Athens: University of Georgia Press.

Salehyan, Idean. 2007. "Transnational Rebels: Neighboring States as Sanctuary for Rebel Groups." *World Politics* 59 (2): 217–42.

——. 2008. "No Shelter Here: Rebel Sanctuaries and International Conflict." *Journal of Politics* 70 (01): 54–66.

——. 2009. *Rebels without Borders: Transnational Insurgencies in World Politics.* Ithaca, NY: Cornell University Press.

Salehyan, Idean, and Kristian Skrede Gleditsch. 2006. "Refugees and the Spread of Civil War." *International Organization* 60 (02): 335–66.

Sarkees, Meredith Reid, Frank Whelon Wayman, and J. David Singer. 2003. "Inter-state, Intra-state, and Extra-state Wars: A Comprehensive Look at Their Distribution over Time, 1816–1997." *International Studies Quarterly* 47 (1): 49–70.

Sasse, Gwendolyn. 2008. "The Politics of EU Conditionality: The Norm of Minority Protection during and beyond EU Accession." *Journal of European Public Policy* 15 (6): 842–60.

Schafer, Joseph L. 2001. "Multiple Imputation with PAN." In *New Methods for the Analysis of Change,* edited by Linda M. Collins and Aline G. Sayer, 357–77. Decade of Behavior. Washington, DC: American Psychological Association.

Scheuermann, Martin. 2000. *Minderheitenschutz contra Konfliktverhütung? Die Minderheitenpolitik des Völkerbundes in den zwanziger Jahren.* Marburg: Verlag Herder-Institute.

Schimmelfennig, Frank. 2000. "International Socialization in the New Europe: Rational Action in an Institutional Environment." *European Journal of International Relations* 6 (1): 109–39.

Schimmelfennig, Frank, and Ulrich Sedelmeier. 2005a. *The Europeanization of Central and Eastern Europe.* Ithaca, NY: Cornell University Press.

——. 2005b. "Introduction: Conceptualizing the Europeanisation of Central and Eastern Europe." In *The Europeanization of Central and Eastern Europe,* edited by Frank Schimmelfennig and Ulrich Sedelmeier, 1–28. Ithaca, NY: Cornell University Press.

Schulze, Jennie L. 2010. "Estonia Caught between East and West: EU Conditionality, Russia's Activism and Minority Integration." *Nationalities Papers* 38 (3): 361–92.

Schwirtz, Michael. 2011. "Latvian Election Shows Gains for Pro-Russia Party." *New York Times,* September 18, sec. World/Europe. http://www.nytimes.com/2011/09/19/world/europe/gains-of-pro-russian-party-show-shift-in-sentiment-in-latvia.html.

Sharp, Alan. 1979. "Britain and the Protection of Minorities at the Paris Peace Conference, 1919." In *Minorities in History,* edited by A. C. Hepburn, 170–88. New York: St. Martin's Press.

Simonsen, Sven G. 2001. "Compatriot Games: Explaining the 'Diaspora Linkage' in Russia's Military Withdrawal from the Baltic States." *Europe-Asia Studies* 53 (5): 771–91. doi:10.1080/09668130120060260.

Singer, J. David, Stuart Bremer, and John Stuckey. 1972. "Capability Distribution, Uncertainty, and Major Power War, 1820–1965." In *Peace, War, and Numbers,* edited by Bruce Russett, 19–48. Beverly Hills, CA: Sage Publications.

Siroky, David S., and John Cuffe. 2014. "Lost Autonomy, Nationalism and Separatism." *Comparative Political Studies* 47: 1738–65.

Sisk, Timothy D. 2009. *International Mediation in Civil Wars: Bargaining with Bullets*. London: Routledge.

Slezkine, Yuri. 1994. "The USSR as a Communal Apartment, or How a Socialist State Promoted Ethnic Particularism." *Slavic Review* 53 (2): 414–52.

Smogorzewski, Casimir. 1934. *Poland's Access to the Sea*. London: G. Allen & Unwin.

Snow, Donald M. 1993. *Peacekeeping, Peacemaking and Peace-Enforcement: The US Role in the New International Order*. Carlisle Barracks, PA: Strategic Studies Institute, U.S. Army War College.

Snyder, Jack. 1993. "The New Nationalism: Realist Interpretations and Beyond." In *The Domestic Bases of Grand Strategy*, edited by Richard N. Rosecrance and Arthur A. Stein, 179–200. Ithaca, NY: Cornell University Press.

Sokalski, Henryk J. 2003. *An Ounce of Prevention: Macedonia and the UN Experience in Preventive Diplomacy*. Washington, DC: U.S. Institute of Peace Press.

Spruds, Andris. 2009. "Latvia's Energy Structure: Between Structural Entrapments and Policy Choices." In *Energy : Pulling the Baltic Sea Region Together or Apart?*, edited by Andris Spruds and Toms Rostoks, 223–49. Riga: Zinātne.

Spuler, Bertold. 1953. *Minister-Ploetz—Regenten und Regierungen der Welt—Teil II: 1492–1953*. Bielefeld: Ploetz Verlagsbuchhandlung.

Stachura, Peter D. 1998. "National Identity and the Ethnic Minorities in Early Inter-war Poland." In *Poland between the Wars, 1918–1939*, edited by Peter D. Stachura. New York: St. Martin's Press.

Stahn, Carsten. 2008. *The Law and Practice of International Territorial Administration: Versailles to Iraq and Beyond*. Cambridge: Cambridge University Press.

Stedman, Stephen John. 1995. "Alchemy for a New World Order: Overselling 'Preventive Diplomacy.'" *Foreign Affairs* 74 (3): 14–20.

——. 1996. "Negotiation and Mediation in Internal Conflict." In *The International Dimensions of Internal Conflict*, edited by Michael Brown, 341–76. Cambridge, MA: MIT Press.

——. 1997. "Spoiler Problems in Peace Processes." *International Security* 22 (2): 5–53.

Steiner, Zara. 1993. "The League of Nations and the Quest for Security." In *The Quest for Stability: Problems of West European Security, 1918–1957*, edited by Rolf Ahmann, Adolf M. Birke, and Michael Howard, 35–70. London: Oxford University Press.

——. 2005. *The Lights That Failed: European International History, 1919–1933*. Oxford: Oxford University Press.

Stojic, Marco. 2008. "Europe and the Serbian Parliamentary Election of May 2008." University of Sussex, European Parties, Elections, and Referendums Network (EPERN), Election Briefing No. 50. May. http://www.sussex.ac.uk/sei/research/europeanpartieselectionsreferendumsnetwork/epernelectionbriefings.

Stone, Julius. 1932. *International Guarantees of Minority Rights: Procedure of the Council of the League of Nations in Theory and Practice*. New York: Oxford University Press.

Straumanis, Andris. 2011. "Cables Show U.S. Embassy Expressed Concern about Harmony Centre." *Latvians Online*, September 3. http://latviansonline.com/cables-show-us-embassy-expressed-concern-about-harmony-centre/.

Strauss, Hannah A. 1949. *The Attitude of the Congress of Vienna toward Nationalism in Germany, Italy, and Poland*. New York: Columbia University Press.

Subotić, Jelena. 2010. "Explaining Difficult States: The Problems of Europeanization in Serbia." *East European Politics & Societies* 24 (4): 595–616.

Suhrke, Astri, and Lela Garner Noble. 1977. *Ethnic Conflict in International Relations*. New York: Praeger.

Suny, Ronald G. 1993. *The Revenge of the Past: Nationalism, Revolution, and the Collapse of the Soviet Union.* Stanford, CA: Stanford University Press.

Svensson, Isak. 2009. "Who Brings Which Peace? Neutral versus Biased Mediation and Institutional Peace Arrangements in Civil Wars." *Journal of Conflict Resolution* 53 (3): 446–69. doi:10.1177/0022002709332207.

Szarka, László. 2004. "The Trianon Peace Treaty and the Minorities." In *Hungary and the Hungarian Minorities: Trends in the Past and in Our Time,* 14–35. New York: Columbia University Press.

Tabuns, Aivars. 2010. "Identity, Ethnic Relations, Language and Culture." In *How Integrated Is Latvian Society? An Audit of Achievements, Failures and Challenges,* edited by Nils Muižnieks, 253–78. Riga: University of Latvia Advanced Social and Political Research Institute.

Tadic, Milka. 2001. "Montenegro: Djukanovic Defies Europe." Institute for War and Peace Reporting, December 14. http://iwpr.net/report-news/montenegro-djukanovic-defies-europe.

Taleski, Dane. 2010. "Internal and External Challenges for Macedonia." In *15 Years of Peace-Building in the Western Balkans—Lessons Learnt and Current Challenges,* edited by Ernst M. Felberbauer, 189–210. Vienna: National Defence Academy.

Taylor, Rupert. 2001. "Northern Ireland: Consociation or Social Transformation?" *Northern Ireland and the Divided World* 1 (9): 37–53.

Taylor, Scott. 2001. "NATO Sleeping with the Enemy: Peacekeepers Disarm Rebels They Tacitly Aid." *Toronto Sun,* August 23.

Thompson, William R. 1995. "Principal Rivalries." *Journal of Conflict Resolution* 39 (2): 195–223. doi:10.1177/0022002795039002001.

Thyne, Clayton L. 2006. "Cheap Signals with Costly Consequences: The Effect of Interstate Relations on Civil War." *Journal of Conflict Resolution* 50 (6): 937.

Tocci, Nathalie. 2007. *The EU and Conflict Resolution: Promoting Peace in the Backyard.* London: Routledge.

Toft, Monica D. 2003. *The Geography of Ethnic Violence: Identity, Interests, and the Indivisibility of Territory.* Princeton, NJ: Princeton University Press.

——. 2009. *Securing the Peace: The Durable Settlement of Civil Wars.* Princeton, NJ: Princeton University Press. http://www.google.com/books?hl=hu&lr=&id=D_8NwzYnb04C&oi=fnd&pg=PR1&dq=toft+civil+wars&ots=m9SWGDXru2&sig=AoXtgIj52Q0d6e4uZ1QfQe3qTB0.

Tolvaišis, Leonas. 2011. "Ethnic Minority Policies and Political Parties' Appeal to Ethnic Voters: A Case Study of Estonia's Russians." *Baltic Journal of Law & Politics* 4 (1): 106–33. doi:10.2478/v10076–011–0005–4.

Torzecki, Ryszard. 1989. *Kwestia ukraińska w Polsce w latach 1923–1929.* Wyd. 1. Kraków: Wydawn. Literackie.

Touval, Saadia. 1975. "Biased Intermediaries: Theoretical and Historical Considerations." *Jerusalem Journal of International Relations* 1 (1): 51–69.

Touval, Saadia, and I. William Zartman. 1985. *International Mediation in Theory and Practice.* Boulder, CO: Westview Press.

Toynbee, Arnold J., and Fred L. Israel. 1967. *Major Peace Treaties of Modern History: 1648–1967.* New York: Chelsea House.

Trbovich, Ana S. 2008. *A Legal Geography of Yugoslavia's Disintegration.* Oxford: Oxford University Press. http://www.google.com/books?hl=hu&lr=&id=Ojur7dVoxIcC&oi=fnd&pg=PR5&dq=trbovich+ana&ots=S8UcPyxZQo&sig=2cmKZx0UsEJLYq_6OKkA_tTx9bw.

Treisman, Daniel. 1997. "Russia's 'Ethnic Revival': The Separatist Activism of Regional Leaders in a Postcommunist Order." *World Politics* 49 (2): 212–49. doi: http://dx.doi.org/10.1353/wp.1997.0006.

U.S. Embassy Tirana, Albania. 2013. "U.S. Ambassador Alexander A. Arvizu's Remarks on Meeting with Red and Black Alliance (January 29, 2013)." http://tirana.usembassy.gov/press-releases2/2013-press-releases/u.s.-ambassador-alexander-a.-arvizus-remarks-on-meeting-with-red-and-black-alliance-january-29-2013.

Vachudova, Milada A. 2005. *Europe Undivided: Democracy, Leverage, and Integration after Communism*. Oxford: Oxford University Press.

Van Cleef, Eugene. 1933. "Danzig and Gdynia." *Geographical Review* 23 (1): 101–7.

Van Evera, Stephen. 1994. "Hypotheses on Nationalism and War." *International Security* 18 (4): 5–39.

Vangeli, Anastas. 2011. "Nation-Building Ancient Macedonian Style: The Origins and the Effects of the So-Called Antiquization in Macedonia." *Nationalities Papers* 39 (1): 13–32. doi:10.1080/00905992.2010.532775.

Vareikis, Vygantas. 2001. "Memellander/Klaipėdiškiai Identity and German-Lithuanian Relations in Lithuania Minor in the Nineteenth and Twentieth Centuries." *Identiteto Raida. Istorija Ir Dabartis* 1 (2): 54–65.

Vermeersch, Peter. 2003. "Ethnic Minority Identity and Movement Politics: The Case of the Roma in the Czech Republic and Slovakia." *Ethnic and Racial Studies* 26 (5): 879–901.

Vollebaek, Knut. 2012. *HCNM at 20: The Challenges of Change—Continued*. OECD. http://www.osce.org/hcnm/92214?download=true.

Von Riekhoff, Harald. 1971. *German-Polish Relations, 1918–1933*. Baltimore: Johns Hopkins University Press.

Wallensteen, Peter. 2014. "International Conflict Resolution, UN and Regional Organizations." In *Regional Organizations and Peacemaking: Challengers to the UN?*, 13–27. London: Routledge.

Wallensteen, Peter, and Anders Bjurner. 2014. *Regional Organizations and Peacemaking: Challengers to the UN?* London: Routledge.

Walter, Barbara F. 1997. "The Critical Barrier to Civil War Settlement." *International Organization* 51 (03): 335–64. doi:http://dx.doi.org/10.1162/002081897550384.

——. 1999. "Designing Transitions from Civil War: Demobilization, Democratization, and Commitments to Peace." *International Security* 24 (1): 127–55. doi:10.1162/016228899560077.

——. 2002. *Committing to Peace: The Successful Settlement of Civil Wars*. Princeton, NJ: Princeton University Press.

Walters, Francis P. 1986. *A History of the League of Nations*. Westport, CT: Greenwood Press. Originally published by Oxford University Press, 1952.

Watson, Cameron J. 1994. "Ethnic Conflict and the League of Nations: The Case of Transylvania, 1918–1940." *Hungarian Studies* 9 (1–2): 173–80.

Wayland, Sarah. 2004. "Ethnonationalist Networks and Transnational Opportunities: The Sri Lankan Tamil Diaspora." *Review of International Studies* 30 (3): 405–26.

Weinberg, Gerhard L. 1995. *Germany, Hitler, and World War II: Essays in Modern German and World History*. Cambridge: Cambridge University Press.

Weiner, Myron. 1996. "Bad Neighborhoods, Bad Neighbors: An Inquiry into the Causes of Refugee Flows." *International Security* 21 (1): 5–42.

Weyland, Kurt. 2012. "The Arab Spring: Why the Surprising Similarities with the Revolutionary Wave of 1848?" *Perspectives on Politics* 10 (4): 917–34.

Wilkinson, Jonathan, Kathleen J. Young, David M. Quinn, and Victor Asal. 2005. *Mediating International Crises.* London: Routledge.

Williams, Rhodri. 2007. "Excluding to Protect: Land Rights and Minority Protection in International Law." In *Den Åländska Hembydgsrätten*, edited by S. Spiliopoulou Åkermark, 91–133. Helsinki: Författarna. https://terra0nullius.files.wordpress.com/2010/02/williams91-1331-copy.pdf.

Wimmer, Andreas. 2012. *Waves of War: Nationalism, State Formation, and Ethnic Exclusion in the Modern World.* Cambridge: Cambridge University Press. http://www.google.com/books?hl=en&lr=&id=jlIhAwAAQBAJ&oi=fnd&pg=PR10&dq=andreas+wimmer&ots=pCEfHqKhQD&sig=G8sjxmLMfdwY_ht93G0ZAJishos.

Wimmer, Andreas, Lars-Erik Cederman, and Brian Min. 2009. "Ethnic Politics and Armed Conflict: A Configurational Analysis of a New Global Data Set." *American Sociological Review* 74 (2): 316–37.

Wingfield, Nancy M. 1989. *Minority Politics in a Multinational State: The German Social Democrats in Czechoslovakia, 1918–1938.* New York: Columbia University Press.

Wippman, David, ed. 1998. *International Law and Ethnic Conflict.* Ithaca, NY: Cornell University Press.

Wiskemann, Elizabeth. 1956. *Germany's Eastern Neighbours: Problems Relating to the Oder-Neisse Line and the Czech Frontier Regions.* London: Oxford University Press.

Włodarska, Agata. 2011. "Russian-Estonian Relations after 2007: Current Status and Development Prospects." *International Studies* 13 (1): 40–47.

Wolff, Stefan. 2008. "Learning the Lessons of Ethnic Conflict Management? Conditional Recognition and International Administration in the Western Balkans since the 1990s." *Nationalities Papers* 36 (3): 553–70.

——. 2010. "Approaches to Conflict Resolution in Divided Societies: The Many Uses of Territorial Self-Governance." *Ethnopolitics Papers* 5.

Wolff, Stefan, and Oya Dursun-Ozkanca. 2012. "Intervening in Civil Wars: Success and Failure of International and Regional Organisations in Managing Violent Conflict." *Civil Wars* 14 (3): 1–53.

Wolff, Stefan, and Marc Weller. 2005. "Self-Determination and Autonomy: A Conceptual Introduction." In *Autonomy, Self Governance and Conflict Resolution: Innovative Approaches to Institutional Design in Divided Societies*, edited by Marc Weller and Stefan Wolff, 1–25. London: Routledge.

Wolff, Stefan, and Christalla Yakinthou, eds. 2012. *Conflict Management in Divided Societies: Theories and Practice.* New York: Routledge.

Young, Oran R. 1972. "Intermediaries: Additional Thoughts on Third Parties." *Journal of Conflict Resolution* 16 (1): 51–65.

Zaagman, Rob. 1999. *Conflict Prevention in the Baltic States: The OSCE High Commissioner on National Minorities in Estonia, Latvia and Lithuania.* ECMI Monograph no. 1. Flensburg, Germany: European Centre for Minority Issues (ECMI).

Zahar, Marie-Joelle. 2005. "Power Sharing in Lebanon: Foreign Protectors, Domestic Peace, and Democratic Failure." In *Sustainable Peace: Power and Democracy after Civil Wars*, edited by Philip G. Roeder and Donald S. Rothchild, 567–97. Ithaca, NY: Cornell University Press.

Zartman, I. William. 2001. "Ripeness: The Hurting Stalemate and Beyond." In *International Conflict Resolution after the Cold War*, 225–50. Washington, DC: National Academy Press.

Zartman, I. William, and Saadia Touval. 2007. "International Mediation." In *Leashing the Dogs of War: Conflict Management in a Divided World*, edited by Chester A. Crocker,

Fen Osler Hampson, and Pamela R. Aall, 437–54. Washington, DC: U.S. Institute of Peace Press.

Zeidler, Miklós. 2003. "A Nemzetek Szövetsége és a Magyar kisebbségi Petíciók" [The League of Nations and the Hungarian Minority Petitions]. In *Ethno Policy: The System of Community Relations, Private and International Interests in Central Europe*, edited by Nándor Bárdi and Csilla Fedinec, 59–83. Budapest: László Teleki Foundation.

INDEX